Migration Law in Montenegro

Migration Law in Montenegro

Miloš Vukčević
Bojan Bugarin

This book was originally published as a monograph in the International Encyclopaedia of Laws/Migration Law.

Founding Editor: Roger Blanpain
General Editor: Frank Hendrickx
Volume Editor: Dirk Vanheule

Wolters Kluwer

Published by:
Kluwer Law International B.V.
PO Box 316
2400 AH Alphen aan den Rijn
The Netherlands
E-mail: lrs-sales@wolterskluwer.com
Website: www.wolterskluwer.com/en/solutions/kluwerlawinternational

Sold and distributed by:
Wolters Kluwer Legal & Regulatory U.S.
7201 McKinney Circle
Frederick, MD 21704
United States of America
Email: customer.service@wolterskluwer.com

ISBN 978-94-035-4780-0

e-Book: ISBN 978-94-035-4790-9
web-PDF: ISBN 978-94-035-4800-5

Migration Law in Montenegro

Miloš Vukčević
Bojan Bugarin

This book was originally published as a monograph in the International Encyclopaedia of Laws/Migration Law.

Founding Editor: Roger Blanpain
General Editor: Frank Hendrickx
Volume Editor: Dirk Vanheule

Wolters Kluwer

Published by:
Kluwer Law International B.V.
PO Box 316
2400 AH Alphen aan den Rijn
The Netherlands
E-mail: lrs-sales@wolterskluwer.com
Website: www.wolterskluwer.com/en/solutions/kluwerlawinternational

Sold and distributed by:
Wolters Kluwer Legal & Regulatory U.S.
7201 McKinney Circle
Frederick, MD 21704
United States of America
Email: customer.service@wolterskluwer.com

ISBN 978-94-035-4780-0

e-Book: ISBN 978-94-035-4790-9
web-PDF: ISBN 978-94-035-4800-5

The Authors

Prof. Miloš Vukčević is Attorney at Law and Associate Professor at the Law Faculty of the Mediterranean University in Podgorica. He was born in 1982 in Podgorica, where he finished Elementary and High School. He graduated from the Law Faculty of the University of Montenegro in shortened period and during his studies he was awarded several times. He received a Master's degree at the Law Faculty of the University of Novi Sad in June 2008. In September 2011, he received PhD degree with distinction at the Law Faculty of the University of Belgrade. He had been working at the Law Faculty of the Mediterranean University as the Assistant (2006–2012), Assistant Professor (2012–2017) and Associate Professor (elected in 2017). From 2017 to 2020, he was Dean of the Law Faculty of the Mediterranean University. He served as the Deputy Director for the prevention of money laundering and terrorism financing (2011–2013) and as the Deputy Minister/General Director of the Ministry of Internal Affairs, the Government of Montenegro (2013–2017). He was a member of working groups for negotiation with European Union (EU) – Chapters 23 and 24 (2012–2017) and the Commission for cooperation with emigrants (2016–2017). His field of interest included international public law and EU law. He has published over twenty papers, studies, chapters and books in the country and abroad. He is a member of the Associate of Lawyers of Montenegro since 2008. During his career, he was doing research abroad at several universities and institutions: in the US (University of Iowa), Luxembourg (EIPA) and in UK (London School of Economist and Political Science).

The Authors

Bojan Bugarin was born in Montenegro in 1979. He graduated from the Faculty of Political Sciences – Department of International Relations, University of Belgrade, the Republic of Serbia. Currently, he is Executive Director of NGO Forum for Euro-Atlantic Perspectives. He was employed at the Montenegrin Ministry of Interior, Asylum Office, where he was working on preparation of asylum applications, conducting procedures and making decisions on asylum applications and termination and revocation of status. From 2013 to 2016 he had been working as the Advisor to the Minister of the Interior, where he performed the most complex tasks within the scope of the Ministry of Interior. He also worked in the Foreigners, Migration and Readmission Department, where he was in charge of implementation of the established migration policy, laws and other regulations and international documents in the field of migration and readmission, preparation of draft laws and other regulations in these areas, participation in the development and implementation of strategies, projects and programmes in the field of migration, etc. He was involved in negotiation process between the EU and Montenegro, as a member of the Working Group for Negotiating Chapter 24 – as a Coordinator for migration area, as well as the occasional member of the Working Group for Negotiating Chapter 2 and the Negotiating Chapter 23. During the Visa Liberalization Dialogue with EU, he was the coordinator of visa and post-visa liberalization process on the national level. He was engaged in Ukraine as an expert/trainer of the International Organization for Migration (IOM) for the Ukrainian state bodies and civil servants. He attended numerous conferences, training and seminars organized by international organizations, national governments of individual countries and non-governmental organizations. He is International Visitor Leadership Program (IVLP) alumni, as well as FRONTEX's certified trainer at the national level for screening and debriefing. He is an author of the Study: 'Montenegrin citizenship and domicile – How to get to an up-to-date Central Voter Register', published by Centre for Monitoring and Research (CeMI).

Table of Contents

Table of Contents

List of Abbreviations

DP	Displaced Person
EASO	European Asylum Support Office
EC	European Commission
EU	European Union
Europol	European Police Office
FRONTEX	European Agency for the Management of Operational Cooperation at the External Borders of the Member States of the European Union
FRY	Federal Republic of Yugoslavia
IBM	Integrated Border Management
ID	Identity Document
IDP	Internally Displaced Person
ILO	International Labour Organization
NGO	Non-governmental Organization
OSCE	Organization of Security and Cooperation in Europe
SAA	Stabilization and Association Agreement (EU)
SAP	Schengen Action Plan
SFRY	Socialist Federal Republic of Yugoslavia
SOCTA	Serious and Organized Crime Threat Assessment
UN	United Nations
UNHCR	United Nations High Commissioner for Refugees

List of Abbreviations

Preface

As of the opening of negotiations with the EU (2012), the Migration Law of Montenegro is rapidly developing, and today it can be rightly said that it has been developed and largely harmonized with the EU acquis communautaire. The process of European integration is aimed at Montenegro becoming a full-fledged member of the EU, and one of the obligations that Montenegro must fulfil along the way is the full harmonization and establishment of the legal framework, as well as further strengthening of the institutional framework enabling effective implementation of migration control policy, in accordance with the EU rules and standards, as well as the establishment of a society with an efficient system and recognizable results in the area of integrated migration management. Although the legal system of Montenegro contains the law of the three federal states of which Montenegro was a member republic (Socialist Federal Republic of Yugoslavia, Federal Republic of Yugoslavia and the State Union of Serbia and Montenegro), Montenegrin migration law started to develop more intensively only after the declaration of independence in 2006. Thus, the most significant activity in the area of migration law in Montenegro in the previous period was the adoption of the new Law on International and Temporary Protection of Foreigners and the Law on Foreign Nationals in 2018, resulting in major transposing of the EU acquis communautaire in the area of migration law to these two laws, and their implementation has triggered a change in terms of the quality of this system and its efficiency. By adopting these laws, Montenegro has introduced a new concept that encourages the successful integration of foreigners into the receptive Montenegrin society, guaranteeing full protection of human, civil, economic, social and cultural and other rights, simultaneously establishing an efficient and unique asylum system in which foreigners seeking international protection are guaranteed, as in the EU countries, equal chances of success in the proceedings, as well as guarantees of the equal treatment. The adoption of these laws is pivotal because the migrant crisis that hit Europe and escalated in the form of a massive influx of refugees and illegal immigrants from Asia, Africa and the Middle East to the EU also partly affected Montenegro, which has been increasingly affected by the migration along the so-called coastal route (Albania – Montenegro – Bosnia and Herzegovina), resulting in a significant increase in the number of asylum seekers annually in Montenegro.

By writing this monograph, the authors aimed not only to present the modern migration law of Montenegro in a practical – informative – manner but also to make an overview of its historical development, as well as theoretical discussions. In addition to legal practitioners (lawyers, consultants, legal advisors), this monograph can be useful to law students, judges, as well as all other citizens and the general public. The monograph mainly analyses the provisions of the current Montenegrin legislation governing the right of immigration (immigration law), but partly also to emigration. It is important to point out that the authors had a critical approach in relation to certain legal solutions, believing that Montenegro should alter the legislation and harmonize it with the EU standards in the field of migration law, and also pointed out the lack of its application in certain cases.

Montenegrin migration law has changed frequently, especially in the last ten years of which the authors are aware. The monograph depicts and takes into account the legislation and its amendments as of 1 June 2020.

General Introduction

§1. Immigration History and Statistical Information

1. Montenegro is a country which may be said to have 'populated others without depopulating itself', which means that it is a country with a significant history, primarily of emigration.[1] Throughout history, the migrations of Montenegrin society have gone through several state-related and territorial phases: the Doclean-Zeta period and the territorial framework of a medieval state, the Montenegrin period – since the last Crnojević's family – fall under the Turkish rule, administration by bishops from various clans, then the periods of restoration and establishment of central government bodies and territorial enlargement of the state under the leadership of the bishops and rulers from the dynasty Petrović-Njegoš, then, Montenegro within the framework of three Yugoslavias, in the State Union with Serbia, and finally, its resurrection as an independent, autonomous, sovereign and internationally recognized state, which is on the verge of joining the European Union (EU).[2]

2. Migrations of population from the territory of the contemporary Montenegro may be reliably monitored as of seventeenth century, while they were intensive in the nineteenth and the first half of the twentieth century, and massive after the Balkan, the First and the Second World Wars.[3] The diaspora of Montenegro, divided into smaller groups and colonies, unfortunately largely lost its identity in the new environment, failed to preserve its ethnic identity, national identity or Montenegrin consciousness. The reason for this is partly due to the fact that Montenegrin emigrants, as members of Orthodoxy, were not able to form their own special ecclesiastical municipalities because they always fell under the jurisdiction of Greek, Serbian, or other Eastern Orthodox churches, or converted, by free choice or force, to Catholicism, Islam or another religion.

3. The leading causes of emigration from Montenegro are the economic conditions and thus impossibility to reach the minimum standard of living, as well as the

1. The area of today's Montenegro in the last five hundred years is highly migratory and that only emigration in various directions and several waves lasts for all time, *see* more in Gordan Stojović, *Crnogorski iseljenici u Novom svijetu,* Matica crnogorska, Podgorica 2016.
2. Marijan Mašo Miljić, *Crnogorsko iseljeništvo kroz istoriju*, Diaspora Administration of Montenegro, http://www.dijaspora.mvpei.gov.me/O_nama/Istorija_crnogorskih_iseljavanja (accessed 1 Nov. 2019).
3. Heinz Fassmann & Munz Rainer, *Migracije Istok-Zapad u Europi od 1918-92* (Migracijske teme 11 1995).

increasing economic stratification of society. A small number of families of chiefs made a fortune at the expense of the largest portion of the population who lived in poverty and in debt. Moreover, blood revenge and various epidemics, as well as conflicts with the Turks, contributed to increasing migration outflows from Montenegro.

4. Montenegrins preferred to move to Serbia and Russia, which was the 'promised land' for Montenegrins, then to the Venetian territory, especially to Istria, to the Kingdom of Naples, to the regions under the Austro-Hungarian rule, but also to Turkey.[4] Montenegrins were for a long time travelling to these and other countries without any documents, until 1751 when the first Montenegrin passports were issued. After 1878, the Muslim population emigrated from the newly liberated regions and towns for political and religious reasons. After the Second Serbian Uprising, liberated Serbia was the most common destination for the poorest Montenegrin families, which exercised its right to direct and resettle the population that settled in, in accordance with its state and national interests. In addition to Russia and Serbia, Montenegrins reached also other more distant countries. Thus, there was a large colony of Montenegrin workers in Constantinople formed by around two thousand persons. Moreover, Montenegrins went to Turkey where they became mercenaries.[5]

5. There are several stages in the history of Montenegrin emigration.[6] The *first stage* of emigration lasted from the end of the fifteenth to the end of the nineteenth century, and during this period there was emigration to Boka and Constantinople, forcing emigrants to serve under the Venetian and Austrian authorities. Emigration to territory ruled by Turkey in Nikšić, Ibarski Kolašin, Herzegovina and Bosnia is also characteristic. Particularly interesting is settling in the Venetian territory: Boka, Dalmatia and Istria. An important segment of this period was the emigration of Montenegrins to the Kingdom of Naples and to Austria, and especially to Serbia and Russia, for which Montenegrins were particularly interested. The *second stage* covers the period from the end of the nineteenth century (recognition of Montenegro in 1878), until the First World War. In the history of Montenegro, this is the time of exceptional economic, cultural, scientific and every other progress and is called for a reason the Montenegrin revival. Unfortunately, the earlier reasons that led to the mass emigration of numerous Montenegrin families have not been routed out. The emigration routes remained largely the same, but there were also new ones. Particularly significant was the colonization of Metohija after the First Balkan War. During this period, Montenegrins began to emigrate to North and South America.[7] It was

---

4. Marijan Mašo Miljić, *Crnogorsko iseljeništvo kroz istoriju*, Diaspora Administration of Montenegro, http://www.dijaspora.mvpei.gov.me/O_nama/Istorija_crnogorskih_iseljavanja (accessed 1 Nov. 2019).
5. Šerbo Rastoder, *Crnogorski iseljenici u Turskoj, odšteta i potraživanja poslije I svjetskog rata* (Matica 1, Cetinje 2000), pp. 227–236.
6. Marijan Mašo Miljić, *Crnogorsko iseljeništvo kroz istoriju*, Diaspora Administration of Montenegro, http://www.dijaspora.mvpei.gov.me/O_nama/Istorija_crnogorskih_iseljavanja (accessed 1 Nov. 2019).
7. *Ibid.*

during this period that the most massive emigrations to Serbia took place, simultaneously entailing a vigorous process of Serbianization of Montenegrins. In addition to economic, this stage also brought political emigrations, especially after the introduction of parliamentarism in Montenegro.[8] The third stage of Montenegrin emigration covers the period between the two world wars. The First World War brought major troubles to Montenegro, where for the first time in its history the Montenegrin government had to capitulate, and the king, the Government and a considerable part of the Montenegrin army had to leave the country. Montenegro lost its independence after the First World War and it was annexed to Serbia under the State of Serbs, Croats and Slovenes, later called the Kingdom of Yugoslavia, in which there was no room for the state, people, or the name of Montenegro. During the interwar period, Montenegrins were resettled to Vojvodina, Metohija and other parts of the country existing at that time. The Second World War also brought major disasters to Montenegro, mass exoduses of population, camps and prisons. The end of the war triggered the emigration of a part of the Montenegrin, Chetnik and Federalist movements.[9] Furthermore, after the conflict of Yugoslavia with the Soviet Union in 1948 and the countries in its political sphere, a considerable number of Montenegrins were sent to the Goli Otok or were forced to emigrate. In that fourth stage of emigration, which occurred after the Second World War, there was a mass emigration – the colonization of Montenegrins into Vojvodina, which requires special scientific analysis.[10] The mass education of Montenegrin youth in the Yugoslav and European centres can be considered somehow one of the factors in the history of emigration from Montenegro, especially since a large part of secondary school and university youth remained to live permanently in other areas. The *fifth period* of Montenegrin emigration began with the dissolution of the Socialist Federal Republic of Yugoslavia (SFRY), the war in the region and a large population of Montenegrins who remained in the republics that became states. Montenegrin associations were established to preserve national and cultural identity. The Montenegrin diaspora in Serbia represents a special case. One part of it lost its Montenegrin national identity, especially the older emigrants, while the other, younger emigrants, split into the Serbian and Montenegrin wing, in the spirit of the nineteenth and early twentieth century, 'thanks' to political situation and interests. The sixth period in the history of Montenegrin emigration begins after the independence of Montenegro was declared based on the referendum on 21 May 2006 and the international recognition of Montenegro. The state of Montenegro again becomes a genuine fatherland to its diaspora. However, it is indisputable that even today there is quite a large Montenegrin diaspora, older or younger provenance, scattered throughout the region or around the world.

6. Thus, in the second half of the twentieth century, Montenegrins massively emigrated abroad in a quest for temporary work, especially to Germany, and other

8. Jovan Đonović, *Ustavne i političke borbe u Crnoj Gori 1905-1910* (Belgrade 1939).
9. Numerous opponents of the regime were in exile, especially communists and other leftists, scattered across European countries, especially in Russia, and federalists and supporters of King Nicholas in Argentina and other South American countries.
10. Slobodan Medojević, *Kolonizacija Crnogoraca u Vojvodini 1945-46* (Matica Crnogorska Cetinje 2010).

European countries. They either brought or formed their families there, and most of them are still in those countries today, and have citizenship in those countries. The civil war in the 1990s, the breakup of the former Yugoslavia, and then of the State Union of Serbia and Montenegro, inevitably affected the migration process of the Montenegrin population. Thus, due to the war in the former Yugoslavia (1992–1997), certain demographic changes occurred. A large number of Montenegrin citizens, regardless of nationality, left Montenegro and went to the developed countries of Western Europe. This fact is especially characterized by members of minorities. The war in Croatia had a direct impact on the position of the Croatian minority in Montenegro, whose members were leaving the Montenegrin territory for security, political and economic reasons.[11] With the war in Bosnia and Herzegovina, members of the Bosniak and Muslim people were leaving Montenegro for the same causes and reasons as well as the Albanian population, especially during the conflict in Kosovo.

7. The full-scale civil war in the neighbouring regions led to a huge influx of refugees from war-torn areas. Furthermore, the North Atlantic Treaty Organization intervention in 1999 contributed to a new wave of migration of the Albanian population from Kosovo, therefore during that period the refugee and displaced population exceeded 130,000, which was a record number of refugees, or over 20% of the total population. Since the restoration of its independence, 8,474 refugees from the Former Yugoslav Republics[12] and 16,250 internally displaced persons (IDPs) from Kosovo[13] have resided in Montenegro. According to the 2007 Report, the total number of refugees amounted to 24,610, which is 4.2% of the total population.

8. In 2005, the Government adopted a Strategy for Durable Solution for Refugees and Internally Displaced Persons in Montenegro envisaging three solutions: repatriation, local integration and departure to third countries.[14] The issue of refugee status is a huge problem for Montenegro in terms of the country's economic power and demographic change. All these years Montenegro is implementing an ongoing socio-economic integration of the displaced population and refugees are included in the regular education system and provided with healthcare. The Government of Montenegro, after the restoration of independence on 20 June 2006, adopted a Decision on the temporary retention of the status and rights of displaced and IDPs in Montenegro defining the temporary retention of the status of these persons in Montenegro, in accordance with the laws governing the issue of asylum and

11. Government of Montenegro, *First Report of the Republic of Montenegro on the Implementation of the Framework Convention for the Protection of National Minorities* (Podgorica 2007), p. 9.
12. Government of Montenegro, *Report on the Readiness of Montenegro for Liberalization of Visa Regime – Block IV: Foreign Affairs and Fundamental Rights – Concise Information* (Podgorica 2009).
13. *Ibid.*
14. Government of Montenegro, *Strategy for Durable Solution for Refugees and Internally Displaced Persons in Montenegro* (Podgorica 2005).

aliens, the Strategy for Durable Solution for Refugees and Internally Displaced Persons in Montenegro and the regional documents on resolving the issues of refugees and displaced persons (DPs).[15]

9. In the years after the restoration of independence, Montenegro, through the process of European integration and by being aware that the integration of these displaced and IDPs could cause significant changes in the structure of the population and core electorate, focused its policy on addressing the status of these persons, on the one hand, as well as on preventing their full integration and obtaining political rights, on the other hand. As a result, the number of refugees decreased over time and they have regulated their legal status in Montenegro, which is to the greatest extent the result of Montenegro's EU accession process and commitments undertaken in this process. Therefore the number of refugees from a record number in 1999 (130,000 or 20% of the total population) decreased to several hundreds of refugees requiring assistance in regulating their legal status (for more detailed information *see* Part III Chapter 7).

10. Defining the overall migration policy of Montenegro is to the greatest extent contingent upon the geopolitical position of Montenegro. Namely, Montenegro is on the path of traditional migration flows of the European continent that lead in the direction east-west and south-north. Montenegro, with an area of 13,817 km^2 and a population of less than 650,000, is one of the small countries, and therefore particularly vulnerable when it comes to uncontrolled migration. The successive development of certain economic branches in Montenegro has conditioned the need to engage the missing labour force, which is absorbed from the countries of the region. Dissolutions of the former SFRY and war events in the area has caused large population movements, and consequently the emergence of a large number of displaced and internally displaced persons. Obtaining the status of a candidate country for EU membership and visa liberalization may affect the recognition of Montenegro as a country of final destination, and less as a transit area.[16]

11. In the light of the above, Montenegro is one of the European countries with a low rate of immigration (in-migration). However, what can be noticed is that the number of foreigners has increased in recent years. In 2018, a total of 1,209 applications for obtaining permanent residence permit were received, which with 987 pending applications from the previous period makes a total of 2,196 applications pending decision.[17] Out of the total number of pending applications in 2018, 1,757 applications have been considered, of which 1,540 applications were granted, 91 applications were dismissed, 81 applications were rejected, and 45 applications

15. Government of Montenegro, *First Report of the Republic of Montenegro on the Implementation of the Framework Convention for the Protection of National Minorities* (Podgorica 2007), p. 10.
16. Government of Montenegro, *Strategy for Integrated Migration Management in Montenegro for the Period 2011-2016* (Podgorica 2010).
17. Government of Montenegro, *Report on the Implementation of the Action Plan for the Implementation of the Strategy for Integrated Migration Management in Montenegro 2017-2020, for 2018* (Podgorica 2019), p. 9.

were suspended or terminated.[18] Moreover, in 2018, a total of 48,715 applications for obtaining temporary residence/work permit were received, which with 217 pending applications from the previous period makes a total of 48,932 pending applications. Out of the total number of applications in 2018, 47,834 applications have been considered. Out of 47,834 considered applications, 44,703 applications were granted, 1,353 applications were dismissed, 646 applications were rejected, and 1,132 applications were suspended/terminated.[19]

12. In 2019, a total of 1,150 applications for obtaining permanent residence permit were received, which with 527 pending applications from the previous period makes a total of 1,677 applications pending decision. Out of the total number of pending applications in 2019, 1,092 applications have been considered, of which 993 applications were granted, 33 applications were dismissed, 48 applications were rejected, and 18 applications were suspended or terminated. Moreover, in 2019, a total of 50,512 applications for obtaining temporary residence/work permit were received, which with 1,627 pending applications from the previous period makes a total of 52,139 pending applications. Out of the total number of applications in 2019, 48,712 applications have been considered. Out of this number, 45,551 applications were granted, 1,457 applications were dismissed, 841 applications were rejected, and 863 applications were suspended/terminated.[20]

13. The largest number of temporary residence permits were issued on the basis of work, and slightly less on the basis of family reunification. Over 95% of temporary residence permits were issued on these two grounds. The Decision on determining the annual number of temporary residence permits and work permits for foreigners for 2018[21] has determined the number of work permits to be issued to the foreigners in 2018 amounting to 23,185. Out of this number, 10,000 work permits may be additionally issued by the Ministry of Labor and Social Welfare, in accordance with the labour market demand. The Ministry of Labor and Social Welfare has decided to allocate 6,218 work permits for the employment of foreigners, while the quota for employment of foreigners in 2018 is 27,5% higher than the quota established in 2017 (23,185:18,185).[22] In 2018, 26,327 permits were issued for work and employment of foreigners (15,132 within the quota and 11,195 out of the quota), which is by 5,358 or 25.55% more than in 2017 (20,969).[23] When it comes to the type of permits issued to foreigners within the quota 77.82% permits were issued for the employment of foreigners (11,776), 18.96% permits were issued

18. *Ibid.*
19. *Ibid.*
20. Government of Montenegro, *Report on the Implementation of the Action Plan for the Implementation of the Strategy for Integrated Migration Management in Montenegro 2017-2020, for 2019* (Podgorica 2020), p. 75.
21. *Odluka o utvrđivanju godišnjeg broja dozvola za privremeni boravak i rad stranaca za 2018. godinu,* 'Official Gazette of MNE', Nos 86/2017 and 56/2018.
22. Government of Montenegro, *Report on the Implementation of the Action Plan for the Implementation of the Strategy for Integrated Migration Management in Montenegro 2017-2020, for 2018* (Podgorica 2019), pp. 9 and 10.
23. *Ibid.*

for seasonal employment of foreigners (2,869) and 3.22% permits were issued for the provision of contracted services (487).[24] When it comes to the quotas used for the employment of foreigners in 2018, four occupational groups have predominant share (80.23%): construction, hospitality services, trade and other hospitality activities.[25]

14. As of 2015, when the migrant crisis hit Europe and escalated in the form of a massive influx of refugees and illegal immigrants from Asia, Africa and the Middle East into EU countries, it has also partly affected Montenegro, which has taken a responsible approach in dealing with migration challenges entailing state involvement for effectively addressing the complex task of safeguarding border security, simultaneously providing adequate conditions for persons seeking international protection. In November 2015, the Government of Montenegro adopted the Activity Plan in the event of a massive influx of migrants and refugees in transit through the territory of Montenegro. In accordance with the Plan, an Operational Team was formed, and the responsibilities of the bodies related to the records of persons at the border, the safety of migrants, reception and accommodation, medical care and hygiene, provision of information to the migrants and the public, etc. After the closure of the Western Balkans transit corridor in 2016 migrants in neighbouring regions or within the Western Balkans region continued to search for travel alternatives along other sub-routes. In that sense in 2017 a new sub-route was opened through the Albania-Montenegro–Bosnia and Herzegovina–Croatia. In connection with the opening of this sub-route, since the beginning of August 2017 and during 2018, Montenegro recorded a higher number of illegal crossings from Albania to Montenegro, as well as exits from Montenegro, mostly towards Bosnia and Herzegovina but also towards the Republic of Croatia. Irregular migrants were entering Montenegro over the green border area around the border crossing Božaj and in smaller extent Sukobin on the border with the Republic of Albania, while in most cases they illegally try to leave Montenegro towards the Bosnia and Herzegovina and in smaller number towards the Republic of Croatia. In most cases, after illegally entering Montenegro, migrants expressed intention for international protection or officially applied for international protection in accordance with the law on international and temporary protection on foreigners, with the aim of avoiding misdemeanour liability, realizing the right to move unhindered across the territory of Montenegro with certificates issued by the asylum office or border police. After expressed intention for international protection or officially submitted application for international protection, most of the migrants did not wait for the decision on application, but after a few days they tried to leave Montenegro also illegally. In 2015, as many as 1,611 persons applied for asylum in Montenegro. As a result of the signing of an EU-Turkey agreement on resolving the migrant crisis and interruption of the Western Balkans route in 2016, the number of asylum seekers in Montenegro dropped significantly to 335 asylum seekers in 2016. Given the fact that since autumn 2017 Montenegro has been increasingly affected by migration along the so-called coastal route (Albania–Montenegro–Bosnia and Herzegovina),

24. *Ibid.*
25. *Ibid.*

there has been a significant increase in the number of asylum seekers on an annual basis, resulting in 849 applications in this year, while as many as 3,104 applications for international protection were filed in 2018, while 1921 applications were filled in 2019 (for more detailed information *see* Part III Chapter 6). In order to control migration movements, the Border Police Department is continuously implementing the Plan for enhanced border control through the increased presence of patrols at the border and checkpoints of major roads to the border.

15. When it comes to legislative activities, in February 2017 Montenegro adopted the Strategy for Integrated Migration Management for the period 2017–2020, with the Action Plan for its implementation. The Strategy envisages the full harmonization and establishment of the legal framework, as well as the further strengthening of the institutional framework enabling an effective implementation of the migration control policy. Montenegro has strengthened its accommodation capacities aimed at better regulation of migration processes and the administrative improvement. All measures have been taken to accommodate migrants and refugees in the event of their arrival, in accordance with all international standards governing this area. Thus, in February 2014, the Center for Asylum Seekers (currently: Directorate for the Reception and Accommodation of Foreigners – Reception Center) was put into operation. Moreover, in December 2013, the Reception Center for Foreigners was put into operation, intended for persons who were found in illegal residence on the territory of Montenegro. Both Centres have decent accommodation facilities, adequate conditions are provided for the stay of foreigners, and training for staff employed by the centres have been continuously organized. In addition, in the event that the Centre's accommodation capacity is full or in the case of a large influx of asylum seekers, alternative accommodation is provided for persons from the asylum system. Regarding the management of migration flows in the territory of Montenegro, it is planned to increase the reception capacity, with the financial support of the EU, by creating a 'transit center' at Božaji (border with the Republic of Albania), for the reception of migrants entering the state for the first time and those who want to apply for asylum in Montenegro.

§2. Overview of National Legal Instruments

I. Historical Overview

16. The Evolution of Mankind has been accompanied by migration. The intensity, direction and form have been changeable, but migration has been and it is even today a very characteristic constancy of mankind.[26]

17. The history of the development of migration legislation in Montenegro can be divided into two periods. The first period covers the time when Montenegro was a Member State within the Federal Republic of Yugoslavia (FRY) (1992–2003) and

26. Mladen Friganović, *Migracija kao konstanta Geoprostora*, Radovi, Vol. 24, 19–30 (Zagreb, 1989), pp. 19.

the State Union of Serbia and Montenegro (2003–2006) and the second period covers the time as of 2006 when Montenegro became an independent state. With regard to the first period, the FRY and Serbia and Montenegro generally applied the legislation of the old SFRY concerning the rights of foreigners, border control, etc., which was quite poor. Thus, the Constitution of the FRY, similar to the Constitution of SFRY, prescribed the jurisdiction of the Federation, court jurisdiction and common policy in matters, *inter alia*, of human rights, citizenship, crossing the border, control of movement of goods, services at the border and the status of foreigners.[27] Moreover, during this period, the Constitution prescribed dual citizenship;[28] thus every citizen of Montenegro was simultaneously a citizen of Yugoslavia. In other words, a Yugoslav citizen was simultaneously a national of a Member State (Montenegro or Serbia). All Yugoslav citizens were guaranteed the freedom of movement and residence, as well as the right to leave and return to the country.[29] Freedom of movement and residence and the right to leave the FRY may be restricted by federal law if considered necessary for conducting criminal proceedings, prevention of the spread of communicable disease or defending the country.[30] Article 66 of the Constitution provides for the right of asylum to foreigners and stateless persons who are persecuted for advocating democratic views and for participating in movements for social and national liberation advocating human rights and freedoms or the freedom of scientific or artistic creation. A foreigner may acquire the right of ownership and the right of employment based on reciprocity principle, in accordance with the law, unlike a stateless person who cannot acquire ownership of a land.[31]

18. The State Union of Serbia and Montenegro was established in 2000 with the signing of the Belgrade Agreement and the adoption of the Constitutional Charter replacing the 1992 FRY Constitution. The Constitutional Charter, which came into force in 2003, stipulates that immigration policy, visa regime and the right to asylum shall be regulated at the level of the State Union of Serbia and Montenegro, and that these policies must be harmonized with the EU acquis, while the responsibility for the implementation of international human rights treaties has been conferred to the Member States. In the light of the above, the Parliament of Serbia and Montenegro adopted the Charter on Human and Minority Rights as an integral part of the Constitutional Charter, which regulates migration policy in detail.

Thus, this Charter stipulates that every citizen shall have the right to free movement and residence throughout and in the territory of the State Union. This Charter also reaffirms the right to asylum. During the first period, i.e., during the FRY and State Union of Serbia and Montenegro (1992–2006), Montenegro applied the following laws governing the migration law and human rights:

27. Article 77 of the Constitution of the Federal Republic of Yugoslavia (*Ustav Savezne Republike Jugoslavije*), 'Official Gazette of the Federal Republic of Yugoslavia', No. 1/1992.
28. Article 17 of the Constitution of the Federal Republic of Yugoslavia.
29. Article 30 of the Constitution of the Federal Republic of Yugoslavia.
30. *Ibid.*
31. Article 70 of the Constitution of the Federal Republic of Yugoslavia.

- Organic Law on registration of permanent and temporary residence and residence of citizens.[32]
- Law on the Movement and Stay of Foreigners.[33]
- Law on crossing the state border and moving within the border zone.[34]
- Law on conditions for the establishment of employment relationship with foreign nationals.[35]
- Law on Yugoslav Citizenship.[36]
- Law on Travel Documents of Yugoslav Nationals.[37]
- Law on Asylum.[38]

19. Following the 2006 referendum, when the majority of Montenegrin citizens voted for an independent state (55%), Montenegro became an autonomous and independent state, which reapplied for membership in international organizations, while Serbia was a successor state to the State Union SAMNE. The Constitutional Charter was repealed and after the declaration of independence, Montenegro commenced an intensive reform of its legislation, including migration legislation and human rights with the objective of their alignment with the EU acquis. Thus, in 2007, the Parliament adopted a new and modern Constitution[39] of Montenegro, which will represent a turning point in the development of modern Montenegrin law, and, of course, within it, migration and human rights laws.

II. Current Applicable Legislation

20. Current applicable legislation governing migrations and human rights in Montenegro is primarily grounded on the Constitution of Montenegro adopted in 2007 and the amendments from I to XVI[40] adopted in 2013, representing an integral part of the Constitution. Thus, the Montenegrin Constitution in Article 6 guarantees and protects rights and liberties of everyone, while everyone shall be obliged

---

32. *Osnovni zakon o evidenciji prebivališta i boravišta građana,* 'Official Gazette of the SFRY', Nos 008/65, 029/71.
33. *Zakon o kretanju i boravku stranaca*, 'Official Gazette of the SFRY', Nos 056/80 of 3.10.1980, 053/85 of 4.10.1985, 030/89 of 16.5.1989, 026/90 of 18.5.1990, 053/91 of 12.7.1991, 'Official Gazette of the SRY', Nos 024/94 of 18.4.1994, 028/96 of 21.6.1996, 068/02 of 19.12.2002, 'Official Gazette of Serbia and Montenegro', No. 012/05 of 25.4.2005.
34. *Zakon* o *prelaženju državne granice i kretanju u graničnom pojasu*, 'Official Gazette of the SFRY', Nos 34/1979, 56/1980 and 53/1985.
35. *Zakon o uslovima za zasnivanje radnog odnosa sa stranim državljanima*, 'Official Gazette of the SFRY', Nos 11/1978, 64/1989, 42/1992, 24/1994 and 28/1996.
36. *Zakon o jugoslovenskom državljanstvu*, 'Official Gazette of the SRY', Nos 33/1996, 9/2001.
37. *Zakon o putnim ispravama jugoslovenskih državljana*, 'Official Gazette of the SRY', Nos 033/96 of 19.7.1996, 049/96 of 25.10.1996, 012/98 of 6.3.1998, 044/99 of 25.6.1999, 015/00 of 7.4.2000, 007/01 of 16.2.2001, 071/01 of 28.12.2001, 023/02 of 27.4.2002, 053/02 of 27.9.2002, 068/02 of 19.12.2002, 005/03 of 25.1.2003.
38. *Zakon o azilu*, 'Official Gazette of SaM', No. 012/05.
39. Constitution of Montenegro *(Ustav Crne Gore)*, 'Official Gazette of Montenegro', Nos 001/07 of 25.10.2007, 038/13 of 2.8.2013.
40. Amendments I to XVI to the Constitution of Montenegro *(Amandmani I do XVI na Ustav Crne Gore),* 'Official Gazette of MNE', No. 038/13 of 2.8.2013.

to respect the rights and liberties of others. Direct or indirect discrimination on any grounds shall be prohibited. Regulations and introduction of special measures aimed at creating the conditions for the exercise of national, gender and overall equality and protection of persons who are in an unequal position on any grounds shall not be considered discrimination.[41] Article 9 of the Constitution guarantees the direct application of ratified and published international treaties and generally accepted rules of international law shall make an integral part of the internal legal order and shall have supremacy over the national legislation. Article 16 stipulates that the law shall regulate the manner of exercise of human rights and liberties, when this is necessary for their exercise, as well as the manner of exercise of special minority rights. Guaranteed human rights and freedoms may be limited only by the law, to the extent necessary to satisfy the purpose for which the limitation has been permitted in an open and free democratic society.[42] During the proclaimed state of war or emergency, the exercise of certain human rights and liberties may be limited, to the necessary extent.[43] The limitations shall not be introduced on the grounds of sex, nationality, race, religion, language, ethnic or social origin, political or other beliefs, financial standing or any other personal feature.[44] Article 44 of the Constitution guarantees the right to asylum in such a way that a foreign national reasonably fearing persecution on the grounds of his/her race, language, religion or association with a nation or a group or due to own political beliefs may request asylum in Montenegro. A foreign national shall not be expelled from Montenegro to where due to his race, religion, language or association with a nation he/she is threatened with a death sentence, torture, inhuman degradation, persecution or serious violation of rights guaranteed by this Constitution, but solely on the basis of the decision of the responsible authority and following the legally prescribed procedure.[45] The ownership right of the foreigner has been guaranteed by Article 61 of the Constitution. The Parliament shall decide with two-thirds majority of votes of all members on the laws that regulate the electoral system and property rights of foreign citizens. Everyone, including foreigners, shall be guaranteed the right to freedom of movement and residence, as well as the right to depart from Montenegro.[46] The freedom of movement, residence and departure from Montenegro may be restricted if required so for conducting the criminal procedure, prevention of communicable diseases spreading and for the security of Montenegro. Political organizing and actions of foreign nationals and political organizations with the seat outside of Montenegro shall be prohibited.[47] Article 79 of the Constitution stipulates a number of rights and liberties guaranteed to persons belonging to minority nationals and other minority national communities:

(1) the right to exercise, protect, develop and publicly express national, ethnic, cultural and religious particularities;

41. Articles 7 and 8 of the Constitution of Montenegro.
42. Article 24 of the Constitution of Montenegro.
43. Article 25 of the Constitution of Montenegro.
44. *Ibid.*
45. Article 44 of the Constitution of Montenegro.
46. Article 92 of the Constitution of Montenegro.
47. Article 54 of the Constitution of Montenegro.

(2) the right to choose, use and publicly post national symbols and to celebrate national holidays;
(3) the right to use their own language and alphabet in private, public and official use;
(4) the right to education in their own language and alphabet in public institutions and the right to have included in the curricula the history and culture of the persons belonging to minority nations and other minority national communities;
(5) the right, in the areas with significant share in the total population, to have the local self-government authorities, state and court authorities carry out the proceedings also in the language of minority nations and other minority national communities;
(6) the right to establish educational, cultural and religious associations, with the material support of the state;
(7) the right to write and use their own name and surname in their own language and alphabet in the official documents;
(8) the right, in the areas with significant share in total population, to have traditional local terms, names of streets and settlements, as well as topographic signs written also in the language of minority nations and other minority national communities;
(9) the right to authentic representation in the Parliament of the Republic of Montenegro and in the assemblies of the local self-government units in which they represent a significant share in the population, according to the principle of affirmative action;
(10) the right to proportionate representation in public services, state authorities and local self-government bodies;
(11) the right to information in their own language;
(12) the right to establish and maintain contacts with the citizens and associations outside of Montenegro, with whom they have common national and ethnic background, cultural and historic heritage, as well as religious beliefs;
(13) the right to establish councils for the protection and improvement of special rights.

Furthermore, forceful assimilation of the persons belonging to minority nations and other minority national communities shall be prohibited. The state shall protect the persons belonging to minority nations and other minority national communities from all forms of forceful assimilation.[48]

21. As of the declaration of independence (2006), Montenegro has assigned priority to the accession process to the EU. Thus, the Parliament adopted a Declaration on Montenegro's accession to the EU in June 2006, and the Stabilization and Association Agreement (SAA)[49] concluded between Montenegro and the EU

48. Article 80 of the Constitution of Montenegro.
49. The Stabilization and Association Agreement is a new type of mixed agreement that the European Community concludes with third countries, different from European accession agreements by which the countries of Central and Eastern Europe have acquired the status of candidate countries for the

entered into force in 2010, whereas Montenegro assumed the obligation of harmonizing all its current and future legislation with EU acquis.[50] Article 83 of the SAA stipulates that the parties shall cooperate in order to prevent and control illegal immigration and that Montenegro and the Member States of the EU shall readmit any of their nationals illegally present on the territory of Montenegro or on the territory of one of the Member States of the European Community. The parties also agree to conclude and fully implement the Readmission Agreement, including the obligation to readmit nationals of other countries and stateless persons. The Member States and Montenegro shall provide their nationals with appropriate identity documents (IDs) and shall extend to them the administrative facilities necessary for such purposes. With a view to the readmission of nationals, third-country nationals and stateless persons, the SAA laid down specific procedures between the European Community and Montenegro on the readmission of persons residing without authorization. Montenegro agrees to conclude readmission Agreements with the Stabilization and Association process countries and undertakes to take any necessary measures to ensure the flexible and rapid implementation of all readmission Agreements referred to in this Article. The Stabilization and Association Council shall establish other joint efforts that can be made to prevent and control illegal immigration, including trafficking and human trafficking and illegal migration networks. In implementing the process of harmonizing national legislation with the EU acquis, the Government has adopted a number of strategies, plans and programmes. Thus, the National Accession Program of Montenegro[51] was adopted, entailing an overview of all laws, strategies and plans to be adopted, as well as all activities to be undertaken, including migration and visa regime policy, human rights in the process of European integration of Montenegro and alignment with the EU acquis.

22. As of 19 December 2009, citizens of Montenegro have been able, with biometric passports, to travel visa-free to the Member States of the EU, in accordance with Regulation 539/20011. The decision to lift the visa obligation was based on a thorough assessment of Montenegro progress in fulfilling the requirements of the visa liberalization roadmap in areas including document security, border and migration management, asylum, the fight against organized crime and corruption, and fundamental rights related to freedom of movement. Visa-free travel remains one of the core achievements of these countries' European integration efforts to date. In a statement made to the Justice and Home Affairs Council on 8 November 2010, the Commission underlined that the integrity of the visa-free travel regime depended on each Western Balkan country continuing to implement the measures set out in its visa roadmap. The Commission established a post-visa liberalization monitoring mechanism, covering all the policy areas set out in the visa roadmaps, to evaluate the sustainability of reforms seeking to uphold the integrity of the visa-free travel regime. The Western Balkan countries adopted a joint declaration on visa-free travel

EU membership, *see* more Miloš Vukčević, *Unutrašnje tržište EU & osnovne slobode*, TRIM MNE – EU Approximation in Trade and Single Market Policies (Podgorica 2009), p. 126.

50. Article 72 of the Stabilization and Association Agreement concluded between the EU and Montenegro.

51. Government of Montenegro, *Montenegro's EU Accession Program 2014-2018* (Podgorica 2013).

that confirmed their resolute commitment to implementing the reforms necessary to maintain the integrity of the visa-free travel regime. In December 2012, each visa-free Western Balkan country began submitting to the Commission monthly statistics on migration flows to the EU. The Commission demanded each Western Balkan state to back up its political commitment to visa-free travel with concrete, effective policies on the ground. The Commission recommended that each visa-free state continues taking action in the following areas:

(1) Increase targeted assistance to minority populations, in particular the Roma, aiming to enhance their long-term socio-economic integration via educational, employment and vocational training programmes, including by implementing national strategies and using domestic assistance, supported by available EU assistance and bilateral assistance offered by EU Member States.
(2) Enhance operational cooperation and information exchange with neighbouring states, EU Member States and Schengen Associated States, the European Commission (EC) and, as appropriate, FRONTEX, Europol and European Asylum Support Office (EASO), in the fields of border management, migration, asylum and readmission, in accordance with EU and national legislation.
(3) Continue efforts to investigate facilitators of irregular migration and prosecute those who enable the abuse of the visa-free regime, in close cooperation with the law enforcement authorities of EU Member States, Schengen Associated States and Europol.
(4) In strict compliance with citizens' fundamental rights, enhance border controls and develop closer cooperation with EU Member States that have a direct responsibility for managing EU external borders.
(5) Enhance targeted information and awareness campaigns aimed at further clarifying to citizens the rights and obligations of visa-free travel, including information on liability for any abuse of rights under the visa-free regime.

In order to avoid abuse of a visa-free regime with EU and Schengen countries, the officers of border police are carrying out preventive checks on meeting the conditions for departure from Montenegro and entry into the EU and Schengen countries, related to:

- the amount of money for intended stay;
- reason for staying (letter of guarantee, tourist voucher, hotel booking, etc.);
- possession of the return ticket (air and maritime traffic);
- possession of passengers' health insurance;
- checking the length of stay in Schengen countries according to the border stamps affixed on passengers' passports;
- mandatory checking through current databases;
- validity of passports;
- other (unregistered residence in Montenegro, minors without escort or parents' consent, invalid documents for the vehicle).

23. The notification and information on the conditions of entry to EU Member States are set at the counters for the purchase of airline and ship tickets, as well as at border crossings where it is their check-in. Also, on the road border crossings with Serbia, Bosnia and Herzegovina and Kosovo, preventive checks on the reasons for travel and the fulfilment of conditions for travel have been increased if it becomes aware that the final destination of their travel is EU Member State. An aggravating circumstance is the fact that a significant number of citizens of Montenegro who seek asylum in EU countries do not travel directly from Montenegro. They travel to neighbouring countries from which they continue their journey to EU. There is no indication that the departure of the citizens of Montenegro towards EU countries with the aim of applying for asylum is organized by the smuggling groups. A significant number of Montenegrin citizens, encouraged by the fact that they have relatives among the Montenegrin diaspora in some EU countries, decide to go to those countries with the intention of seeking asylum. During the asylum procedure, these persons are getting social assistance and they are provided accommodation in collective centres. Aware that their applications will be rejected, a significant number of these people manage to find a job and gain income with which they return to Montenegro. Because of this, Montenegrin diplomats are trying, in their communication with representatives of Montenegrin diaspora associations in some EU countries, to send an appeal to Montenegrin emigrants to give the contribution from their side by not encouraging Montenegrin citizens in seeking an asylum.

24. The most important strategies of Montenegro adopted in the migration law area are as follows:

- Strategy for Integrated Migration Management in Montenegro for the period 2017–2020.[52]
- Schengen Action Plan.[53]
- Strategy for combating trafficking in human beings 2019–2024.[54]

52. Government of Montenegro, *Strategy for Integrated Migration Management in Montenegro for the Period 2017-2020* (Podgorica 2016). The new Integrated Border Management Strategy (IBM) for the period 2020–2024, which includes the new European concept of IBM is drafted and will be adopted in the 2020. IBM's new concept (in accordance with Art. 4 of the Regulation of the European Parliament and of the Council of 14 September 2016 on the European Border and Coast Guard, which obliges Member States to prepare their national IBM strategies in a uniform manner) should contribute to the uniform and harmonized implementation of border control rules and standards in accordance with the provisions of the Schengen Borders Code and European Union standards for border management. Present Integrated Border Management Strategy was mainly based on the IBM model from 2006 and the recommendations given by EU experts at various stages of its development.
53. The Government of Montenegro, at its session held on 23 February 2017, adopted the *Schengen Action Plan*, at the proposal of the Ministry of interior. The Schengen Action Plan (SAP) is an umbrella document covering the entire relevant Schengen acquis, and the concept of IBM and the Strategy (including the Action Plan) as an important element in this comprehensive process. It is necessary to avoid overlapping IBM Strategy and SAP in the future, which will be a challenge for all services involved in the concept of Integrated Border Management. The implementation of the new IBM Strategy in line with the new European concept of IBM will also be a challenge.
54. Government of Montenegro, *Strategy for Combating Trafficking in Human Beings 2019-2024* (Podgorica 2018). The establishment of the Working Group for Monitoring the Implementation of Strategy for combating trafficking in human beings 2019–2024, as well as the establishment of the

– Reintegration Strategy for persons returned under the Readmission Agreements for the period 2016–2020.[55]
– Strategy for permanent resolution of the problems of displaced and IDPs in Montenegro, with special reference on the Konik area, for the period 2017–2019.[56]
– Integrated Border Management Strategy for 2014–2018.[57]

25. The Strategy for Integrated Migration Management in Montenegro for the period 2017–2020 aims at full harmonization and establishment of the legal framework, as well as further strengthening of the institutional framework providing an effective implementation of the migration control policy in accordance with EU rules and standards, as well as the establishment of a monitoring system to monitor the Strategy and the implementation of action plans.[58] The ultimate objective of the Strategy is to establish a society with an efficient system and recognizable results in the field of integrated migration management, which will contribute to regional and overall stability in accordance with EU rules and standards.[59]

26. The basic goal of the Strategy of the Reintegration of Persons Returned under Agreement on the Readmission in the period 2016–2020 is the creation of preconditions for adequate access to the process of return and reintegration at all levels, through further improvement of the institutional framework, efficient process of assistance, education and established monitoring system for monitoring the Strategy and realizing the Action Plan for its implementation. Montenegro is determined to develop and improve the legal framework, institutions and administrative capacities, to cooperate with other states and international organizations, as well as to use all available capacities in the view of organizing human return and creating conditions for sustainable reintegration of returnees. The ultimate goal of the Strategy is the establishment of a society with an efficient system and recognizable results in the areas of return and reintegration.

Anti-Trafficking Task Force (consisting of representatives of the Ministry of Interior, the Police Directorate, the Prosecutor's Office and the Ministry of Justice) has taken a good step in strengthening institutional capacity. These two coordination bodies in charge for coordination and monitoring of implementation of the Strategy operate in a multisectoral manner and should enable better coherence between investigative and judicial bodies in the identification and investigation of cases of trafficking in human beings. Within the Ministry of Interior, the National Anti-Trafficking Office functions as a separate organizational unit, headed by the National Coordinator/Head of the National Office who is, at the same time, head of the Working Group for Monitoring the Implementation of the Strategy.

55. Government of Montenegro, *Reintegration Strategy for Persons Returned under the Readmission Agreements for the Period 2016-2020* (Podgorica 2015).
56. Government of Montenegro, *Strategy for Permanent Resolution of the Problems of Displaced and Internally Displaced Persons in Montenegro, with Special Reference on the Konik Area, for the Period 2017-2019* (Podgorica 2016).
57. Government of Montenegro, *Integrated Border Management Strategy for 2014-2018* (Podgorica 2013).
58. Government of Montenegro, *Report on the Implementation of the Action Plan for the Implementation of Strategies for Integrated Migration Management in Montenegro for the Period 2017-2020* (Podgorica 2018), p. 2.
59. *Ibid.*

27. With regard to the legal framework of migration, the EC in its Non-paper[60] stated, 'The legal framework for legal and irregular migration has been largely established since the entry into force of the new Law on Foreign Nationals in March 2018. The Law lays down the provisions on entry, exit, movement, residence, rights and work of foreigners in Montenegro, as well as irregular residence, return (including voluntary returns) and entry bans aiming at aligning the legal framework with the EU migration acquis governing the legal and irregular migrations.' Therefore, it can be concluded herein that the most significant activity in the field of migration in Montenegro in the previous period was the adoption of the new Law on International and Temporary Protection of Foreigners and the Law on Foreign Nationals. The EU acquis communautaire in the field of migration has been largely transposed into both these laws, and its implementation will trigger changes in the quality of this system and its efficiency.

28. The Law on International and Temporary Protection of Foreigners[61] started to apply in January 2018, which has been fully harmonized with the EU legislation and whereby Montenegro has introduced a new concept encouraging successful integration of foreigners into a receptive Montenegrin society, guaranteeing foreigners full protection of human, civil, economic, social and cultural and other rights. The enactment of this Law has established an efficient and unique asylum system in which foreigners seeking international protection are guaranteed, as in the EU countries, equal chances of success in the procedure, as well as guarantees of equal treatment. However, regardless of the law being implemented in Montenegro, there is still a lack of interest from foreigners seeking international protection to obtain protection in Montenegro. The statistics clearly indicate that these persons continue perceiving Montenegro as a transit country, and in most cases the procedures upon application are terminated since these persons do not wish to take part in the procedure; i.e., they leave Montenegro in the course of the proceedings. At the end of 2018, the Government of Montenegro adopted a new Decree on the Organization and Functioning of Public Administration, which, *inter alia*, created formal conditions for unifying competences for all persons in the international protection system, in such a way that the accommodation and assistance in the integration process into the Montenegrin society of persons with approved international protection have been transferred from the Ministry of Labor and Social Welfare to the jurisdiction of the Ministry of Interior.

29. On 26 December 2018, the Parliament adopted the Law on Amendments to the Law on International and Temporary Protection.[62] The reason for the adoption of this Law is primarily to create the prerequisites for the full integration of foreigners with approved international protection into the Montenegrin society. In 2017,

60. European Commission, *Non Paper for Montenegro* (Brussels 2019).
61. *Zakon o međunarodnoj i privremenoj zaštiti stranaca*, 'Official Gazette of Montenegro', Nos 002/17 of 10.1.2017, 003/19 of 15.1.2019.
62. *Zakon o izmjenama i dopunama Zakona o međunarodnoj i privremenoj zaštiti stranaca*, 'Official Gazette of Montenegro', No. 3/19.

849 applications for international protection were submitted to the Asylum Directorate, while in 2018, 3,104 applications for international protection were submitted.[63] In 2018, the highest number of applications was submitted by persons who, according to their statement, came from Syria (1,199), Pakistan (657) and Algeria (304). Moreover, in 2018, 28 complaints were brought before the Administrative Court[64] against decisions of the first-instance authority, 13 of which were dismissed as without merits, 7 complaints were accepted, while 8 complaints are pending decision before the Administrative Court. Furthermore, in 2018, a total of 4,570 foreigners seeking international protection were accommodated in the Reception Center, of which 2,424 were accommodated in the Centre and 2,146 were alternatively accommodated, which is a far greater number of foreigners seeking international protection than in 2017, when a total of 799 persons were accommodated, of which 518 were accommodated at the Centre and 281 in the alternative accommodations. The most common countries of origin of foreigners seeking international protection in 2018 were as follows: Syria, Pakistan, Morocco, Algeria, Palestine, Iraq, Libya, Iran, Afghanistan, and in 2017 Algeria, Morocco, Syria, Pakistan, Iraq, Afghanistan, Cuba, Iran, Tunisia, Russia, Armenia, Eritrea *(for more detailed information see* Part III Chapter 6*).*

30. Pursuant to the Law on International and Temporary Protection of Foreigners, a total of seven subordinate regulations have been adopted, the most important of which are the following:

- Rulebook on the layout and content of the form and the manner of issuing documents for foreigners who have applied for international protection, asylum seekers and foreigners under subsidiary protection.[65]
- Rulebook on the residence rules and house rules at the Reception Center.[66]
- Rulebook on the conditions of accommodation and the manner of providing accommodation for asylum seekers and foreigners under subsidiary protection.[67]
- Rulebook on determining the list of safe countries of origin of foreigners seeking international protection.[68]
- Decree on the amount of financial assistance to a foreigner seeking international protection and to an asylum seeker and a foreigner under subsidiary protection.[69]

63. Government of Montenegro, *Report on the Implementation of the Action Plan for the Implementation of the Strategy for Integrated Migration Management in Montenegro 2017-2020, for 2018* (Podgorica 2019), p. 6.
64. *Ibid.*
65. *Pravilnik o bližem načinu uzimanja otisaka prstiju i fotografije od stranca koji izražava namjeru za podnošenje zahtjeva za međunarodnu zaštitu*, 'Official Gazette of Montenegro', No. 072/17 of 1.11.2017.
66. *Pravilnik o pravilima boravka i kućnom redu u Prihvatilištu za strance,* 'Official Gazette of Montenegro', Nos 061/17 of 2.10.2017, 040/19 of 19.7.2019.
67. *Pravilnik o uslovima smještaja i načinu obezbjeđivanja smještaja azilanata i stranaca pod supsdijarnom zaštitom*, 'Official Gazette of Montenegro', No. 087/17 of 22.12.2017.
68. *Pravilnik o utvrđivanju liste sigurnih zemalja porjekla stranaca koji traže međunarodnu zaštitu*, 'Official Gazette of Montenegro', No. 069/19 of 18.12.2019.
69. *Uredba o visini novčane pomoći strancu koji traži međunarodnu zaštitu i azilantu i strancu pod subsdijarnom zaštitom*, 'Official Gazette of Montenegro', No. 028/18 of 27.4.2018.

31. When it comes to legislation activities, by adopting a new Law on Foreign Nationals, which entered into force on 3 March 2018, Montenegro has significantly improved the legislative framework in terms of regular and irregular migration, since it has been aligned with most EU directives governing this area, thereby EU migration standards are largely transposed into this Law. The new Law on Foreign Nationals, which superseded the Law on Foreign Nationals from 2008,[70] has been aligned with EU directives relating to the entry, exit, movement, stay and work of nationals of EU Member States and their families, studies, exchange of students, non-profit training or volunteer services, the stay and work of highly qualified third-country nationals, as well as the illegal stay and return of foreigners, the obligation to issue a return decision, a voluntary return. Among other things, this Law establishes clear, transparent and fair rules in the policy of return of persons illegally residing in Montenegro, representing an integral part of a well-managed migration policy. Persons who are illegally residing in Montenegro in the return procedure will be respected with their basic rights and dignity. The voluntary departure of Montenegro takes precedence over the forced return of a foreigner. Foreigners who are detained will be treated in accordance with international and national laws. The most significant changes enshrined in the new Law on Foreign Nationals relate to the entry, exit, movement, stay and work of nationals of EU Member States and their families. These provisions will apply from the day of Montenegro's accession to the EU, and it is crucial that these persons have equal rights as the citizens of Montenegro. In order to recruit highly qualified third-country nationals, the Law prescribes the procedures for obtaining temporary residence and work permits. By facilitating the regulation of residence and work of highly skilled workers and their families, our country will become more inciting, thus maintaining its competitiveness and economic growth. These norms will apply from the day of Montenegro's accession to the EU. The Parliament of Montenegro adopted the Law on Amendments to the Law on Foreign Nationals,[71] in order to simplify the procedure for issuing temporary residence and work permits for employment and seasonal employment. Specifically, there is a need to amend the Law on Foreign Nationals in order to provide the necessary personnel in the future – foreign workers, above all, in the fields of construction, tourism and hospitality services. A key new thing laid down in the Law pertaining to the work of foreigners is that the annual quota is set only by industry and not by occupation in which foreigners can be employed. In addition to this new thing, the deadlines for resolving the submitted application are shortened from twenty to fifteen days, foreigner is allowed to perform the duties of executive director at several employers, a foreign entrepreneur and executive director in companies in which they are the sole owners or owners of more than 51% of the capital can obtain a work permit even though they are over 67 years of age. Moreover, when applying for a temporary residence and work permit, a foreigner/employer is not required to obtain an excerpt from the systematization act with the employer. In addition, this Law has enabled the introduction of an electronic visa,

70. Law on Foreign Nationals, 'Official Gazette of Montenegro', Nos 082/08 of 31.12.2008, 072/09 of 30.10.2009, 032/11 of 1.7.2011, 053/11 of 11.11.2011, 027/13 of 11.6.2013, 061/13 of 30.12.2013.
71. *Zakon o izmjenama i dopunama Zakona o strancima,* 'Official Gazette of Montenegro', No. 3/2019.

which enables a greater degree of security, easier connection of the Visa Information System with the systems of the Schengen Member States and other security institutions, which is also Montenegro's obligation in the process of accession to the EU. A foreigner may apply for a visa to enter Montenegro electronically. The electronic visa application is fed into the Visa Information System, managed by the Ministry of Foreign Affairs. The visa application is processed in accordance with Article 19 of the Law on Foreign Nationals; i.e., the opinion of the Ministry of interior/Police Administration and the National Security Agency has to be obtained. After obtaining the opinion of the authorities responsible for the provision of opinions, the visa may be issued through the information system, in the manner that an appropriate form will be provided to the applicant, containing the bar code, photo and personal data of the applicant.

32. With the objective of implementing the Law on Foreign Nationals, twenty-six subordinate legislations have been adopted, which have been submitted to the EC for review after being translated into the English language. Following the positive opinion of the EC, the aforementioned subordinate legislation entered into force after its publication in the Official Gazette of Montenegro. The most important are as follows:

– Decision on determining the annual number of permits for temporary residence and work of foreigners in 2020.[72]
– Rulebook on more detailed manner and procedure of forced removal of foreigners.[73]
– Rulebook on more detailed manner and implementation of the special protection procedure for juvenile foreigners in ensuring the implementation of return measures.[74]
– Rulebook on more detailed manner of submitting the application and cancellation of the residence of foreigners through a tourist organization, or a competent local government authority.[75]
– Rulebook on more detailed conditions and manner of issuing a temporary residence permit for conducting scientific research work.[76]

72. *Odluka o utvrđivanju godišnjeg broja dozvola za privremeni boravak i rad stranaca za 2020. godinu,* 'Official Gazette of Montenegro', No. 069/19 of 18.12.2019.
73. *Pravilnik o bližem načinu i postupku prinudnog udaljenja stranca,* 'Official Gazette of Montenegro', No. 043/18 of 3.7.2018.
74. *Pravilnik o bližem načinu i sprovođenju postupka posebne zaštite maloljetnih stranaca prilikom obezbjeđenja primjene mjera za povratak,* 'Official Gazette of Montenegro', No. 073/18 of 19.11.2018.
75. *Pravilnik o bližem načinu podnošenja prijave i odjave boravka stranaca preko turističke organizacije, odnosno nadležnog organa lokalne uprave,* 'Official Gazette of Montenegro', No. 070/18 of 31.10.2018.
76. *Pravilnik o bližim uslovima i načinu izdavanja dozvole za privremeni boravak radi naučno istraživačkog rada,* 'Official Gazette of Montenegro', No. 073/18 of 19.11.2018.

- Rulebook on more detailed conditions and manner of issuing a temporary residence permit for participation in international student fellowship and student exchange programmes or other youth programmes.[77]
- Rulebook on more detailed conditions for issuing a work registration certificate of foreigners and application forms for registering work and the certificate on registration of work of foreigners.[78]
- Rulebook on the voluntary departure of foreigners.[79]
- Rulebook on the manner of issuing and the form of a permanent residence permit.[80]
- Rulebook on the rules of stay and house rules at the Foreigners Reception Center.[81]
- Rulebook on implementation of the procedure on the application for determining whether the applicant is a stateless person.[82]
- Decree on the criteria and procedure for determining the annual number of permits for temporary residence and work of foreigners.[83]
- Visa Regime Decree.[84],[85]

33. The new Law on Foreign Nationals[86] adopted on 1 April 2015 superseded the Law on Employment and Work of Foreigners.[87] Prior to its adoption, the normative framework governing the employment and work of foreign nationals was such that a foreign national first had to obtain a work permit, pursuant to the Law

77. *Pravilnik o bližim uslovima i načinu izdavanja dozvole za privremeni boravak radi učestvovanja u programima međunarodne razmjene učenika i studenata ili drugim programima mladih,* 'Official Gazette of Montenegro', No. 077/18 of 30.11.2018.
78. *Pravilnik o bližim uslovima za izdavanje potvrde o prijavi rada stranaca i obrascima prijave rada i potvrde o prijavirada stranaca*, 'Official Gazette of Montenegro', No. 043/18 of 3.7.2018.
79. *Pravilnik o dobrovoljnom odlasku stranaca*, 'Official Gazette of Montenegro', No. 068/18 of 19.10.2018.
80. *Pravilnik o načinu izdavanja i obrascu dozvole za stalni boravak*, 'Official Gazette of Montenegro', No. 020/19 of 4.4.2019.
81. *Pravilnik o pravilima boravka i kućnom redu u Prihvatilištu za strance*, 'Official Gazette of Montenegro', Nos 061/17, 040/19 of 19.7.2019.
82. *Pravilnik o sprovođenju postupka po zahtjevu za utvrđivanje da je podnosilac zahtjeva lice bez državljanstva*, 'Official Gazette of Montenegro', No. 072/18 of 13.11.2018.
83. *Uredba o kriterijumima i postupku za utvrđivanje godišnjeg broja dozvola za privremeni boravak i rad stranaca*, 'Official Gazette of Montenegro', No. 020/19 of 4.4.2019.
84. *Uredba o viznom režimu*, 'Official Gazette of Montenegro', No. 033/19 of 14.6.2019.
85. When it comes to the visa policy of Montenegro, it is not fully harmonized with the EU policy, especially in the part of the list of countries whose citizens need a visa; i.e., no visa is required. Due to the tourist interest of Montenegro, citizens of Russia, Armenia, Kazakhstan, Azerbaijan, Belarus, Cuba, Ecuador, Kuwait and Turkey are allowed to enter and stay for a short time without a visa, predominantly on a seasonal basis. Also, measures related to exemptions from the obligation to obtain seasonal visas (during the summer tourist season) are not in line with EU regulations and standards. The 2019 EC Progress Report stresses that Montenegro is still exempting the nationals of previous mentioned countries from the obligation of holding a short-stay visa – either seasonally for tourism or permanently. Seasonal exemption from visa requirements is not in line with the EU acquis and these countries are on the EU list of countries whose nationals are required to have an EU visa.
86. *Zakon o strancima*, 'Official Gazette of Montenegro', No. 56/14.
87. *Zakon o zapošljavanju i radu stranaca*, 'Official Gazette of Montenegro', Nos 22/08 and 32/11.

on Employment and Work of Foreigners, and only then submit a request to the Ministry of Interior for temporary residence on the basis of work and employment, pursuant to the Law on Foreign Nationals. So these were two separate proceedings. One of the most significant change brought by the Law on Foreign Nationals, which included all provisions regarding the employment and work of foreign nationals, was the introduction of a single and unique procedure for issuing work and residence permits, as a single document, in accordance with Directive 2011/98/EU of the European Parliament and of the Council of 13 December 2011 on a single application procedure for a single permit for third-country nationals to reside and work in the territory of a Member State and on a common set of rights for third-country workers legally residing in a Member State.

34. In addition to the two umbrella Laws – the Law on Foreign Nationals and the Law on International and Temporary Protection of Foreigners – it is important to mention the following laws that are relevant to migration law:

- Labor Law ('Official Gazette of Montenegro', Nos 49/08, 26/09, 88/09, 26/10 and 59/11).
- Law on Travel Documents ('Official Gazette of Montenegro', Nos 021/08 from 27.3.2008, 025/08 from 10.4.2008, 040/11 from 8.8.2011, 039/13 from 7.8.2013, 054/16 of 15.8.2016).
- Law on Employment and Exercise of Rights from Unemployment Insurance ('Official Gazette of Montenegro', Nos 14/10, 45/12, 61/13 and 20/15).
- Law on Pension and Disability Insurance ('Official Gazette of the Republic of Montenegro', Nos 54/03, 39/04, 61/04, 79/04, 80/04, 29/05, 14/07, 47/07, and the 'Official Gazette of Montenegro', Nos 12/07, 13/07, 79/08, 14/10, 78/10, 34/11, 40/11, 66/12, 38/13, 61/13 and 6/14), Law on Montenegrin Citizenship ('Official Gazette of Montenegro', Nos 13/08, 40/10 and 28/11).
- Law on the Central Population Register ('Official Gazette of the Republic of Montenegro', No. 49/07 and 'Official Gazette of Montenegro', No. 41/10) – Law on Travel Documents ('Official Gazette of Montenegro', Nos 21/08 and 25/08).
- Law on Business Environment Improvement ('Official Gazette of Montenegro', No. 40/10), Law on Foreign Affairs ('Official Gazette of Montenegro', No. 46/10).
- Law on Border Control ('Official Gazette of Montenegro', No. 72/09).
- Criminal Code ('Official Gazette of the Republic of Montenegro', Nos 70/03 and 47/06 and the 'Official Gazette of Montenegro', Nos 40/08, 25/10 and 32/11), Criminal Procedure Code ('Official Gazette of Montenegro', No. 57/09).
- Law on Misdemeanors ('Official Gazette of Montenegro', Nos 01/11, 06/11 and 39/11).
- Law on Health Care ('Official Gazette of the Republic of Montenegro', Nos 39/04 and 14/10), Law on Health Insurance ('Official Gazette of Montenegro', No. 06/16).
- Law on Internal Affairs ('Official Gazette of Montenegro', No. 44/12).
- Law on the recognition of foreign educational certificates and the equalization of qualifications ('Official Gazette of Montenegro', No. 57/11).

– Law on national professional qualifications ('Official Gazette of Montenegro', Nos 80/08 and 14/09).

35. The Law on Montenegrin Citizenship[88] (2008), which has been amended on several occasions, regulates the manner and conditions for the acquisition and loss of Montenegrin citizenship, as well as the keeping of the register of Montenegrin citizens. Montenegrin citizenship is acquired by origin, birth on the territory of Montenegro, admission, under international treaties and agreements. Acquisition of Montenegrin citizenship by admission requires discharge from the citizenship of the applicant's nationality. A person who has applied for Montenegrin citizenship but does not have the discharge certificate from the citizenship of another state may be issued with a guarantee that he will acquire Montenegrin citizenship if he meets certain conditions.[89] Therefore, dual citizenship is an obstacle to the acquisition of Montenegrin citizenship.

36. Along with becoming a United Nations (UN) member in 2006, Montenegro succeeded to all UN treaties ratified by its preceding countries as of 3 June 2006, including the 1954 Convention Relating to the Status of Stateless Persons. In 2007, Montenegro joined the Council of Europe and on 11 May 2007 signed the Council of Europe Convention on the Avoidance of Statelessness in relation to State Succession, which was eventually ratified on 2 March 2010, together with the 1997 European Convention on Nationality. In general, Law on Montenegrin Citizenship does not allow for dual citizenship since one of the conditions for acquiring Montenegrin citizenship is release from a citizenship of another state. However, there are several exceptions to this rule:

– Montenegrin emigrant and a member of his or her family up to the third degree of consanguinity in lineal terms may be granted Montenegrin citizenship if he or she takes up lawful and habitual residence for a minimum of two years and if basic legal conditions of this Law are satisfied.
– A person who has been married to a Montenegrin citizen for at least three years and who takes up lawful and habitual residence in Montenegro for at least five years may be granted Montenegrin citizenship.
– A person may be granted Montenegrin citizenship if it represents the economic, scientific, cultural, sport, national or other interest to Montenegro, without his or her release from another citizenship.
– Moreover, Montenegrin citizen who also had another citizenship on 3 June 2006 can retain citizenship of Montenegro.

37. Apart from the above-mentioned cases, dual citizenship can be acquired based on the ratified international agreements and treaties signed by Montenegro, subject to reciprocity. In 2009, the Government of Montenegro had set up grounds

88. *Zakon o crnogorskom državljanstvu*, 'Official Gazette of Montenegro', Nos 013/08 of 26.2.2008, 040/10 of 22.7.2010, 028/11 of 10.6.2011, 046/11 of 16.9.2011, 020/14 of 25.4.2014, 054/16 of 15.8.2016, 073/19 of 27.12.2019.
89. Article 9 of the Law on Montenegrin Citizenship.

for negotiations and for entering into bilateral agreements on dual citizenship between Montenegro and other states. Negotiations were initiated and the Government of Montenegro, in 2009, delivered the Draft of Agreement to competent authorities in the Republic of Serbia, the Republic of Macedonia, the Republic of Slovenia, the Republic of Croatia and Bosnia and Herzegovina and proposed beginning of negotiations on concluding of Bilateral Agreements on Dual Citizenship. Four rounds of negotiations were organized with the Delegation of the Republic of Serbia and the text of the Agreement is not harmonized. Delegation of the Government of Montenegro and Delegation of the Government of the Republic of Croatia had just one round of negotiations on concluding the Agreement on Dual Citizenship. There were no negotiations with competent authorities of the Republic of Slovenia and Bosnia and Herzegovina. Montenegro and Macedonia have entered Agreement on Dual Citizenship, dated 6 March 2009.

38. In November 2018, the Government adopted a Decision[90] introducing a citizenship by investment scheme. The Decision specified the criteria, method and procedures for the selection of investors who could obtain Montenegrin citizenship. This 'Economic Citizenship' programme was launched in January 2019 and aims at the implementation of development projects in a number of sectors – tourism, agriculture and manufacturing, as well as fostering development, especially in less developed municipalities. Applicants must meet the criteria of depositing EUR 450,000 in the coastal region and Podgorica in the account of the State of Montenegro, or EUR 250,000 in the northern region and central region except Podgorica, as well as EUR 100,000 for less developed areas. In addition, the applicant must deposit EUR 15,000 for himself, EUR 10,000 each for up to four family members, and EUR 50,000 for each subsequent family member as specified by the Minister for Sustainable Development and Tourism. However, this programme also carries certain risks to the European integration process, therefore in its 2019 Progress Report; the EC stated, 'Montenegro should put in place robust monitoring systems to counter the risks posed by such schemes, in particular to counter security risks, money laundering, tax evasion, terrorist financing, corruption and infiltration of organized crime. As a candidate country, Montenegro should refrain from any measure that could jeopardize attainment of the EU's objectives, when using its prerogatives to award nationality'[91] (for more detailed information *see* Part III Chapter 4 §4. Investment Activities).

39. The Law on Border Control[92] (2009) regulates border control and checks, as well as international border police cooperation. It is a modern Law drafted with the

90. Decision on the criteria, manner and procedure for selection of persons who can acquire Montenegrin citizenship by admission for the purpose of implementation of a special investment programme of special importance for the business and economic Interest of Montenegro (*Odluka o kriterijumima, načinu i postupku izbora lica koje može steći crnogorsko državljanstvo prijemom radi realizacije posebnog programa ulaganja od posebnog značaja za privredni i ekonomski interes Crne Gore*), 'Official Gazette of Montenegro', Nos 079/18 of 7.12.2018, 012/20 of 11.3.2020.
91. European Commission, *Montenegro Progress Report* (Brussels 2019).
92. *Zakon o graničnoj kontroli*, 'Official Gazette of Montenegro', Nos 072/09 of 30.10.2009, 020/11 of 15.4.2011, 040/11 of 8.8.2011, 039/13 of 7.8.2013, 017/19 of 19.3.2019.

expert support of the EC. Border control, under this Law, encompasses border control, border checks and assessment of threats to the security of the state border and is carried out in order to: secure the state border; protection of life and health of people and the environment; preventing the commission and detection of criminal offences and misdemeanours and finding and apprehending their perpetrators; prevention of illegal migration; preventing and detecting other activities and actions threatening the state border security, public order and public health.[93] Border control is carried out by the Police, which in the exercise of border control activities exercises the powers established by the law, attaining the objectives with the least harmful consequences. In the light of the above, the police are authorized to set up and use technical and other means of communication, service dogs, as well as other means under the Law. This Law provides for the cooperation of the police, customs, sanitary, health and other services in order to achieve the freedom of movement of persons and goods across the border (integrated border management (IBM)).

40. The Criminal Code of Montenegro, *inter alia*, prescribes criminal offences of relevance to migrants and their rights. Thus, the Criminal Code prescribes in Article 405 the criminal offence of 'Illegal crossing of the state border and smuggling of persons' falling under the group of crimes against public law and order. The offence of trafficking in human beings[94] has been prescribed as a separate offence other than smuggling under the Heading 'Criminal offences against humanity and other values guaranteed by international law.' In this chapter, along with the criminal offence of trafficking in human beings, there is also the criminal offence of 'Racial and other discrimination',[95] punishing anyone who on grounds of a difference in race, ethnic origin or affiliation violates basic human rights. There are also the criminal offences of 'Trafficking in Children for Adoption', 'Submission to Slavery and Transportation of Enslaved Persons',[96] 'Endangering Persons under International Protection'.[97] Moreover, criminal offences against freedoms and rights of persons and citizens that might be relevant to migrants are as follows: 'Violation of the right to use language and alphabet',[98] 'Violation of Equality',[99] 'Violation of freedom of expression of national or ethnic affiliation',[100] 'Violation of the freedom of movement and residence'.[101]

41. Regarding the alignment of migration legislation with the EU acts, the following are the most important:

Directives:

93. Article 2 of the Law on Border Control.
94. Article 444 of the Criminal Code.
95. Article 443 of the Criminal Code.
96. Article 445 of the Criminal Code.
97. Article 448 of the Criminal Code.
98. Article 158 of the Criminal Code.
99. Article 159 of the Criminal Code.
100. Article 160 of the Criminal Code.
101. Article 163 of the Criminal Code.

- 2000/43/EC implementing the principle of equal treatment between persons irrespective of racial or ethnic origin.
- 2000/78/EC establishing a general framework for equal treatment in employment – 2001/40/EC on the mutual recognition of decisions on the expulsion of third-country nationals – 2002/90/EC defining the facilitation of unauthorized entry, transit and residence.
- 2003/11/EC on assistance in case of transit for the purpose of removal by air.
- 2003/109/EC of 25 December 2003 concerning the status of third-country nationals who are long-term residents.
- 2003/86/EC of 22 September 2003 on the right to family reunification.
- 2004/57/EC on the organization of removal of third-country nationals from the territory of two or more Member States.
- 2004/81/EC on the residence permits issued to third-country nationals who are the victims of trafficking in human beings or who have been subject of an action to facilitate illegal migration, who cooperate with the competent authorities.
- 2004/114/EC of 13 December 2004 on the conditions of admission of third-country nationals for the purposes of study, pupil exchange, unremunerated training or voluntary service.
- 2004/38/EC of 29 April 2004 on the right of citizens of the Union and their family members to move and reside freely within the territory of the Member States.
- 2005/71/EC of 12 October 2005 on a specific procedure for admitting third-country nationals for the purposes of scientific research.
- 2008/115/EC of 16 December 2008 on common standards and procedures in Member States for returning illegally staying third-country nationals.
- 2009/50/EC of 25 May 2009 on the conditions of entry and residence of third-country nationals for the purposes of highly qualified employment.
- 2009/52/EC of the European Parliament and of the Council of 18 June 2009 providing for minimum standards on sanctions and measures against employers of illegally staying third-country nationals – 2014/36/ EU of 26 February 2014 on the conditions of entry and stay of third-country nationals for the purpose of employment as seasonal workers.
- 2014/66/EU of 15 May 2014 on the conditions of entry and residence of third-country nationals in the framework of an intra-corporate transfer; 2003/86/EC of 22 September 2003 on the right to family reunification (OJ L 251, 3 October 2003).
- 2011/95/EU of the European Parliament and of the Council of 13 December 2011 on standards for the qualification of third-country nationals or stateless persons as beneficiaries of international protection, for a uniform status for refugees or for persons eligible for subsidiary protection, and for the content of the protection granted (recast) (OJ L 337, 20 December 2011).
- 2013/32/EU of the European Parliament and of the Council of 26 June 2013 on common procedures for granting and withdrawing international protection (recast) (OJ L 180, 29 June 2013) – 2013/33/EU of the European Parliament and of the Council of 26 June 2013 laying down standards for the reception of applicants for international protection (recast) (OJ L 180, 29 June 2013).

- (EU) 2016/801 of the European Parliament and of the Council of 11 May 2016 on the conditions of entry and residence of third-country nationals for the purposes of research, studies, training, voluntary service, pupil exchange schemes or educational projects and au pairing.

Regulations:

- 1560/2003 of 2 September 2003 laying down detailed rules for the application of Council Regulation (EC) No. 343/2003 establishing the criteria and mechanisms for determining the Member State responsible for examining an asylum application lodged in one of the Member States by a third-country national (OJ L 222, 5 September 2003).
- 603/2013 603/2013 of the European Parliament and of the Council of 26 June 2013 on the establishment of 'Eurodac' for the comparison of fingerprints for the effective application of Regulation (EU) No 604/2013 establishing the criteria and mechanisms for determining the Member State responsible for examining an application for international protection lodged in one of the Member States by a third-country national or a stateless person and on requests for the comparison with Eurodac data by Member States' law enforcement authorities and Europol for law enforcement purposes, and amending Regulation (EU) No. 077/2011 establishing a European Agency for the operational management of large-scale IT systems in the area of freedom, security and justice (recast) (OJ L 180, 29 June 2013).
- 604/2013 of the European Parliament and of the Council of 26 June 2013 establishing the criteria and mechanisms for determining the Member State responsible for examining an application for international protection lodged in one of the Member States by a third-country national or a stateless person (recast) (OJ L 180, 29 June 2013).
- 118/2014 of 30 January 2014 amending Regulation (EC) No. 1560/2003 laying down detailed rules for the application of Council Regulation (EC) No. 343/2003 establishing the criteria and mechanisms for determining the Member State responsible for examining an asylum application lodged in one of the Member States by a third-country national (OJ L 222, 5 September 2003).
- 377/2004, of 19 February 2004, on the creation of an immigration liaison officer's network – 2252/2004, of 13 December 2004 on standards for security features and biometrics in passports and travel documents issued by Member States.

III. Administrative and Judicial Authorities

42. The organization and competence of the state administration are regulated primarily by the Decree on the Organization and Functioning of the State Administration,[102] which defines the competence of a number of authorities in charge of the adoption and application of regulations governing migration law, as well as the

102. *Uredba o organizaciji i nadležnosti državne uprave*, 'Official Gazette of Montenegro', Nos 087/18 of 31.12.2018, 002/19 of 11.1.2019, 038/19 of 5.7.2019.

already mentioned umbrella laws: the Law on Foreign Nationals, Law on international and temporary protection of foreigners, as well as other laws and subordinate legislation. Pursuant to the Law on Public Administration,[103] it is necessary to distinguish between public administration authorities, which may be under the ministries or bodies independent from the ministries. At the end of December 2018, the Government of Montenegro adopted a new Decree on the Organization and Functioning of the Public Administration, which stipulates that the Ministry of Interior, *inter alia*, carries out administrative tasks related to the accommodation of foreigners granted with the asylum or subsidiary protection and assistance in their integration into the society; provision of financial assistance to foreigners seeking international protection; coordinating the exercise of the legal rights of foreigners granted asylum or subsidiary protection; provision of support for inclusion in social, economic and cultural life; implementation of national, regional and international documents for resolving refugee issues; assistance in exercising the rights of Montenegrin citizens upon their return to Montenegro in accordance with the obligations laid down in the readmission agreement. These competences were taken over from the Ministry of Labor and Social Welfare. Persons with approved protection are under the competences of the Ministry of Internal Affair, which is obliged to provide them with accommodation for two years and to issue an Integration Plan ensuring full inclusion of persons with approved protection into the Montenegrin society.

43. In addition, the Ministry of Interior is competent to carry out administrative tasks relating to: citizenship, travel documents, immigration, granting asylum, naturalization, identity cards, residence and, in reference therewith, keeping of prescribed registers; personal identification number; personal name; birth registry. The Police Administration, *inter alia*, performs tasks related to: surveillance and security of the state border and exercising border control and control of the movement and stay of foreigners.

44. At the end of December 2018, the Government adopted a new Decree on Organization and Functioning of State Administration, which stipulates that the Ministry of Interior, among other things, performs administrative tasks related to accommodation of foreigners granted asylum or subsidiary protection and assistance with integration into society; providing financial assistance to foreigners seeking international protection; coordination in exercising the legally prescribed rights of foreigners who have been granted asylum or subsidiary protection; providing support for inclusion in social, economic and cultural life; implementation of national, regional and international documents for resolving refugee issues; assistance in exercising the rights of Montenegrin citizens upon their return to Montenegro in accordance with the obligations set out in the readmission agreements. These are jobs that have been transferred from the previous competence of the Ministry of Labor and Social Welfare to the competence of the Ministry of Interior. Persons

103. *Zakon o državnoj upravi*, 'Official Gazette of Montenegro', No. 078/18 of 4.12.2018.

with approved protection have passed into the competence of the Ministry of Interior, which is obliged to provide them with accommodation for two years and to adopt an Integration Plan that ensures persons with approved protection full inclusion in Montenegrin society.

45. The Ministry of Foreign Affairs and European Integration, *inter alia*, performs administrative tasks related to: representing Montenegro in relations with other countries, international organizations and other international institutions, as well as with their representations in Montenegro; communication and coordination of communication of other bodies with diplomatic and other missions of other countries and missions of international organizations in Montenegro; diplomatic-consular affairs and other professional affairs related to the fostering of political, economic, cultural-informative and other relations with other countries and international organizations; visa system; coordinating the harmonization of national regulations with the EU legal order, as well as the certification of the form and table of compliance with EU regulations; protection of the interests of Montenegro, its citizens and legal entities abroad. The Ministry of Foreign Affairs and European Integration shall keep a record of the visa applications submitted and a record of the visa issued.

46. The Ministry of Education, *inter alia*, carries out administrative tasks related to: student and academic staff mobility and international cooperation in the field of higher education, recognition of foreign educational certificates for completed primary, secondary and higher education and development and implementation of the National Qualifications Framework and compliance with the European Qualifications Framework.

47. The Ministry of Science, *inter alia*, carries out administrative tasks relating to: implementation of programmes of general interest integrating scientific research institutions and researchers into the European Research Area and international programmes in science; training and mobility of Montenegrin researchers with the objective of facilitating their work in research centres and institutes in Montenegro and abroad; regional cooperation and infrastructure integration in research; implementation of national and international scientific research projects; centres of excellence; upgrading the infrastructure necessary to carry out research; fostering scientific productivity; provision of incentives to publishing activities and organizing scientific congresses; inclusion of the scientific diaspora in scientific research activity in Montenegro; inclusion of internationally recognized scientists from other countries in research programmes and projects in Montenegro.

48. Ministry of Sustainable Development and Tourism, *inter alia*, carries out administrative tasks related to: coordination of activities for the preparation and monitoring of tourist seasons; keeping records of the number of tourists, accommodation capacities, financial effects and results of tourism operations; organizing tourist information activities; enhancing cooperation between the tourism and complementary sectors; cooperation with the National Tourism Organization and organization of tourist missions in other countries.

49. Ministry of Health, *inter alia*, carries out administrative tasks related to: healthcare, health insurance and provision of public healthcare. As of 3 June 2006, after the declaration of independence, Montenegro has taken over international agreements concluded by the former State Union. Pursuant to the aforementioned, twenty-two international social security agreements are effective.

50. Ministry of Human and Minority Rights, *inter alia*, carries out administrative tasks related to: protection of human rights and freedoms if such protection is not within the competence of other ministries, as well as the protection against discrimination.

51. The Ministry of Labor and Social Welfare, *inter alia*, carries out administrative tasks related to: labour relations, protection at work, wages and other income from and on the basis of labour; labour market, employment and adult education for the needs of the labour market in all forms of work except in government bodies; employment of persons with disabilities; protection of Montenegrin citizens at work abroad; international cooperation and international treaties within the competence of the Ministry; pension and disability insurance system and the field of war veterans' and disability protection; the protection of war veterans, war invalids, families of fallen combatants, civilian war invalids and their families; social protection, child protection, protection of persons with disabilities, protection of the elderly; social protection of asylum seekers, persons to whom the refugee status and subsidiary protection has been granted; family protection; cooperation with local government bodies on the development of services needed in municipalities; cooperation with the Red Cross of Montenegro, non-governmental organisations (NGOs), UN agencies and other international organizations; administrative procedure within the competence of the Ministry; keeping a register of General and Branch Collective Agreements, keeping the registers of trade union organizations, representative trade unions and the register of representative organizations of employers' associations; issuing authorizations for performing tasks in the field of occupational safety and keeping a register of issued authorizations; recognition of foreign certificates in non-formal and informal education, keeping the register of licensed providers of social and child welfare services, administrative oversight in the areas for which the ministry was established; as well as other assigned tasks.

52. Employment Agency is an institution that develops key innovative employment programmes for all job seekers. Office for Combating Trafficking in Human Beings operates under the General Secretariat of the Government of Montenegro and coordinates activities on the implementation of the National Strategy for Combating Trafficking in Human Beings, with the objective of providing high-quality protection of victims, prevention and prosecution of perpetrators.

53. Statistical Office (MONSTAT) carries out tasks related to the organization and conduct of statistical surveys, collection, processing, statistical analysis and publication of statistical data, production and development of methodologies for statistical surveys. Local self-government performs tasks related to meeting the needs of direct and common interest for the citizens of the municipality, i.e., local self-government.

54. An appeal may be lodged with the competent ministry against the decisions of state administration authorities, after which a party not satisfied with the decision of a ministry may lodge a complaint before the Administrative Court in Podgorica. The decisions of ministries may be appealed to the Appeals Commission, representing a professional authority established by the Law on Civil Servants and State Employees. If a party is not satisfied with the decision of the Appeals Commission, it may contest it before the Administrative Court (administrative dispute) by filing a complaint for annulment. An appeal may be filed against the judgments of the Administrative Court for the protection of legality to the Supreme Court of Montenegro. In case of violation of human and other constitutional rights, a constitutional complaint may be lodged with the Constitutional Court. A constitutional complaint may be filed by any physical person or legal entity, organization, settlement, group of persons and other forms of organization that do not have the legal entity status if they believe that their human rights or freedoms guaranteed by the Constitution have been violated by a specific act, action or inaction of a state authority, local self-government authority, or local government body, legal entity or other entity exercising public competences.[104] A constitutional appeal is allowed after exhausting all effective legal remedies, implying that the complainant has exhausted all legal remedies to which he was entitled. Migration law is often the subject of disputes before misdemeanour courts, of which there are three in Montenegro: Podgorica, Budva and Bijelo Polje. The party not satisfied with the result of the procedure may lodge an appeal before the Higher Misdemeanor Court in Podgorica.

55. The Ombudsman is an independent state institution governed by the Law on the Protector of Human Rights and Freedoms.[105] The Protector independently and autonomously, based on the principles of justice and fairness, undertakes measures for the protection of human rights and freedoms, when they have been violated by an act, activity or omission of state bodies, state administration bodies, local self-government bodies and local authorities, public services and other holders of public authorizations, as well as measures to prevent torture and other forms of inhuman or degrading treatment and punishment and anti-discrimination measures. The Protector has no authority in relation to the work of the courts, except in the cases stipulated by this Law.[106] Anyone who believes that his/her rights or freedoms have been

104. Law on Constitutional Court of Montenegro *(Zakon o Ustavnom sudu Crne Gore)*, 'Official Gazette of Montenegro', Nos 011/15 of 12.3.2015, 055/19 of 27.9.2019, Art. 68.

105. *Zakon o zaštitniku ljudskih prava i sloboda*, 'Official Gazette of Montenegro', Nos 042/11 of 15.8.2011, 032/14 of 30.7.2014, 021/17 of 31.3.2017.

106. Article 2 of the Law on the Protector of Human Rights and Freedoms.

violated by an act, activity or omission of a body may address to the Protector. The Protector also acts at its own initiative. The proceedings before the Protector are free of charge.[107]

§3. OVERVIEW OF INTERNATIONAL LEGAL INSTRUMENTS

56. Montenegro is a signatory party to almost all legal instruments of the UN and the Council of Europe concerning migration, freedom of movement and human rights. Many of these instruments were in force in Montenegro while it was a part/member of the Kingdom of Yugoslavia (1918–1943), SFRY (1945–1992), FRY (1992–2003), State Union of Serbia and Montenegro (2003–2006), when these instruments were ratified by these states. Following the declaration of independence in 2006, Montenegro as a successor state had to reclaim membership in the aforementioned organizations and to ratify the legal instruments herein. In June 2012, Montenegro opened accession negotiations with the EU and, at the time of writing this monograph, Montenegro has opened all negotiation chapters, including Chapter 24 'Justice, Freedom and Security' covering, *inter alia*, migrations, asylum, as well as the freedom of movement, with the exception of Chapter 8 (Competition), while the three negotiation chapters have been temporarily closed. Although it did not close Chapter 24, in seven years of negotiations, most of the regulations governing migration area have been aligned with the EU acquis communautaire, as evidenced by the latest European Commission Progress Report on Montenegro:[108]

> The legal framework was further strengthened with the entry into force of the new Law on Foreign Nationals in March 2018, and the adoption of 20 pieces of secondary legislation. This important legal package, largely in line with the EU acquis, regulates key aspects of legal and irregular migration. With the adoption of the secondary legislation for the Law on asylum, Montenegro is now equipped with a largely EU-compliant legal framework.

Furthermore, it is also important to emphasize that ratified and published international agreements are directly applicable to the legal order of Montenegro under Article 9 of the Constitution and have supremacy in case of the conflict of national and international laws.

I. UN/League of Nations

57. Montenegro has ratified the following UN conventions and protocols important for the status and fundamental rights of migrants:

– 1951 Geneva Conventions and the 1967 Refugee Status Protocol.

107. Article 3 of the Law on the Protector of Human Rights and Freedoms.
108. European Commission, *Montenegro Progress Report* (Brussels 29 May 2019).

- 1984 Convention against Torture, Torture and Other Cruel, Inhuman or Degrading Treatment or Punishment.
- 1989 Convention on the Rights of the Child.
- 1965 Convention on the Elimination of All Forms of Racial Discrimination.
- 1966 International Covenant on Civil and Political Rights.
- 1966 International Covenant on Economic, Social and Cultural Rights.
- 1979 Convention on the Elimination of All Forms of Discrimination against Women.
- 2006 Convention on the Rights of Persons with Disabilities.
- 1960 Convention against Discrimination in Education.
- Convention on the Status of Stateless Persons, 1954.
- European Convention on Human Rights, 1950.
- 1995 Framework Convention for the Protection of National Minorities.
- United Nations Convention on the Reduction of Statelessness.
- Convention on Migration for Employment.
- Refugee Status Protocol.
- Convention on Migrant Workers (Supplementary Provisions).
- European Convention on the Legal Status of Migrant Workers.
- Schengen Implementation Convention.
- International Convention for the Protection of the Rights of Migrant Workers and Members of Their Families.
- Protocol against the smuggling of migrants by land, sea and air.
- Protocol for the Prevention, Suppression and Punishment of Trafficking in Human Beings, in particular Women and Children, as amended by the Convention against Transnational Organized Crime.
- Convention for the Suppression of Trafficking in Human Beings – European Social Charter International Convention for the Suppression of the Traffic in Women and Children (League of Nations, ratification date: 28 February 1929).
- International Convention for the Suppression of the 'White Slave Traffic' (League of Nations, entered into force: 1929).
- Convention for the Suppression of the Traffic in Persons and of the Exploitation of the Prostitution of Others (UN, ratification date: 28 December 1950).
- Supplementary Convention on the Abolition of Slavery, the Slave Trade, and Institutions and Practices Similar to Slavery (UN, ratification date: 14 January 1958).
- Convention Relating to the Status of Refugees (UN, ratification date: 29 September 1959).
- Convention Related to the Status of Stateless Persons (UN, entered into force: 6 June 1960).
- International Convention on the Elimination of All Forms of Racial Discrimination (UN, entered into force: 1 June 1967).
- Additional Protocol on the Status of Refugees of 1967 – 'New York Protocol' (UN, ratification date: 11 October 1967).
- Convention on the Elimination of All Forms of Discrimination against Women (UN, entered into force: 11 November 1967).
- UN International Covenant on Civil and Political Rights (UN, ratification date: 30 January 1971).

- Convention on the Rights of the Child (UN, ratification date: 18 December 1990).
- Convention against Torture and Other Cruel, Inhuman or Degrading Treatment or Punishment (UN, ratification date: 20 June 1991).
- Amendment to Article 43, paragraph 2, of the Convention on the Rights of the Child (UN, ratification date: 26 June 1997).
- Optional Protocol to the International Covenant on Civil and Political Rights (UN, ratification date: 22 June 2001).
- Second Optional Protocol to the International Covenant on Civil and Political Rights, Aiming at the Abolition of the Death Penalty (UN, ratification date: 22 June 2001).
- Protocol against the Smuggling of Migrants by Land, Sea and Air, supplementing the United Nations Convention against Transnational Organized Crime (UN, ratification date: 6 September 2001).
- Optional Protocol to the Convention on the Rights of the Child on the Sale of Children, Child Prostitution and Child Pornography (UN, ratification date: 2 July 2002).
- Protocol to Prevent, Suppress and Punish Trafficking in Persons, especially Women and Children, supplementing the United Nations Convention against Transnational Organized Crime (UN, entered into force: 25 December 2003).
- Convention on the Protection on the Rights of All Migrant Workers and Members of Their Families (UN, signed: 11 November 2004).
- Optional Protocol to the Convention against Torture and other Cruel, Inhuman or Degrading Treatment or Punishment – OPCAT (UN, ratification date: 1 December 2005).
- Convention on the Reduction of Statelessness (UN, signed: 7 December 2011).

II. Council of Europe

58. Montenegro acceded to the Council of Europe in 2006 and ratified the following migration legal instruments:

- European Convention on Extradition (date of ratification: 30 September 2002; entered into force: 29 December 2002).
- Additional Protocol to the European Convention on Extradition (date of ratification: 30 September 2002; entered into force: 29 December 2002).
- European Convention on Mutual Legal Assistance in Criminal Matters (date of ratification: 30 September 2002; entered into force: 29 December 2002).
- Convention on the Transfer of Sentenced Persons (date of ratification: 30 September 2002; entered into force: 1 January 2003).
- First Additional Protocol to the European Convention on Mutual Legal Assistance in Criminal Matters (date of ratification: 23 June 2003; entered into force: 21 September 2003).
- Additional Protocol to the Convention on the Transfer of Sentenced Persons (date of ratification: 30 September 2002; entered into force: 1 January 2003).

- European Convention for the Protection of Human Rights and Fundamental Freedoms (date of ratification: 3 March 2004).
- Protocol No. 2 to the Convention for the Protection of Human Rights and Fundamental Freedoms concerning the possibility of the European Court of Human Rights to provide advisory opinions (date of ratification: 3 March 2004).
- Protocol No. 3 to the Convention for the Protection of Human Rights and Fundamental Freedoms which are changed on 29, 30 and 34 Convention Article (date of ratification: 3 March 2004).
- Protocol No. 4 to the Convention for the Protection of Human Rights and Fundamental Freedoms, securing certain rights and freedoms other than those already included in the Convention and in the first Protocol thereto (date of ratification: 3 March 2004; entered into force: 3 March 2004).
- Protocol No. 5 to the Convention for the Protection of Human Rights and Fundamental Freedoms amending Articles 22 and 24 of the Convention (date of ratification: 3 March 2004).
- Protocol No. 6 to the Convention for the Protection of Human Rights and Fundamental Freedoms, concerning the abolition of the death penalty (date of ratification: 3 March 2004).
- Protocol No. 7 to the Convention for the Protection of Human Rights and Fundamental Freedoms (date of ratification: 3 March 2004; entered into force: 6 January 2004).
- Protocol No. 8 to the Convention for the Protection of Human Rights and Fundamental Freedoms (date of ratification: 3 March 2004; entered into force: 3 March 2004).
- Protocol No. 11 to the Convention for the Protection of Human Rights and Freedoms, amending the control system established by the Convention (date of ratification: 3 March 2004; entered into force: 3 March 2004).
- Protocol No. 12 to the Convention on the Protection of Human Rights and Fundamental Freedoms (date of ratification: 3 March 2004; entered into force: 1 April 2005).
- Protocol No. 13 to the Convention on the Protection of Human Rights and Fundamental Freedoms, concerning the abolition of the death penalty in all circumstances (date of ratification: 3 March 2004; entered into force: 1 July 2004).
- Protocol No. 14 to the Convention on Human Rights and Fundamental Freedoms, amending the control system established by the Convention (date of ratification: 9 June 2005; entered into force: 9 June 2005).
- Convention for the Protection of Individuals with regard to Automatic Processing of Personal Data regarding supervisory authorities and transborder data flows (date of ratification: 9 June 2005; entered into force: 1 January 2006).
- Additional Protocol to the Convention for the Protection of Individuals with regard to Automatic Processing of Personal Data regarding supervisory authorities and transborder data flows (date of ratification: 9 June 2005; entered into force: 1 January 2006).
- Second Additional Protocol to the European Convention on Mutual Legal Assistance in Criminal Matters (date of ratification: 26 April 2007; entered into force: 1 August 2007).

- Convention on Action against Trafficking in Human Beings (signed: 16 May 2005).
- Convention on the Protection of Children against Sexual Exploitation and Sexual Abuse (signed on 25 October 2007).
- First Additional Protocol to the Convention on the Protection of Individuals with regard to Automatic Processing of Personal Data, regarding supervisory authorities and the transborder data flows (signed: 2 February 2008).

III. International Labour Organization

59. As one of the successors to SFRY, Montenegro is also applying the following International Labour Organization (ILO) Conventions:

- Convention No. 97, Migration for Employment Convention (date of ratification: 5 November 1962).
- Convention No. 143, concerning Migrations in Abusive Conditions and the Promotion of Equality of Opportunity and Treatment of Migrant Workers (date of ratification: 1 December 1980).

IV. Hague Conference on Private International Law

60. Montenegro applies the following conventions of the Hague Conference on Private International Law relevant to migration matters:

- Convention Abolishing the Requirement of Legalization for Foreign Public Documents of 5 October 1961.
- Convention on the Service Abroad of Judicial and Extrajudicial Documents in Civil or Commercial Matters of 15 November 1965.
- Convention on the Civil Aspects of International Child Abduction of 25 October 1980.
- Convention on International Access to Justice of 25 October 1980.

61. Montenegro has acceded to but pending signature of the following conventions of the Hague Conference on Private International Law:

- Convention relating to the settlement of the conflicts between the law of nationality and the law of domicile of 15 June 1955.
- Convention on the law applicable to maintenance obligations towards children of 24 October 1956.
- Convention concerning the powers of authorities and the law applicable in respect of the protection of infants of 5 October 1961.
- Convention on Protection of Children and Co-operation in Respect of Intercountry Adoption of 29 May 1993.

V. European Union

62. The Agreement between Montenegro and the European Community on readmission (return and admission) of persons without residence permit entered into force on 1 January 2008, and represents a major legal instrument governing readmission issues in the context of relations with the EU. It aims at facilitating the return of irregular migrants, i.e., persons residing illegally in an EU Member State or in Montenegro. It applies not only to nationals of the requesting country but also to any individual who illegally entered the requesting country after his stay or transit in the requesting country. Montenegro is an area with significant population movements both inside and outside the country, and the reasons for these movements rested on political, religious, ethnic, economic and demographic circumstances. Visa liberalization for Montenegrin citizens travelling to Schengen countries has been in force since as of 19 December 2009; thus, the readmission agreements are getting their full significance. The SAA between Montenegro and the EU, which has been in force as of May 2010, recognizes the issue of migration and readmission as priority issues, which occupy a high place in the Agreement itself. Thus, Title VII – Justice, Freedom, Security, Article 83 of the SAA provides:

> The Parties shall cooperate in order to prevent and control illegal immigration. To this end, Montenegro and the Member States shall readmit any of their nationals illegally present on their territories and the Parties agree to conclude and fully implement an Agreement for readmission, including an obligation for the readmission of nationals of other countries and stateless persons. The Member States and Montenegro shall provide their nationals with appropriate identity documents and shall extend to them the administrative facilities necessary for such purposes. Specific procedures for the purpose of readmission of nationals, third country nationals and stateless persons shall be laid down in the Agreement between the Community and Montenegro on the readmission of persons residing without authorization. Montenegro agrees to conclude readmission Agreements with the Stabilization and Association process countries. Montenegro undertakes to take any necessary measures to ensure the flexible and rapid implementation of all readmission Agreements referred to in this Article. The Stabilization and Association Council shall establish other joint efforts that can be made to prevent and control illegal immigration, including trafficking and illegal migration networks.

63. The conclusion and implementation of readmission agreements, i.e., readmission of persons who do not have a residence permit, are one of the obligations of Montenegro, which, *inter alia*, represents the basis for controlling and preventing illegal migration. Readmission agreements represent an important policy instrument for the return of migrants and asylum seekers from the EU Member States, which defines the obligation of States Parties to readmit their nationals as well as third-country nationals and stateless persons. Montenegro has concluded, and since January 2008 has been implementing with the European Community an agreement on the readmission of persons without residence permits, on the basis of which the implementation protocols have been concluded with the Republic of Slovenia,

Malta, the Republic of Austria, Bulgaria, the Czech Republic, the Republic of Germany, the Benelux States, the Slovak Republic, the Republic of Estonia, Hungary and the Kingdom of Spain. Montenegro has signed and applies readmission agreements with: Albania, Bosnia and Herzegovina, Serbia, Kosovo, Macedonia, Moldova, Turkey, Azerbaijan, the Kingdom of Norway and the Swiss Confederation. Activities on concluding a readmission agreement with Georgia, Iceland, Ukraine, and China are also underway.

64. In April 2016, the Government of Montenegro adopted a Reintegration Strategy for persons returned on the basis of a readmission agreement for the period 2016–2020, in line with European standards in this area and tasked the Ministry of Interior to report the Government thereof. Pursuant to the Decision of the Minister of Internal Affairs of 30 August 2017, the intersectoral working group for monitoring the strategy implementation has been established. In addition to the representatives of the Ministry of Interior, the members of this working group are also the representatives of the Ministry of Labor and Social Welfare, Ministry of Foreign Affairs, Ministry of Education, Ministry of Health, Police Administration, the Directorate for the Care of Refugees, Directorate for Inspection Affairs, Tax Administration, Association of Municipalities of Montenegro, Statistical Office of Montenegro, Employment Agency of Montenegro, Red Cross of Montenegro and the International Organization for Migration (IOM). The intersectoral working group was tasked with managing, organizing and coordinating the activities of state administration bodies and other competent organizations in the implementation of the Strategy and Action Plan for its implementation; establishing priorities, dynamics and timelines for implementation; evaluating the results achieved; and proposing an Action Plan for the implementation of the Strategy. In March 2018, the Government adopted the 2018 and 2019 Action Plans for the implementation of the Reintegration Strategy for persons returned on the basis of a readmission agreement for the period 2016–2020. The most significant activities implemented during 2018 pertained to the establishment of teams to support the reintegration of returnees in local communities. The Government of Montenegro at the end of December 2018 adopted a new Decree on the Organization and Functioning of Public Administration, transferring the competence of assisting in the exercise of the rights of Montenegrin citizens upon their return to Montenegro in accordance with the obligations set out in the readmission agreement from the Ministry of Labor and Social Welfare to the Ministry of Interior.[109] In the light of the above, in order to create a functioning, efficient and comprehensive system of international protection, in addition to the implementation of international readmission agreements, the tasks of assisting in the exercise of the rights of Montenegrin citizens upon their return to Montenegro are currently the responsibility of one state authority (Ministry of Interior). This solution guarantees the successful and quality implementation of standards and policies governing this area. Of course, the most significant in the previous period is the decrease in the number of Montenegrin nationals who are seeking consent to return

109. Government of Montenegro, *Report on the Implementation of the Action Plan for the Implementation of the Strategy for Reintegration of Persons Returned on the Basis of Readmission Agreements for the Period 2016-2020*, for 2018, p. 2.

to Montenegro, thus in 2016 readmission requests were submitted by 965 persons, in 2017 by 756 persons, while in 2018 the readmission requests were submitted by 619 persons, which means that this number has decreased by 35% compared to 2016.[110]

65. In the Non-paper of the EC[111] from November 2018, it was concluded that the 'Readmission Agreements with neighboring countries continued to be implemented satisfactorily, except with Albania. Despite the fact that irregular migrants enter Montenegro mainly through the Albanian-Montenegrin border, Montenegro reports that Albania's acceptance rate for readmission requests from Montenegro is very low: in the period January-September 2018 Montenegro reported that only 14 people were readmitted by Albania, out of 159 requests (under both the regular and the accelerated procedures). This creates an additional challenge for Montenegro's reception capacity, as, on the outward side of the migration route; the country smoothly fulfils its readmission obligations vis-à-vis Bosnia and Herzegovina. Montenegro accepted 471 migrants from neighboring countries during the reporting period, including 455 from Bosnia and Herzegovina.' Furthermore, in this Non-paper, the EC concluded that the 'the Readmission Agreement with the EU continued to be implemented smoothly, with a return rate for Montenegrin nationals higher than 100% in 2016 and 2017 and relatively low absolute numbers (730 return decisions issued towards Montenegrin nationals in 2017)'. According to Montenegrin national statistics, all readmission requests sent by EU Member States between January and June 2018 concerning Montenegrin citizens (230 cases) were accepted. A total of 92% of these requests came from Germany. As regards EU readmission, requests for third-country nationals, refused requests mostly concern citizens from the Roma community with an invalid passport from the former Yugoslavia, for which the evidence of stay in Montenegro prior to their departure to an EU Member State is not recognized by Montenegro.

66. In 2018, as in previous years, the largest number of requests was received by the competent authorities of the Federal Republic of Germany, followed by France, Sweden, Switzerland, Austria; thus the total number of persons who submitted return request to Montenegro is 619, and Germany, 539 or 87%.[112]

67. The Agreement on Cooperation with FRONTEX was signed in October 2019, and it will enable the engagement of FRONTEX teams in Montenegro, i.e., the implementation of joint border controls at border crossings, border surveillance, interviewing and determining the nationality of migrants. The new Agreement is another step forward in controlling migration flows, combating irregular migration and cross-border crime, including migrant smuggling, human trafficking and terrorism. All activities will be carried out by FRONTEX staff in cooperation with the Montenegrin border police.

---

110. *Ibid.*
111. European Commission, *Montenegro Non – Paper* (Brussels 2018).
112. *Ibid.*, str. 6.

Table 1 presents statistics on the implementation of the Readmission Agreements related to the number of accepted readmission requests from EU Member States, as well as the number of accepted readmission requests from neighbouring countries and the number of readmission requests submitted by Montenegro to neighbouring countries. As can be seen from Table 1, the number of readmission requests from EU Member States is declining from year to year, while the number of readmission requests coming from neighbouring countries and the number of readmission requests submitted by Montenegro to neighbouring countries are growing from year to year as a result of the transit of migrants through the Western Balkans on their way to EU countries.

Table 1 Statistics on the Implementation of the Readmission Agreements[113,114]

Given Consent for Acceptance of Persons from EU Member States					
2017		**2018**		**2019**	
553		415		274	
Given Consent for Acceptance and Hand Over (By Number of Persons) from Neighbouring Countries					
2017		**2018**		**2019**	
acceptance	**hand over**	**acceptance**	**hand over**	**acceptance**	**hand over**
498	105	727	135	2,098	385

113. Ministry of Interior work reports for 2017, 2018 and 2019.
114. *Ibid.*

Part I. Border Control and Entrance

Chapter 1. Organization of Border Control

§1. General Framework

68. The borders of Montenegro with the former republics of the former SFRY were determined and defined in accordance with the 1974 SFRY Constitution, and as such, after the restoration of independence, were recognized and confirmed as the national borders. The state border of Montenegro extends over land, sea, lakes and rivers and its depth is due to the indeterminacy of the border line with neighbouring countries – is set at approximately 840.4 km. The land border (hereinafter referred to as 'the green border') is 571.6 km long, 50.5 km lake border and 81.3 km river border and 137 km sea border (hereinafter referred to as 'the blue border'). The length of the state border with the Republic of Croatia amounts to about 41.7 km, Bosnia and Herzegovina 254.4 km, the Republic of Serbia 168.5 km, the Republic of Kosovo 75.6 km and the Republic of Albania 207.2 km. The state border is established only with the Republic of Albania.

69. There are twenty-eight border crossing points in the territory of Montenegro, being as follows: road nineteen, air two, maritime five and railway two, of which two border crossing points with the Republic of Croatia, eight with Bosnia and Herzegovina, six with the Republic of Serbia, one with the Republic of Kosovo and four with the Republic of Albania.

70. Upon accession to the EU, Montenegro will share internal borders with the Republic of Croatia and take control of the EU's external land borders with Bosnia and Herzegovina, the Republic of Serbia, the Republic of Kosovo and the Republic of Albania. Moreover, the number of border crossing points will be reviewed along the future external borders (Bosnia and Herzegovina, the Republic of Serbia, the Republic of Kosovo and the Republic of Albania), and border crossing points will be determined for international and border traffic. Following the process of recategorization of border crossings and the signing of agreements with neighbouring countries, border crossing points will be divided into the following categories: border crossing points for international passenger traffic and goods traffic with all inspection services; border crossing points for international passenger traffic and goods traffic; border crossing points for international passenger traffic and border crossing points for border traffic.

71. In order to meet its border management commitment and to further strengthen partnership, stability and economic growth and reduce security risks, Montenegro established IBM in 2006 and continued to improve this system in line with recommendations and best EU practice. The last and currently effective IBM Strategy 2014–2018 was adopted in 2014, as well as the Action Plan for its implementation. The main objective of the Strategy is to meet the criteria for Montenegro's accession to the EU and the Schengen Area; thus it is necessary to ensure the efficient work of the border police and other competent border services for the purpose of preserving the national security and security of the EU, especially with regard to combating illegal migration and cross-border crime. The Montenegrin Strategy will follow the concept of the EU IBM and will be grounded on a four-tier access control model (four control filters). The 2019 Action Plan for the Implementation of the Integrated Border Management Strategy was developed on the basis of the Strategy and the Framework Action Plan for the Implementation of the Integrated Border Management Strategy for the period 2014–2018, as well as on the progress made in 2014, 2015, 2016, 2017 and 2018, with reference to the unimplemented measures from the Framework Action Plan and in accordance with the recommendations of the Expert Mission for External Borders and Schengen from June 2018. The current Integrated Border Management Strategy 2014–2018 follows the concept of the EU IBM and has been grounded upon the four-tier access control model (four control filters). The new Regulation (EU) 2016/1624 of 14 September 2016 on the European Border and Coast Guard[115] has amended the structure of the European IBM concept, establishing eleven strategic components, which requires the development of a new strategy, as well as compliance with the new EU IBM concept. The recommendations issued in the Report of the Border Management Expert Mission,[116] held in the period from 25 to 29 June 2018, emphasized, *inter alia*, that the new IBM Strategy should be developed in compliance with the EU processes. Therefore, the new Strategy should be developed in accordance with the new European IBM concept laid down in the aforementioned Regulation and in accordance with the main elements for developing the European IBM Strategy of 14 March 2018. A key recommendation is that a development of a new Strategy should be started, but that it should be finalized after the European Border and Coast Guard Agency (FRONTEX) prepares an EU IBM technical and operational strategy and adopts a new IBM concept. Based on the Opinion of the EC that the effectiveness of the current IBM Strategy should be extended until the end of 2019 to allow for enough time for the development of a new Strategy in compliance with the

---

115. Regulation (EU) 2016/1624 of the European Parliament and of the Council of 14 September 2016 on the European Border and Coast Guard and amending Regulation (EU) 2016/399 of the European Parliament and of the Council and repealing Regulation (EC) No. 863/2007 of the European Parliament and of the Council, Council Regulation (EC) No. 2007/2004 and Council Decision 2005/267/EC.

116. Government of Montenegro, *Action Plan for the Implementation of the Integrated Border Management Strategy for 2019, with the Report on the Implementation of the Action Plan for 2018* (Podgorica, 2019), p. 6.

revised EU IBM concept, the Government of Montenegro has extended the effectiveness of the Strategy until the end of 2019.[117] The new Integrated Border Management Strategy will be significantly different from the current one, bearing in mind that the Government of Montenegro, at its session of 23 February 2017, adopted the Schengen Action Plan, for avoiding the overlapping of measures envisaged in these two strategic documents.

72. Montenegrin legislation governing the IBM is permanently aligned with the EU acquis communautaire and the IBM best practice. The legal and administrative framework for the preparation of external border management, i.e., border control, is harmonized with the EU standards in this area. In order to improve the situation in the IBM area, the concept of EU IBM is continuously monitored and the Montenegrin IBM adapted thereof, especially in the implementation of procedures, technical equipment and border infrastructure. In March 2019, the Parliament of Montenegro adopted the amendments to the Law on Border Control,[118] primarily due to the need to align the Law with the EU acquis. The EC gave a positive opinion, emphasizing that the Law has been fully aligned with the Regulation of the European Parliament and of the Council of 9 March 2016 on a Union Code on the rules governing the movement of persons across borders (Schengen Borders Code), commending that at this stage the Law has entirely fulfilled all that was requested by the EC. In the development of this Law, in the period from 14 to 18 May 2018, an external support of twenty experts from the Slovenian Border Police was used, engaged by the TAIEX. The Law has improved the comprehensive control of green and blue borders, but it requires the continued development of this system.

§2. Organization of Border Control

73. Border control is under the competence of the Police Administration and is carried out by the Border Police Sector.[119] Border control encompasses state border control, border checks and assessment of threats to the security of the state border, all with the aim of protecting the life and health of people and the environment, preventing and detecting criminal offences and administrative offences, preventing illegal migration and other activities. The following organizational units have been established within the Border Police Sector for caring out these tasks:[120]

- Department for the surveillance of state border.
- Department for border checks.
- Department for operational work and risk analysis.
- Department for Foreigners, Visas and Suppression of Illegal Migration.

117. *Ibid.*
118. Law on Amendments to the Law on Border Control *(Zakon o izmjenama i dopunama Zakona o graničnoj kontroli)*, 'Official Gazette of Montenegro', No. 017/19 of 19.3.2019.
119. Article 24 of the Law on Border Control.
120. Government of Montenegro, *Rulebook on Organization and Systematization of Employees Posts in the Ministry of Interior* (*Pravilnik o organizaciji i sistematizaciji radnih mjesta u Ministarstvu unutrašnjih poslova*) Ministry of Interior, www.mup.gov.me.

– Border Security Departments established in: Berane, with border police stations in Rozaje and Plav; Pljevlja, with border police stations in Pljevlja and Boljanići; Bijelo Polje; Podgorica, with border police stations in Tuzi, at Podgorica Airport; Nikšić, with border police stations in Vilusi, Banjani and Pluzine; Bar, with border police stations in Bar and Ulcinj; Herceg Novi, with border police stations in Sutorina and Tivat; and the Border Maritime Police Department, with Border Police Stations in Podgorica, Bar and Herceg Novi.

74. Police Administration – The Border Police Sector is the primary authority responsible for implementing the Integrated Border Management Strategy. The Department for Integrated Border and Border Management was established pursuant to the Rulebook on Internal Organization and Systematization of the Ministry of Interior as an organizational unit, which carries out tasks related to state border security, IBM, border management, coordination, organization and synchronization of activities of border services in carrying out border procedures. Pursuant to the provisions of Article 4 of the Law on Border Control,[121] the tasks of demarcation and the establishment of the state border, as well as preparations for the conclusion of an international agreement on the state border, are carried out by the Commission established by the Government of Montenegro.

121. *Zakon o graničnoj kontroli*, 'Official Gazette of Montenegro', Nos 072/09 of 30.10.2009, 020/11 of 15.4.2011, 040/11 of 8.8.2011, 039/13 of 7.8.2013, 017/19 of 19.3.2019.

Chapter 2. Right to Enter the Country

§1. Conditions for the Right to Enter

75. The Law on Border Control and the Law on Foreign Nationals regulate the conditions for entry into Montenegro. The border control encompasses the control of persons and their travel documents, vehicles and objects in the border crossing zone or immediately after crossing the state border, as well as other controls on movement of persons, capital, transport services, animals and plants across the state border. When entering or leaving Montenegro, a foreigner is subject to the border check procedures. Border checks, as well as the protection of state borders, are carried out in accordance with the Law on Border Control.[122]

76. When conducting a border check of a person, a police officer is authorized to inspect travel documents, take information thereof, determine the identity of persons crossing the state border and check the records kept by the Police Administration, Ministry and other state administration bodies, as well as international organizations.[123] The police officer is also authorized to take fingerprints and palm prints of persons and other biometric data if there is a suspicion about the identity, i.e., the authenticity of the travel or other documents requested for crossing the state border, checks whether the person fulfils the conditions for entering Montenegro, i.e., leaving the country; certifies the crossing of the state border, i.e., enters into the travel or other document required for crossing the state border information on entry and exit, as well as data on the prohibition of entry into the country, data on the entry and transfer of firearms and ammunition, and other data relevant for the border check, checks the purpose of the travel of the person, performs the examination and search of the person that does not include the examination of the body cavities, if it is not otherwise possible to perform the check of the person, and detains the person for the time necessary to carry out the check, for a maximum of six hours.[124] A police officer is authorized to require a person crossing the state border to show things and objects he/she has with him or in a vehicle if there are grounds for suspecting possession of prohibited items.[125] The police officer is also authorized to carry out an internal and external visual inspection of the vehicle, as well as a search of the vehicle, including the dismantling of certain parts of the vehicle if there are grounds for suspecting that the person operating the vehicle is smuggling persons and prohibited things indicating their identity or the identity of other passengers in the vehicle to prevent the illegal crossing of the state border.[126] In performing border control tasks, the police officer shall exercise the powers established by the law, attaining objectives with least harmful consequences. The police officer is also

122. Articles 29 and 30 of the Law on Border Control.
123. Article 25 of the Law on Border Control.
124. *Ibid.*
125. Article 32 of the Law on Border Control.
126. *Ibid.*

authorized to set up and use technical and other means of communication, service dogs, and other means in accordance with the law.[127]

77. The border check is carried out in the area of the border crossing points on the first (border crossing point at which the border check is usually carried out) or the second line of checks (especially the designated border crossing point at which the border check is carried out outside the usual place).[128] Deviation from the border check regime is possible in the case of exceptional and unforeseen circumstances that led to traffic of such magnitude that the waiting time at the border crossing points becomes too long, despite the use of all organizational and other possibilities, which implies the omission of certain actions during performing border checks. It is introduced gradually and lasts for the duration of the circumstances that caused it.[129] In this case, the police officer puts the stamp on the travel documents at the entrance to Montenegro and at the exit from Montenegro.[130]

78. A temporary border crossing point[131] may be established for the purpose of conducting exercises for the prevention of natural and other disasters; organization of cultural, religious, scientific, professional, sports and tourism activities; need to divert traffic, perform activities arising from international treaties, agricultural and economic activities, with the consent of the Minister of the Internal Affairs and with the consent ministers of finance, transport and maritime affairs, spatial planning and construction of structures and foreign affairs.

79. The entry regime of the nationals of EU Member States is regulated by a special Chapter IX of the Law on Foreign Nationals 'Entry, exit, movement and stay and work of the nationals of the EU Member States', referred to in Article 150 prescribing that a national of an EU Member State may enter Montenegro without a visa or granted temporary residence. If a national of an EU Member State does not have the travel document, the police must provide him/her with the opportunity to acquire necessary documents or otherwise prove that he/she is a national of the EU Member State.[132] A national of an EU Member State with the valid travel document or personal identity card issued by the competent authority of such state shall have the right to leave Montenegro for travelling to another Member State.[133]

§2. Administrative Procedure and Documents

80. Whenever entering Montenegro and exiting from it, a foreign national shall be under an obligation to undergo the border control pursuant to the Law regulating

127. Article 24 of the Law on Border Control.
128. Article 29 of the Law on Border Control.
129. Article 34 of the Law on Border Control.
130. *Ibid.*
131. Article 16 of the Law on Border Control.
132. Article 150 of the Law on Foreign Nationals.
133. *Ibid.*

border control.[134] A foreigner may enter, move and reside in Montenegro with a valid foreign travel document to which a visa is affixed or a valid foreign travel document with a temporary residence permit, temporary residence permit and work permit or permanent residence permit.

81. A foreigner applying for a short-stay visa (visa C) for one or two entries into Montenegro must prove that he/she has adequate and valid travel medical insurance to cover the costs that may be incurred in reference to the return to the country of origin.[135]

82. When a minor travels accompanied by one of the parents, it is necessary to have a valid travel document, which is issued with the consent of both parents. If a minor travels without parents, with a third party, it is necessary to obtain consent from both parents or social services if it is a minor without parents.

83. Pursuant to Article 6 of the Law on Foreign Nationals, foreign travel document means any personal, family, collective, diplomatic and service passport, and any seaman's book, shipping book or any other travel document recognized under international treaties, according to which the identity of its holder can be confirmed and which has been issued pursuant to the regulations on issuing travel documents of another state. A foreign travel document issued in the last ten years and whose validity shall not expire at least three months after the planned date of departure from the territory of Montenegro shall be deemed valid.[136]

84. A foreign national whose name is entered in the foreign travel document of another person may enter into and exit from Montenegro only accompanied by the person holding the foreign travel document in which his name is entered. Moreover, foreign nationals holding either a collective passport or another collective foreign travel document may enter into and exit from Montenegro only if they are together. Each of the foreign nationals whose name is in the travel document referred to in paragraph 2 above must hold also another document – with his personal photo in it – to serve as his own identification. The leader of such group of foreign nationals must hold his personal passport.[137]

85. The border may be crossed both outside the border crossing point and outside the fixed working hours of the border crossing point in case of crossing of persons or groups authorized to cross the state border if such crossing is necessary for justified reasons and is not contrary to international agreement. The Police, with the consent of the Customs Administration and the Harbor Master's Office, with a term of validity of up to one year at the request of persons intending to cross the state border issues a crossing permit. Approval may be withdrawn prior to its expiry date

134. Article 7 of the Law on Foreign Nationals.
135. Article 23 of the Law on Foreign Nationals.
136. Article 9 of the Law on Foreign Nationals.
137. Article 12 of the Law on Foreign Nationals.

if it has been misused, and if it is not used for the purpose for which it was issued and upon termination of the reason for which it was issued.[138]

86. Crossing the state border is verified in the travel document by stamping the seal. At the request of a person crossing the state border with an ID card, a police officer is obliged to issue a certificate that serves as proof of entry into Montenegro, i.e., exit from Montenegro, while the foreigner whose travel document has no stamp of entry stamp, which proves that he entered Montenegro legally, the police may issue a certificate of legal residence on the prescribed form.[139]

87. The police are authorized to collect personal and other data from persons subject to a thorough inspection and to enter and process such data in the records it maintains. The police may also collect the aforementioned information using technical and other means. The data shall be destroyed upon the expiration of five years from the date of its collection, and the data collected through video surveillance, after the expiration of thirty days from the day of the recording, unless they are necessary for conducting criminal and misdemeanour proceedings.[140]

88. For the needs of border control, the Police shall keep the records of:

(a) persons and vehicles subject to border checks;
(b) persons and vehicles not allowed to cross the state border;
(c) persons subjected to identification procedure;
(d) persons who have been granted the authorization referred to in Article 11 paragraph 3, Article 42 paragraph 2 and Article 57 paragraph 1 of this Law;
(e) persons to whom the identification marks referred to in Article 22a of this Law have been issued;
(f) persons who have violated the inviolability of the state border;
(g) persons who announced hunting or fishing along the border line;
(h) persons bringing, transferring and bringing firearms and ammunition across the state border;
(i) persons who maintain an operational database;
(j) derogation from the border checks regime referred to in Article 34 of this Law;
(k) persons caught attempting to commit or committing criminal offences and misdemeanours, which endanger the security of the state border by this act;
(l) persons and means of transport maintained by the data collections generated by video surveillance.

89. Border checks shall include measures and actions carried out at the border crossing point at the intended or shortly after crossing the state border in order to control the lawful entry of persons into Montenegro, i.e., exit from Montenegro.[141]

138. Article 11 of the Law on Foreign Nationals.
139. Article 43 of the Law on Foreign Nationals.
140. Article 61 of the Law on Foreign Nationals.
141. Article 28 of the Law on Border Control.

Border checks include checks of persons, things and means of transport.[142] There are two types of border checks: basic and detailed one. The basic border check is intended for the nationals of Montenegro, nationals of the EU, nationals of the countries signatories to the Treaty on the European Economic Area and nationals of the Swiss Confederation, unless otherwise stipulated by this law, and includes verification of the identity of the person, authenticity and validity of the travel document, as well as the traffic check.[143] Detailed border control encompasses all other persons not covered by the basic check, as well as persons who are suspected of endangering the state border security, public order and public health.[144]

90. Pursuant to Article 87 of the Rulebook on the manner of carrying out certain police tasks and the exercise of powers in carrying out these tasks,[145] a police officer may check means of transport, passengers and baggage when performing border control tasks. An inspection of a means of transport is considered to be an inspection of all open and closed spaces of the means of transport and of the goods being transported, and before the inspection, the police officer shall inform the person of the reasons why the inspection is carried out and invite him/her to show the objects which he/she has with him or in the means of transport, except if this would jeopardize the performance of an official assignment.[146] If the person refuses inspection or to show the objects in the vehicle, the police officer may, with prior warning, forcibly open the closed vehicle and carry out the inspection in the presence of the person who operated the vehicle or the person whose objects or baggage are inspected.[147] When inspecting means of transport, a police officer may remove passengers from that mean until an inspection has been carried out, and an official annotation shall be developed by the police officer on the inspection of the means of transport, passengers and baggage.[148] Where upon examination, a police officer determines that there are circumstances that necessitate a search of vehicles, passengers and baggage, he/she shall proceed in accordance with the Criminal Procedure Code and conduct a search without a court order.[149]

91. In the case of exceptional and unforeseen circumstances that led to traffic of such magnitude that the waiting time at the border crossing becomes too long, and despite the utilization of all organizational and other possibilities, it is possible to depart from the border check regime, which entails the failure of certain actions during the carrying out of the border checks. This is introduced gradually and lasts for

---

142. Article 30 of the Law on Border Control.
143. Article 36 of the Law on Border Control.
144. Article 38 of the Law on Border Control.
145. Rulebook on the manner of carrying out certain police tasks and the exercise of powers in carrying out these tasks *(Pravilnik o načinu obavljanja određenih policijskih poslova i primjeni ovlašćenja u obavljanju tih poslova)*, 'Official Gazette of Montenegro', Nos 021/14 of 6.5.2014, 066/15 of 26.11.2015.
146. *Ibid.*, Arts 88 and 89.
147. *Ibid.*, Art. 89.
148. *Ibid.*, Art. 90.
149. *Ibid.*, Art. 91.

the duration of the circumstances, which gave rise to it.[150] The decision to derogate from the border check regime is made by the police officer who manages the border check at the border crossing point.[151]

§3. Visa Regime of Montenegro

92. A foreign national may enter, move throughout and stay in Montenegro if he holds a valid foreign travel document with a visa affixed to it, or a valid foreign travel document accompanied by a temporary residence permit. A foreign national whom Montenegro is under an obligation to admit pursuant to an international treaty and where it is required for humanitarian, or internal security or public health reasons may enter Montenegro without a valid foreign travel document.[152] Moreover, it is important to emphasize that the nationals of certain countries can enter Montenegro without a visa with a valid identity card, or another document on the basis of which their identity and citizenship can be determined if so prescribed by the international treaty or visa regime of Montenegro, adopted by the Government at the proposal of the Ministry of Foreign Affairs.[153]

93. A visa is the permission ensuring a foreign national to enter, stay in and transit the territory of Montenegro.[154] The Law on Foreign Nationals recognizes three types of visas: airport-transit visa (A visa), short-stay visa (C visa) and long-stay visa (D visa).

94. A foreign national shall be issued an airport-transit visa (A visa) for single or multiple transiting through an international transit terminal of an airport during a layover or a transfer between two international flight legs, without actually entering the territory of Montenegro. A foreign national who does not leave an aeroplane or international transit terminal of an airport of Montenegro during his stopover at the airport shall not be required to have a visa.[155]

95. A short-stay visa (C visa) shall be issued for the purpose of transiting through Montenegro or for entering as well as for staying in the territory of Montenegro, whereas such stay may not be longer than 90 days within a time period of 180 days counted as of the first day of entry. A foreign national coming for a private or a business visit to a natural person or a legal entity in Montenegro may be required to present an affidavit of support, i.e., a letter of invitation or any other evidence corroborating that the natural person or the legal entity will bear his stay in Montenegro-related costs, including also his accommodation and support costs and those for his departure from Montenegro.[156]

---

150. *Law on Border Control,* Art. 34.
151. *Ibid.*
152. Article 9 of the Law on Foreign Nationals.
153. *Ibid.*
154. Article 14 of the Law on Foreign Nationals.
155. Article 16 of the Law on Foreign Nationals.
156. Article 17 of the Law on Foreign Nationals.

96. A foreign national intending to stay in Montenegro for longer than 90 days – for performing business activities or work or serving in foreign accredited diplomatic and consular missions and representative offices of international organizations in Montenegro – but not for longer than 180 days – counted as of the first entry day – in a time period of one year, shall be issued a long-stay visa (D visa). This visa shall be issued as a single- or multiple-entry visa for entering Montenegro and may be issued to a foreign national holding an affidavit of support, i.e., a letter of invitation issued by either a natural person or a legal entity, or other evidence corroborating that the natural person or the legal entity will bear his stay in Montenegro-related costs, including also his accommodation and support costs and those for his departure from Montenegro.[157]

97. A visa is obtained prior to entering Montenegro, and shall be issued by the Ministry of Foreign Affairs via diplomatic-consular representative offices,[158] to whom a visa application is also submitted. The visa application is decided within ten days from the date of application. This deadline can be extended up to thirty days if further consideration is required, whereas exceptionally, when additional documentation is required for visa issuing, the deadline may be extended up to sixty days.[159]

98. A competent authority shall not issue visa to a foreign national if:

(1) he has enclosed a damaged, forged or somebody else's travel document with his visa application;
(2) he has not supplied evidence justifying the purposes and circumstances of the intended stay;
(3) he has not submitted evidence of either his possession of sufficient resources for his support during the time of his intended stay in Montenegro, for his return to his country of origin or residence or for his transiting to a third country that admits him or he cannot obtain such resources in a legal manner;
(4) he stayed in Montenegro for 90 days, whereas 180 days have not passed as of the day of his first entry;
(5) he has been imposed the entry and stay ban in Montenegro, or he has been subjected to international measures for entry restrictions which bind Montenegro;
(6) if so is required by the Montenegrin national, i.e., internal security, or public health reasons;
(7) he has not submitted the evidence of travel medical insurance;
(8) there are grounds for suspicions about the authenticity of submitted evidence and their respective contents, trustworthiness of statements of the foreign national, or about his intention to leave Montenegro prior to the expiration of the requested visa validity period.[160]

157. Article 18 of the Law on Foreign Nationals.
158. Article 19 of the Law on Foreign Nationals.
159. Article 25 of the Law on Foreign Nationals.
160. Article 17 of the Law on Foreign Nationals.

In the aforementioned events, a competent authority shall issue a decision on rejecting to issue visa to a foreign national. An appeal against this decision may be submitted to the Ministry of Foreign Affairs via the diplomatic or consular mission within eight days as of the day of receiving the decision.[161] Exceptionally, also where there are the reasons referred to in paragraph 1 above and if so required by humanitarian reasons, Montenegro's interests or undertaken international commitments, a foreign national may be issued a visa and in that case, a foreign national may be allowed to enter only at a certain border crossing point.[162]

99. A short-stay visa (C visa) validity may be extended for humanitarian or force majeure reasons, as well as for serious personal reasons. A visa extension application shall be submitted to the Police in the place of a foreign national's stay, prior to the visa validity expiration, and the police shall issue a decision within seven days.[163]

100. Nationals of all twenty-eight Member States of the EU, as well as the Republic of Albania, Principality of Andorra, Bosnia and Herzegovina, the Republic of Iceland, the Republic of Kosovo, the Kingdom of Liechtenstein, the Republic of Northern Macedonia, Principality of Monaco, the Kingdom of Norway, the Republic of San Marino, the Republic of Serbia, Holy See and the Swiss Confederation may enter, cross the territory and stay in Montenegro for up to thirty days, without a visa, with a valid identity card issued by the competent authority of those states.[164] In other words, nationals of these countries are not required to show their passports when checking at the border crossing point, but may enter with an ID card issued in their respective countries. Moreover, visa is not required for the nationals of the following countries: the Republic of Albania, Principality of Andorra, Antigua and Barbuda, Argentine Republic, Aruba, Azerbaijan, State Union of Australia, the Republic of Austria, Bahamas, Barbados, the Kingdom of Belgium, Bermuda, Bosnia and Herzegovina, Federal Republic of Brazil, Brunei Darussalam, the Republic of Bulgaria, the Czech Republic, the Republic of Chile, the Kingdom of Denmark, Dominican Republic, the Republic of Estonia, the Republic of Finland, French Republic, Grenada, Georgia, the Republic of Guatemala, Hellenic Republic, the Kingdom of the Netherlands, Netherlands Antilles, the Republic of Honduras, the Republic of Croatia, the Republic of Ireland, the Republic of Iceland, the Republic of Italy, State of Israel, Japan, Canada, Qatar, the Republic of Cyprus, Kiribati, Colombia, the Republic of Korea, the Republic of Kosovo, the Republic of Costa Rica, Kuwait, the Republic of Latvia, Principality of Liechtenstein, the Republic of Lithuania, Grand Duchy of Luxembourg, Hungary, the Republic of Northern Macedonia, Malaysia, the Republic of Malta, Mauritius, the Republic of Marshall Islands, Micronesia, United States of Mexico, the Republic of Moldova, Principality of

161. Article 27 of the Law on Foreign Nationals.
162. *Ibid.*
163. Article 28 of the Law on Foreign Nationals.
164. Visa Regime Decree, 'Official Gazette of Montenegro', No. 033/19 of 14.6.2019, Art. 2.

Monaco, the Republic of Nicaragua, the Kingdom of Norway, New Zealand, Federal Republic of Germany, Palau, the Republic of Panama, the Republic of Paraguay, the Republic of Poland, Portugal, Romania, the Republic of El Salvador, Samoa, the Republic of San Marino, Seychelles, the Republic of Singapore, United States of America, Slovak Republic, the Republic of Slovenia, Solomon Islands, the Republic of Serbia, Saint Lucia, Saint Christopher and Nevis, Saint Vincent and the Grenadines, Holy See, the Kingdom of Spain, the Kingdom of Sweden, the Swiss Confederation, Taiwan, Timor-Leste, Tonga, Trinidad and Tobago, the Republic of Turkey, Tuvalu, the United Arab Emirates, Vanuatu, the United Kingdom of Great Britain and Northern Ireland, Ukraine, Eastern Republic of Uruguay and the Bolivarian Republic of Venezuela, the Hong Kong Special Administrative Region of the People's Republic of China and Macau of the People's Republic of China.[165] Citizens of these countries can enter, cross the territory and stay in Montenegro for up to ninety days, but they must have passports. Moreover, citizens of the Republic of Ecuador, the Republic of Cuba, the Republic of Peru and the Russian Federation may enter and stay without a visa for up to thirty days with a valid travel document issued by those countries.[166]

101. Nationals of all other countries not mentioned in the text or with whom an international treaty on entry, crossing or stay in the territory of Montenegro has not been concluded may enter, cross the territory and stay in Montenegro on the basis of a valid foreign travel document to which visa is affixed.[167]

102. The 2019 EC Progress Report stresses that Montenegro continues to align its visa policy with the EU acquis, and has added Georgia to the list of countries with which it has a free visa regime.[168] However, Montenegro is still exempting the nationals of Russia, Armenia, Kazakhstan, Azerbaijan, Belarus, Cuba, Ecuador, Kuwait and Turkey from the obligation of holding a short-stay visa – either seasonally for tourism or permanently. Seasonal exemption from visa requirements is not in line with the EU acquis, and these countries are on the EU list of countries whose nationals are required to have an EU visa.[169] Montenegro must take concrete steps aimed at full compliance of its visa policy with the EU visa regime. At present, twenty-four Montenegrin consular missions are connected to the national visa information system, and another six are pending connection in 2019. Web portal enabling electronic application for Montenegrin visa has been created and linked to the national visa information system. In the post-visa liberalization process, Montenegro continued to implement relevant measures aimed at preventing the misuse of the free visa regime with the EU and to submit monthly reports thereof. A particular focus should be placed on the successful reintegration of returnees, especially the most vulnerable ones, such as the Roma and Egyptians.

165. *Ibid.,* Art. 1.
166. *Ibid.,* Art. 3.
167. *Ibid.,* Art. 4.
168. European Commission, *Montenegro Progress Report* (Brussels, 2019).
169. *Ibid.*

103. The visa application, electronically, comes to the Visa Information System managed by the Ministry of Foreign Affairs. After obtaining the opinion of the authorities responsible for giving opinions (Ministry of Interior; Police and Agency for National Security), the visa can be issued through the information system, by submitting to the applicant, electronically, an appropriate form containing a bar code, photo and personal data of the applicant. By the way, according to the Law on Foreign Nationals, the Ministry of Foreign Affairs, as the body responsible for issuing visas, received a total of 4,092 visa applications in 2019, of which 3,424 were approved, while 668 applications were rejected, 16.32%.[170]

170. Government of Montenegro, *Report on the Implementation of the Action Plan for the Implementation of the Strategy for Integrated Migration Management for 2019* (Podgorica 2020) p. 74.

Chapter 3. Refusal of Entry

§1. Reasons for Refusal of Entry

104. The possession of a passport or other travel document or temporary residence permit does not automatically mean that a foreign national will be allowed to enter Montenegro. Even if the aforementioned conditions are met, the entry may be refused. Thus, a foreign national shall not be allowed to enter Montenegro if he/she does not have a valid travel document or has enclosed somebody else's invalid, or forged travel or other document constitutes a criminal offence.[171] Crossing the border without a passport or other valid travel document constitutes a misdemeanour for which a monetary fine may be imposed ranging from EUR 200 to EUR 1,200.[172]

The entry of a foreigner into Montenegro shall be also refused when he/she does not possess proof that justifies the purpose and conditions of the intended stay. Therefore, the foreigner shall be refused entry if he/she is not able to provide evidence of the purpose, or intention of his/her entry and stay (work, study, tourism, research, training, etc.). In a vast number of situations, the border police conclude from an interview with a foreigner that his/her purpose of entry is not the one he/she stated in the application. One of the reasons for refusal is when a foreigner lacks sufficient resources to support himself during the intended stay in Montenegro and for returning to the state from which he has come or for a travel to a third country.[173]

A specific reason why a foreigner shall not be allowed to enter the EU is where national or internal security or public health reasons require that.[174] Thus, a foreigner shall not be allowed to enter if he/she comes from an area affected by an epidemic or communicable disease, and he/she does not have proof that he/she has been vaccinated or has not been infected. Such a decision shall be made by the Ministry of Health and based on a report by the World Health Organization.[175] In case a foreigner comes from a country that is at high risk of spreading epidemics and communicable diseases, he or she may be subject to medical surveillance and quarantine if there is a risk of spreading the infection.[176] The Ministry of Health, at the suggestion of the Institute of Public Health, may prohibit the entry of foreigners from a country affected by the epidemic of communicable disease.

105. A foreigner shall not be allowed to enter where national security requires that.[177] The Ministry of Interior, or the Police, shall adopt the decision on the refusal of entry, based on the opinion of the National Security Agency. Therefore, the

171. This refers to the criminal offence '*Counterfeiting documents*' referred to in Art. 412 of the Criminal Code.
172. Article 213 of the Law on Foreign Nationals.
173. Article 8 of the Law on Foreign Nationals.
174. *Ibid.*
175. Article 33 of the Law on protection of population against Communicable Diseases.
176. Article 55 of the Law on protection of population against Communicable Diseases.
177. Article 8 of the Law on Foreign Nationals.

National Security Agency shall determine the existence of threat to national security, which exists if a foreigner is carrying out or has carried out activities that could lead to the commission of criminal offences against humanity or other assets protected by international law or against the constitutional order and security of Montenegro, or if a foreigner belongs to, or has belonged to, organizations advocating violent changing of the constitutional order or acting in a manner that threatens human rights and freedoms established by the Constitution; or if he/she publicly advocates and disseminates ideas that incite national, religious or racial discrimination; belongs to or has belonged to organizations and organized criminal groups planning or committing criminal offences and in any other way provides support to these organizations and groups; has or has had or has been in contact with or maintains contacts with persons who illegally collect secret and other information, terrorists, saboteurs, members of organized criminal groups or persons who are reasonably suspected of belonging to such groups; does not respect the state of Montenegro and its symbols, does not execute decisions of courts, state administration bodies and other bodies or where circumstances indicate that a person, after being issued a temporary residence permit, temporary residence and work permits and permanent residence permit, would not respect the legal order of Montenegro.[178] When the Ministry of Interior or the Police bring a decision/decision on the refusal of entry based on the opinion of the Agency on the existence of the threat to national security, then it does not state these reasons in the operative part of the decision.[179]

106. A foreigner may also not be allowed to enter if the competent state authorities (Agency, Police, Prosecutors Service) have determined that he/she may violate public law and order, jeopardize the security of persons or if there is a reasonable suspicion that the person concerned is member of an international organized crime group, or based on information from national or international organization, there is a suspicion that a person is a member of or affiliated with a terrorist organization or participates in the financing, planning of an act of terrorism against another country or its citizens.

107. One reason for not allowing a foreign national to enter is where he lacks sufficient resources to support himself during the intended stay in Montenegro and for returning to the state from which he has come or for a travel to a third country.[180] Sufficient funds are considered to be at least EUR 5,000 per day, and a foreigner can prove it by a statement from the bank about his savings, credit card or guarantee letter in which the other person guarantees that he will bear the costs of a foreigner's stay.

A competent authority shall not issue visa to a foreign national if:

(1) he has enclosed a damaged, forged or somebody else's travel document with his visa application;

178. Article 95 of the Law on Foreign Nationals.
179. *Ibid.*
180. Article 8 of the Law on Foreign Nationals.

(2) he has not supplied evidence justifying the purposes and circumstances of the intended stay;
(3) he has not submitted evidence of either his possession of sufficient resources for his support during the time of his intended stay in Montenegro, for his return to his country of origin or residence or for his transiting to a third country that admits him or he cannot obtain such resources in a legal manner;
(4) he stayed in Montenegro for 90 days, whereas 180 days have not passed as of the day of his first entry;
(5) he has been imposed the entry and stay ban in Montenegro, or he has been subjected to international measures for entry restrictions which bind Montenegro;
(6) he does not hold evidence satisfying the purpose and requirements of the intended stay;
(7) within a 180-day period, he already stayed for 90 days in the territory of Montenegro;
(8) he lacks sufficient resources both to support himself during the intended stay in Montenegro and for returning to the state from which he has come or for a travel to a third country;
(9) where there is the expulsion of a foreign national from the country as a security measure or the expulsion of a foreign national from the territory of Montenegro as a protection measure or the measure is in force, or an entry ban has been imposed on him;
(10) where national, i.e., internal security or public health-related reasons require that.

108. The Police shall adopt the decision on the refusal of entry, which shall be made without hearing the foreign national concerned.[181] An appeal may be lodged against the decision on the refusal of entry via the nearest diplomatic or consular mission of Montenegro abroad (hereinafter referred to as 'the Diplomatic and Consular Mission'), within eight days as of the day of receiving the decision, which shall be decided by the Ministry of Interior. The appeal does not postpone the decision enforcement. Exceptionally, the appeal referred to in paragraph 4 of this article shall postpone the decision enforcement if the police estimate that the life or freedom of the foreign national are jeopardized in the country of origin due to his racial, religious or national affiliation, due to the affiliation to a particular social group or due to political opinion, or where he could be subject to torture or inhuman and degrading treatment or punishment, or he could be subject to a death penalty, as well as his returning to a country where there is danger of him being forcibly returned to the country of origin.[182] The refusal of entry shall be affixed to the foreign national's travel document.[183] The Police shall keep records on the refusal of entry imposed on foreign nationals, while a separate Rulebook of the Ministry of Interior regulates the form and manner for affixing the refusal of entry.[184]

181. *Ibid.*
182. *Ibid.*
183. *Ibid.*
184. Rulebook on registering entry ban and cancellation of stay of a foreign national in a foreign travel document, 'Official Gazette of Montenegro', Nos 043/18 of 3.7.2018, 044/18 of 6.7.2018.

Part II. Right of Residence

Chapter 1. General Provisions

109. The right of a foreigner to stay in Montenegro is regulated primarily by the Law on Foreign Nationals and its subordinate legislation, as well as the Law on International and Temporary Protection of Foreigners. Pursuant to the Law on Foreign Nationals, the general rule is that a foreigner may enter and stay in Montenegro on the basis of a valid travel document and issued visa or residence permit, unless otherwise provided by this Law or an international treaty.[185] The exception to this general rule where a foreigner can enter without a valid travel document is the case when Montenegro is obliged to accept a foreigner on the basis of an international treaty and where is required for humanitarian or international security or public health reasons.[186] Furthermore, nationals of certain countries can enter Montenegro with a valid ID card issued by the competent authority of another country, or another document on the basis of which their identity and citizenship can be determined, in accordance with an international treaty or the Visa Regime Decree of the Government of Montenegro.[187] Therefore, the Government of Montenegro is authorized to determine by its decision/decree the countries whose nationals can enter the country on the basis of an identity card or other document on the basis of which the identity can be determined. Thus, the citizens of EU Member States and countries in the region (Arabia, Albania, Bosnia and Herzegovina, the Republic of Northern Macedonia) can enter and stay for up to thirty days with a valid ID card.[188]

110. Legal entry into Montenegro shall be considered the crossing of the state border at the border crossing point where the border check shall be carried out in accordance with the Law on Border Control. The stay of a foreigner in the transit area of the airport and the anchorage of the port or pier, under this Law, shall not be considered the entry into Montenegro.

111. A valid foreign travel document, which constitutes a basic condition for entry and stay of a foreigner, shall mean a passport, family passport, joint passport, diplomatic passport, official passport, seaman's book, shipping book and other

---

185. Article 9 of the Law on Foreign Nationals.
186. *Ibid.*
187. Visa Regime Decree, 'Official Gazette of Montenegro', No. 033/19 of 14.6.2019.
188. Visa Regime Decree, Art. 2.

travel documents recognized in accordance with international treaties, based on which identity of its holder can be determined and which is issued in accordance with the regulations on the issuance of travel documents of another state, and which has not expired. A foreign travel document issued in the last ten years and whose validity shall not expire at least three months after the planned date of departure from the territory of Montenegro shall be deemed. Exceptionally, in a justified emergency, the period of validity of a foreign travel document may be shorter, but may not expire before the planned date of departure from the territory of Montenegro.[189]

112. The Law on Foreign Nationals specifies three types of residence of foreign national in Montenegro:[190]

(1) stay of up to ninety days;
(2) temporary residence;
(3) permanent residence.

189. Article 9 of the Law on Foreign Nationals.
190. Article 33 of the Law on Foreign Nationals.

Chapter 2. Short Stay

§1. Condition for Short Stay

113. Pursuant to the Law on Foreign Nationals, a foreign national may stay in Montenegro for up to ninety days based on a short-stay visa (C visa) or without a visa, according to the Decree on Visa Regime regulation, or he may stay longer than ninety days based on a long-stay visa (D visa). For stay up to ninety days, it is necessary for a foreign citizen to possess a valid travel document. A foreigner may reside in Montenegro for a maximum of ninety days within a period of six months, counting from the day of the first entry, unless otherwise has been provided for by this Law or an international treaty. A foreigner, who has resided in Montenegro for ninety days, may re-enter and reside in Montenegro upon expiry of the time period of six months, counting from the day of the first entry. For stay up to ninety days, it is necessary for a foreign citizen to possess a valid travel document. Also, citizens of certain countries may enter and reside in Montenegro up to thirty days with a valid personal ID card, or other document based on which their identity and citizenship may be determined, in accordance with the Decree on Visa Regime. In other words, the foreigner who has entered Montenegro lawfully, and who meets the general preconditions for entry and stay as defined in the Law on Foreign Nationals, may freely stay in the country in accordance with the declared purposes of stay. A specific exception to this general rule can be found in Article 10 of the Law on Foreign Nationals which stipulates that movement within a certain region of Montenegro shall be restricted or banned where national, i.e., internal security or public health reasons require so, according to the law.[191]

114. A short-stay visa (C visa) shall be issued for the purpose of transiting through Montenegro or for entering as well as for staying in the territory of Montenegro, whereas such stay may not be longer than 90 days within a time period of 180 days counted as of the first day of entry and shall be issued as single-, double- or multiple-entry visa for entering Montenegro. Multiple-entry–short-stay visa (C visa) validity shall range from six months to five years if a foreigner has proved a need for travelling or has justified his intention to travel frequently, i.e., regularly, while particularly for business or family reasons, and has proved that he will not misuse an issued visa, in particular by using visas previously issued according to the Law, having funds he has in the country of origin and by his actual intention to leave the territory of Montenegro prior to the expiration of the visa he requested. The short-stay visa validity shall include also the additional fifteen-day period. A foreigner coming for a private or a business visit to a natural person or a legal entity in Montenegro may be required to present an affidavit of support, i.e., a letter of invitation or any other evidence corroborating that the natural person or the legal

191. Article 34 of the Law on Foreign Nationals.

entity will bear his stay in Montenegro-related costs, including also his accommodation and support costs and those for his departure from Montenegro. An issued short-stay visa shall not be any guarantee that a foreign national will be permitted to enter Montenegro.[192]

115. The Law on Foreign Nationals also recognizes another type of visa – long-stay visa (D visa). According to this provision, a foreigner intending to stay in Montenegro for longer than 90 days for performing business activities or work or serving in foreign accredited diplomatic and consular missions and representative offices of international organizations in Montenegro, but not for longer than 180 days counted as of the first entry day in a time period of one year, shall be issued a long-stay visa (D visa). A long-stay visa (D visa) shall be issued as single- or multiple-entry visa for entering Montenegro. A foreigner holding an affidavit of support, i.e., a letter of invitation issued by either a natural person or a legal entity, or other evidence corroborating that the natural person or the legal entity will bear his stay in Montenegro-related costs, including also his accommodation and support costs and those for his departure from Montenegro, may be issued a long-stay visa.[193]

§2. Administrative Procedures and Documents for Short Stay

116. As a general rule, a foreign national is obliged to submit a visa application personally. In exceptional, justified cases, a foreign national does not have to apply for a visa personally, but does need to appear at the diplomatic or consular representative office once it is issued. For a foreign national who is minor, i.e., legally incapable, visa application shall be filed by a parent or his legal representative. In addition to the visa application, he/she is obliged to submit:

- valid travel document (the period of validity of the travel document should exceed that of the visa's by three months);
- one colour photo 35 × 45 mm;
- proof of the purpose of stay in Montenegro (letter of guarantee by a physical person or letter of invitation by a legal entity, state authority in Montenegro or organizer of an international conference or event);
- proof of ensured accommodation (receipt from a tourist arrangement, hotel or other type of accommodation reservation that has been paid in);
- proof of possession of means for sustenance during his stay in Montenegro, as well as for return into the country where he comes from or for travel into a third state (cash, a bank account, traveller's checks, credit cards, etc.);
- proof of the means of travel and intention to return into the state where a foreigner comes from or into a third state (a return aeroplane or other transportation ticket, a driving licence);
- proof of health insurance;
- proof that the consular fee has been charged;

192. Article 17 of the Law on Foreign Nationals.
193. Article 18 of the Law on Foreign Nationals.

– as well as other corresponding documents based on which the purpose and ensured accommodation in Montenegro can be determined.[194]

117. Ministry of Foreign Affairs is the competence authority for issuing visas through a diplomatic and consular mission. Prior to issuing a visa, Ministry of Foreign Affairs is obliged to obtain prior consent of the National Security Agency of Montenegro and the Police, for finding out whether there are any national and/or internal security reasons preventing a visa issuing, and for a long-stay visa (D visa) issuing for work purposes, the consent of the Ministry of Interior. A visa is granted in the form of a visa sticker affixed to the valid foreign travel document. A short-stay visa (C visa) validity may be extended for humanitarian or force majeure reasons or extended for serious personal reasons. A visa extension application of a short-stay visa (C visa) shall be submitted to the Police in the place of a foreign national's stay, prior to the visa validity expiration and in the required form.

118. A visa will not be issued if:

– a foreign national has enclosed a damaged, forged or used somebody else's travel document with his visa application;
– a foreign national has not supplied evidence justifying the purposes and circumstances of the intended stay;
– a foreign national has not submitted evidence of either his possession of sufficient resources for his support during the time of his intended stay in Montenegro, for his return to his country of origin or residence or for his transiting to a third country that admits him or he cannot obtain such resources in a legal manner;
– a foreign national stayed in Montenegro for 90 days, whereas 180 days have not passed as of the day of his first entry;
– a foreign national has been imposed the entry and stay ban in Montenegro, or he has been subjected to international measures for entry restrictions which bind Montenegro;
– so is required by the Montenegrin national, i.e., internal security, or public health reasons;
– a foreign national has not submitted the evidence of travel medical insurance;
– there are grounds for suspicions about the authenticity of submitted evidence and their respective contents, trustworthiness of statements of the foreign national or about his intention to leave Montenegro prior to the expiration of the requested visa validity period.[195]

119. The general rule is that the foreign national who intends to reside in Montenegro for a short time (up to ninety days) does not have to undergo any administrative procedures apart from the regular border formalities and registration of residence. A foreign national will be requested to present at the border his/her travel

194. Rulebook on Visas and Visa Forms, 'Official Gazette of Montenegro', No. 36/2015.
195. Article 27 of the Law on Foreign Nationals.

document and a visa unless he/she is exempted from the visa requirement. Sometimes (i.e., not necessarily, and not always) foreign national may be asked to present documents that indicate the purpose of his intended stay and to prove that he meets the requirements for entry and short stay, most often that he has sufficient funds to finance his entire stay.

120. A foreign national who has been issued a long-stay visa (visa D) or who stays in Montenegro for up to ninety days in accordance with Article 34 of the Law on Foreign Nationals is obliged to file to the police the application for registration of residence on a prescribed form, in the place where he or she intends to stay, within twenty-four hours from his or her arrival to the place of residence as well as the application for deregistration of residence, on a prescribed form, within twenty-four hours prior to leaving the place of residence.

§3. Legal Position in the Event of Short Stay

121. All foreign nationals legally residing in Montenegro are entitled to the protection of basic rights guaranteed in the Constitution and in the international conventions to which Montenegro is a party. Generally, foreign nationals are provided with equal access to the judicial system, without discrimination in relation to Montenegrin citizens. The Constitution of Montenegro and ratified international agreements provide equal protection of all persons in a general way, regardless of whether they are foreign or Montenegrin citizens. Everyone has the right to equal legal protection, without discrimination, and to use maternal language in the proceedings before the court and other state bodies or institutions.

122. For the use of healthcare, foreign nationals pay a fee to the health institution according to the price list of the health institution, and if their country is a signatory of an international agreement with Montenegro, according to the type of agreement, they are entitled to reimbursement of the said costs according to national regulations. Healthcare facilities and healthcare providers are obliged to provide emergency medical assistance to a foreign national.

123. A foreign national who does not have a regulated status in Montenegro can be educated as Montenegrin citizen under the conditions of reciprocity. Education is compulsory and free of charge for all children.

124. A foreign national who resides for up to ninety days may work under the work registration certificate. Under the work registration certificate issued in Montenegro, the following foreign nationals may reside and work for up to ninety days, within the time period of one year:

– those who perform business activities in Montenegro under international agreements concluded between Montenegro and an international organization or the EU on the professional and technical assistance or under the other ratified international treaties;

- founders, members of controlling and managing bodies and executive bodies of a company as well as auditors engaged by such company;
- those invited to participate in a scientific and research project of importance for Montenegro as professors or lecturers and scientists;
- lecturers participating in organized professional meetings and seminars;
- civil and military servants of governments of other countries coming to Montenegro under a cooperation agreement with the Government;
- those performing the services for which higher education or specialized knowledge and experience is required, provided that a prior approval was obtained from the state administration authority in charge of business activity for which the service is rendered;
- those performing research activities in Montenegro approved by the Government;
- correspondents accredited in Montenegro or foreign media reporters;
- artists and technical staff for opera, ballet, theatre, concerts, fine arts and other cultural events, if they do not stay in Montenegro for longer than thirty days, i.e., three months a year, with interruptions;
- authors and performers in the area of film, television, music, music and performing, dancing and ballet industry, as well as accompanying technical staff, if they do not stay in Montenegro for longer than thirty days, i.e., three months a year, with interruptions;
- employees of a foreign company who conduct additional training and professional development of employees, as well as employees who take additional training and professional development in a legal entity with the seat in Montenegro which is connected with a foreign company by business or ownership;
- those coming to Montenegro for the participation in sports competitions;
- those carrying out the activities of delivery, assembly, and servicing of machinery and equipment, if their work does not last longer than thirty days uninterruptedly, i.e., three months a year in total, with interruptions;
- those participating in fair or exhibition events where their employer exhibits;
- pupils or students who carry out their apprenticeship in Montenegro under the international pupil, i.e., student, exchange agreement;
- those active in registered humanitarian organizations;
- service providers negotiating the sale of services or concluding service agreements;
- staff of a circus or an amusement park.

125. Legal entities and natural persons using the services of foreign nationals shall have a concluded agreement or other evidence of doing business with a foreign national or foreign employer who posts a foreign national to Montenegro for work, prior to coming of such foreign national to Montenegro. Under the issued work registration certificate, a foreign national may work on the entire territory of Montenegro for the same employer or service recipient.[196]

196. Article 85 of the Law on Foreign Nationals.

§4. Position of Family Members

126. Family members should meet individually all the above-mentioned requirements for a short stay. Accordingly, each family member must hold a passport or ID and a visa unless he/she has one of the categories (citizenship) that are exempted from these requirements.

Chapter 3. Temporary Residence

§1. Conditions for Temporary Residence

127. A temporary residence may be granted to a foreign national intending to stay in Montenegro for longer than ninety days for the purposes of:

- family reunification;
- schooling;
- participation in international student exchange programmes or in other youth programmes;
- specialization, professional competence training or practical training of foreign nationals;
- scientific research work;
- medical treatment;
- humanitarian reasons;
- exercising the right to enjoy as well as to dispose of a real property owned in Montenegro;
- religious service;
- volunteering in the European Voluntary Service Programme;
- a stateless person's stay;
- work;
- other events, according to the law and an international treaty.

128. As a result of granted temporary residence, Ministry of Interior is issuing a temporary residence permit or temporary residence and work permit. A foreign national to whom temporary residence permit has been issued on grounds of the above-listed reasons is obliged to stay in Montenegro in accordance with the purpose for which the residence has been approved. In other words, it is not allowed to change the purpose of residence during the permitted temporary residence.[197]

129. The general rule is that a foreign national may be issued a temporary residence permit and a temporary residence and work permit if:

- he/she possesses sufficient funds to support himself/herself;
- he/she has provided accommodation;
- he/she holds health insurance;
- he/she holds either a valid foreign travel document or identity card;
- he/she has not been imposed an entry and stay ban in Montenegro;
- in Montenegro he/she has not been pronounced a final judgment sentencing him/her to an effective imprisonment longer than six months, for a criminal offence that is pursued ex officio, or a judgment legal effects ceased (does not apply to a foreign national under the age of 16);

197. Articles 38, 39 and 40 of the Law on Foreign Nationals.

– in his/her country of origin he/she has not been pronounced a final judgment sentencing him/her to an effective imprisonment longer than six months, for a criminal offence that is pursued ex officio, or a judgment legal effects *ceased (does not apply to a foreign national under the age of 16)*;
– national and/or internal security or public health-related restrictions do not exist;
– he/she has submitted evidence justifying his/her permit application.[198]

130. In relation to the purposes of temporary residence, a foreign national who is applying for temporary residence also needs to meet conditions which depend on the declared purpose of residence, in addition to the general conditions.

131. Evidence of the justification of an application for issuing a temporary residence permit for the purpose of work is considered to be written offer of an employer for the employment of a foreign national at a particular job position, evidence of the acquired level of education and qualifications, evidence of medical fitness, excerpt from the document on job description of the employer.[199]

132. Evidence of the justification of an application for issuing a temporary residence permit for the purpose of family reunification is considered to be the document issued by a competent authority proving that a foreigner is a member of the immediate family of a Montenegrin citizen or a member of the immediate family of a foreigner who has been granted permanent residence or temporary residence in Montenegro.[200]

133. Evidence of the justification of an application for issuing a temporary residence permit for the purpose of schooling is considered to be his schooling certificate.[201]

134. Evidence of the justification of an application for issuing a temporary residence permit for the purpose of participation in international student exchange programmes or in other youth programmes is considered to be certificate of the state administration authority responsible for the implementation of international treaties on pupil or student exchange programmes, corroborating the participation of the foreign national in the international exchange programme and certificate of a competent authority or institution of financing the costs of schooling or study, support, accommodation and health insurance as well as the costs of return of the foreign national back to the country whose citizen he is.[202]

135. Evidence of the justification of an application for issuing a temporary residence permit for the purpose of specialization, professional competence training or

198. Article 43 of the Law on Foreign Nationals.
199. Article 69 of the Law on Foreign Nationals.
200. Article 44 of the Law on Foreign Nationals.
201. Article 47 of the Law on Foreign Nationals.
202. Article 48 of the Law on Foreign Nationals.

practical training of foreign nationals is considered to be certificate of the competent authority, institution, or other legal entity in Montenegro that his/her specialization, professional training or practical course was approved, as well as the curriculum of the specialization, professional training or practical training also defining the duration thereof.[203]

136. Evidence of the justification of an application for issuing a temporary residence permit for the purpose of scientific research work is considered to be the contract concluded with a scientific or research institution or institution of higher education or with another legal entity or natural person, in accordance with the Law.[204]

137. Evidence of the justification of an application for issuing a temporary residence permit for the purpose of medical treatment is considered to be certificate issued by healthcare institution in which he or she is to be treated, and which shall also contain the time required for treatment.[205]

138. Evidence of the justification of an application for issuing a temporary residence permit for the purpose of exercising the right to enjoy as well as to dispose of a real property owned in Montenegro is considered to be real estate folio in the land register or other evidence confirming the ownership of such real estate, in accordance with the law governing the real estate cadastre.[206]

139. Evidence of the justification of an application for issuing a temporary residence permit for the purpose of religious service is considered to be the confirmation that the religious community in which he or she intends to perform a religious ceremony and religious affairs has registered its activities and seat in Montenegro in accordance with the regulations governing the legal status of religious communities.[207]

140. Evidence of the justification of an application for issuing a temporary residence permit for the purpose of volunteering in the European Voluntary Service Programme is considered to be concluded contract on volunteer service signed for the purpose of participation in the volunteer programme.[208]

§2. Administrative Procedures and Documents for Residence

141. A foreign national personally applies for temporary residence permit to the Ministry of Interior in the place of residence and he/she may remain in Montenegro

203. Article 49 of the Law on Foreign Nationals.
204. Article 50 of the Law on Foreign Nationals.
205. Article 51 of the Law on Foreign Nationals.
206. Article 56 of the Law on Foreign Nationals.
207. Article 57 of the Law on Foreign Nationals.
208. Article 58 of the Law on Foreign Nationals.

until the issuing of an enforceable decision. He/she is obliged to submit the evidence of the fulfilment of conditions, such as:

- sufficient funds to support himself/herself *(evidence of possession of means of subsistence for the issuance of a temporary residence permit shall be as follows: evidence of possession of funds in a bank account (credit card, savings book, confirmation of a commercial bank on account transactions), evidence of personal income from work engagement in the last three months, evidence of the amount of the scholarship, evidence of the provision of treatment costs, evidence that the means of subsistence have been provided on the basis of the lease of immovable property that a foreign national owns in Montenegro or a statement by which a natural or legal person shall be obliged to bear the costs of the stay of a foreign national. A foreign national shall be deemed to have the means of subsistence if he possesses cash in the amount of at least EUR 1,000 for each day of requested stay. Evidence of possession of means of subsistence for the issuance of a temporary residence and work permit shall be considered to be the written offer of an employer for employment of a foreign national at a particular job position, in which the minimum amount of net earnings in the amount of EUR 31,000 is stated)*;[209]
- he/she has provided accommodation *(evidence of secured accommodation shall mean a property right certificate in a residential area or a concluded lease agreement, i.e., a written statement of the person where a foreign national has secured accommodation, a certificate from the employer about the provided collective accommodation or a certificate of accommodation at a business entity or entrepreneur or a natural person registered for providing accommodation services)*;[210]
- he/she holds health insurance *(the evidence of health insurance shall mean travel health insurance provided by an authorized insurance company, health insurance provided in accordance with international agreements or health insurance realized under the conditions and in the manner determined by a special law)*;[211]
- he/she holds either a valid foreign travel document or identity card issued to him/her by another country's competent authority, the validity period of which must be at minimum three months longer than the period of his/her granted stay, or a stateless travel document;
- in his/her country of origin, he/she has not been pronounced a final judgment sentencing him/her to an effective imprisonment longer than six months, for a criminal offence that is pursued ex officio, or a judgment legal effects ceased.

---

209. Article 9 of the Rulebook on Forms, More Detailed Conditions and Manner of Issuing the Temporary Residence Permit and the Temporary Residence and Work Permit, 'Official Gazette of Montenegro', No. 25/2019.
210. Article 10 of the Rulebook on Forms, More Detailed Conditions and Manner of Issuing the Temporary Residence Permit and the Temporary Residence and Work Permit, 'Official Gazette of Montenegro', No. 25/2019.
211. Article 11 of the Rulebook on Forms, More Detailed Conditions and Manner of Issuing the Temporary Residence Permit and the Temporary Residence and Work Permit, 'Official Gazette of Montenegro', No. 25/2019.

In addition to all the above, a foreign national is obliged to submit evidence justifying his permit application, in regard to the purpose of residence he is applying for.

142. Ministry of Interior is obliged to obtain opinion from the Agency for National Security and the Police on the existence of any obstacles for the issuing of a temporary residence permit for the reasons of national or internal security. The Ministry makes a decision within forty days from the date when the application was duly filed. Temporary residence permit may be issued for the validity period of up to one year and may be extended for the same period.[212]

143. A foreign national is obliged to file to the Ministry of Interior the application for the extension of a temporary residence permit personally, in the place of residence, not later than within thirty days prior to the expiry of the validity period of the temporary residence permit. In the event that the application for the extension of the permit is approved, a temporary residence permit shall be issued with a new validity period of up to one year. In addition to the application for the extension of the permit, a foreign national is obliged to submit a valid foreign travel document or a personal identity card and the evidence of the grounds of application for the issuing of a temporary residence permit.[213]

144. In the event that the foreign national who has been issued a temporary residence permit intends to temporarily stay in another place in Montenegro for longer than three days, he or she has to file the application for registration of residence. He or she has to file the application for registration of residence also in the event when he or she intends to stay in another place in Montenegro for longer than twenty-four hours. He or she has to file to the police the application for previous registration, within twenty-four hours from his or her arrival to the place of residence. Also, he or she is obliged to file to the police the application for deregistration of residence, on a prescribed form, within twenty-four hours prior to leaving the place of residence. For a child, the registration and deregistration of the previous mentioned residence shall be filed by a parent, adoptive parent, guardian, foster parent or the persons to whom the child is entrusted for care, raising, upbringing and education.[214]

§3. Legal Position of Residents

145. Generally, foreign nationals are provided with equal access to the judicial system, without discrimination in relation to Montenegrin citizens. The Constitution of Montenegro and ratified international agreements provide equal protection

212. Articles 61, 62 and 63 of the Law on Foreign Nationals.
213. Article 64 of the Law on Foreign Nationals.
214. Article 96 of the Law on Foreign Nationals.

of all persons in a general way, regardless of whether they are foreign or Montenegrin citizens. Everyone has the right to equal legal protection, without discrimination, and to use maternal language in the proceedings before the court and other state bodies or institutions.

146. Rights to social security (pension and disability insurance, social protection and financial support to families and children) are regulated in accordance with bilateral agreements on social security with other countries. These agreements cover the basic principles and rules, such as: the principle of aggregation of insurance and residence periods necessary for establishing the right to social security benefits, equal treatment of citizens of the contracting states, the principle of preservation of the acquired rights, and the principle of payment of pensions within the territory of another contracting state.

147. According to the Law on Social and Child Protection,[215] the rights in the area of social and child protection established by this Law and international treaty may be exercised by a foreign national with granted temporary residence in the state, in accordance with a special law. Material benefits from social care are the following: material securing, personal disability benefit, allowance for care and assistance, funeral costs, single monetary assistance, allowance for a parent or guardian beneficiary of personal disability benefit. Material benefits from child protection are as follows: allowance for newborn child, child allowance, nutrition costs in preschool institutions, assistance for upbringing and education of children and youth with special educational needs, reimbursement of salary compensation and salary compensation for maternity, i.e., parental leave, compensation based on childbirth, reimbursement of salary and salary compensation for work with half of full-time.

148. Primary education is obligatory for all children from the age of 6 to 15 and it lasts nine years. For the acquisition of general secondary education (high school) and vocational secondary education in an institution financed by the Budget of Montenegro, if a foreign national is a full-time student, he/she does not pay tuition fees. If he/she is a part-time student, he/she pays the appropriate tuition fees. Recognition of the certificate of acquired or commenced education (primary school, secondary vocational or secondary general school or higher education), in order to continue education, is carried out in the appropriate educational institution in which you wish to continue your education. The same is relevant for the higher education that has been commenced; i.e., the recognition is given by the institution of higher education where the education is to be continued. Foreign nationals who have a temporary or permanent residence in Montenegro are equal in exercising their right to education (preschool, primary, secondary) with Montenegrin citizens.

149. For the acquisition of vocational education and general secondary education (gymnasium) in a publicly funded institution, a full-time student (Montenegrin

215. *Zakon o socijalnoj i dječijoj zaštiti*, 'Official Gazette of Montenegro', Nos 27/13, 01/15, 42/15, 47/15, 56/16, 66/16, 01/17, 31/17, 42/17, 50/17.

citizen and foreign national) does not pay tuition fees, while the part-time student pays tuition fees in accordance with the regulations. Ministry of Education may determine the number of places of enrolment in high schools and vocational schools for foreign nationals who are educated on the principle of reciprocity in accordance with an international agreement, as well as the number of places under the student exchange programme.

150. Foreign nationals and Montenegrin citizens are completely equal in terms of the amount of tuition, i.e., the amount of tuition is the same for foreign students and for domestic students who pay for tuition. Students who are funded by the Budget may exercise the right to home and board accommodation, student loans and scholarships and transportation participation. However, students who self-finance (domestic and foreign nationals) can also enjoy the right to accommodation and food at an economical cost if there are vacancies left after the allocation of places in the dorm.

151. An educational document on the basis of which a foreign citizen enrols in a certain grade of primary and secondary school or enrols in a higher education institution acquired abroad is subject to the procedure of recognition, in accordance with the Law on the Recognition of Foreign Educational Documents and the Equalization of Qualifications.[216]

152. According to the Law on Health Care,[217] a foreign national is entitled to healthcare in accordance with this Law and international treaty. The healthcare institution and healthcare professionals are obliged to provide a foreign national with urgent medical assistance. A foreign national shall bear the costs of the emergency medical care or other healthcare provided, according to the price list of the health institution, unless otherwise regulated by an international treaty. So, a foreign national pays a fee to the health institution according to the price list of the health institution, and if their country is a signatory of an international agreement with Montenegro, according to the type of agreement, they are entitled to reimbursement of the medical costs according to national regulations.

153. Given the way international agreements regulate healthcare, the agreements can be grouped into three groups, namely:

(1) Healthcare with following countries is regulated under the insurance principle, which implies that each state bears the cost of healthcare for its policyholders, with foreign nationals using healthcare under the agreement not directly paying the fee for the health services provided, but rather the cost of healthcare are calculated and reimbursed between the competent insurance carriers of the two countries (Austria, Belgium, Germany, the Netherlands, Luxembourg, France, Romania, the Czech Republic, Italy, Macedonia,

216. *Zakon o priznanju stranih obrazovnih isprava i kvalifikacija*, 'Official Gazette of Montenegro', Nos 57/2011, 42/2016, 56/2018.

217. *Zakon o zdrastvenoj zaštiti*, 'Official Gazette of Montenegro', Nos 03/16, 39/16, 02/17.

Croatia, Bosnia and Herzegovina, Serbia and Hungary). In order to exercise the right to healthcare in Montenegro, the insures of these states must obtain from their competent health insurance providers a bilingual certificate of the right to use healthcare during their temporary stay in our country.

(2) Healthcare with following countries is regulated on the principle of reciprocity, which means that foreign nationals who use healthcare under the agreement do not pay the fee for the health services provided, but the healthcare costs fall on the country of the healthcare provider (UK, Bulgaria, Slovakia, Poland). In order for nationals of these countries to exercise their right to healthcare, they need to have a valid travel document and proof that they are insured in their own country.

(3) The insures of the following countries are entitled to healthcare in the same way and under the same conditions as Montenegrin insures, with the direct payment of costs for the use of health services (Switzerland, Sweden, Denmark and Norway). Healthcare institutions are obliged to issue invoices to them in which they are entitled to reimbursement in their own country under national regulations.

154. According to the Law on Health Insurance,[218] the insured persons, for the purposes of this Law, are: a foreigner national who works in Montenegro with domestic legal entities, or individuals, on the basis of special agreements and agreements on international technical cooperation; a foreign national employed in Montenegro by international organizations and institutions and other foreign legal and natural persons, unless otherwise stipulated by an international treaty or insured under the regulations of another country.

§4. Position of Family Members of Residents

155. The Law on Foreign Nationals stipulates that one of the purposes of applying for a temporary residence is family reunification. A foreign national residing in Montenegro under a temporary residence permit or a permanent residence permit has the right to family reunification with his/her close family members or as defined in the Law – 'immediate family members'. According to the Law, as immediate family members are considered spouses, their minor children born in or out of wedlock, underage adopted children or underage stepchildren, parents or adoptive parents of minor children. Exceptionally, another relative may also be considered as an immediate family member if there are distinct, personal or humanitarian reasons for family reunification in Montenegro. In the case of a polygamous marriage, family reunification is to be allowed only to one spouse. Temporary residence permit for family reunification may be extended where the Montenegrin citizen has deceased, as well as in an event of the dissolution of marriage that lasted continuously for at minimum three years in Montenegro, as well as to a child who has attained the age of majority, where he or she fulfils the requirements of the Law and where he or she

218. *Ibid.*

had a granted temporary residence in Montenegro for a continuous three-year period for the purpose of family reunification.[219]

156. According to the Law on Foreign Nationals, temporary residence permit for family reunification shall not be granted to a foreign national if it has been found that the marriage was concluded as one of convenience. A marriage of convenience is considered to be the marriage that a foreign national entered into with the sole aim of obtaining an entry into or residence in Montenegro contrary to this Law. Circumstances that may indicate that a marriage is one of convenience are: spouses do not observe the marital community; spouses fail to fulfil marriage obligations; spouses have not met before the conclusion of their marriage; spouses do not speak a language they both understand; spouses do not provide true personal data; funds were given to conclude the marriage, however, not as a custom of giving dowry, where the spouses come from the countries cherishing the tradition of the dowry; where there is evidence that the spouses used to conclude marriages of convenience before either in Montenegro or in a foreign country.[220]

219. Articles 44 and 45 of the Law on Foreign Nationals.
220. Article 46 of the Law on Foreign Nationals.

Chapter 4. Long-Term Residence

§1. Conditions for Long-Term Residence

157. The Law on Foreign Nationals specifies conditions for granting permanent residence to foreign nationals. Permanent residence may be granted to a foreign national who, until the date of filing the application for the permit issue, has legally resided in Montenegro, for uninterrupted five years, based on:

- granted temporary residence;
- granted asylum or subsidiary protection in accordance with the law governing international and temporary protection of foreign nationals.

158. Exceptionally, a permanent residence permit may be issued to a foreign national who, until the date of filing the application for the issuing of permit, had a granted temporary residence in Montenegro for less than five years uninterruptedly, if so required by humanitarian reasons or if that is in the interest of Montenegro. If a foreign national previously had the temporary residence granted in Montenegro for schooling or specialization, professional training or practical training, only half of the time spent under the granted temporary residence shall be taken into account as the time necessary for granting a permanent residence. For the time necessary for granting permanent residence to a foreign national to whom asylum or subsidiary protection has been granted in accordance with the law governing international and temporary protection of foreign nationals, a half of the time that has passed from the filing of application for international protection until the issuing of the decision under which the international protection is granted shall be taken into account. If the time from the filing of application for international protection until the issuing of the decision under which the international protection is granted was longer than eighteen months, such entire time shall be taken into account.[221]

159. A permanent residence permit may be granted to a child:

- whose one parent, at the time of his or her birth, is a Montenegrin national and domiciled in Montenegro;
- whose both parents, at the time of his or her birth, have a granted permanent residence;
- whose one parent, at the time of his or her birth, has a granted permanent residence, whereas the other parent is either unknown or dead.[222]

160. A foreign national may be granted a permanent residence permit if he/she has a valid travel document; permanent, regular and sufficient funds to support himself/herself; health insurance; accommodation provided and knowledge of the

221. Article 86 of the Law on Foreign Nationals.
222. Article 87 of the Law on Foreign Nationals.

Montenegrin language at the level which enables elementary communication. A foreign national shall not be issued a permanent residence permit in the case of the existence of reasons/obstacles in terms of national/internal security.

§2. Administrative Procedures and Documents for Long-Term Residence

161. A foreign national personally applies for permanent residence permit to the Ministry of Interior in the place of residence on the prescribed form. At the moment of filing the application for the issuing of permanent residence permit, a foreign national must have a granted temporary residence, asylum or subsidiary protection in accordance with the law governing international and temporary protection of foreign nationals. Together with the application, a foreign national shall submit evidence on possession of permanent, regular and sufficient funds to support himself (evidence on the incomes based on the work engagement in the last three months, or incomes based on the pension, evidence of earning revenues based on agriculture, handcraft or other activities in amount necessary for the support); on possession of health insurance (health insurance provided in accordance with international agreements and health insurance provided under conditions and in a manner stipulated by a special law) and on accommodation provided (real estate folio in the land register or other evidence proving ownership over housing in accordance with the law governing land registry of real estate or signed contract on lease, or right to use the accommodation).[223]

162. The Ministry of Interior is obliged to obtain opinion from the Agency for National Security and the Police on the existence of any obstacles for the issuing of a permanent residence permit for the reasons of national or internal security. The Ministry of Interior makes a decision within six months from the date when the application was duly filed.[224]

163. A foreign national is entitled to permanent residence in Montenegro for an indefinite period. A permanent residence permit is issued with a validity period of five years, with the obligation of extension. The application for extension of the residence permit shall be submitted within eight days from the date of expiry of permit validity. To a foreign national younger than four years of age, a permanent residence permit is issued with a validity period of two years.[225]

164. In the event that the foreign national who has been issued a permanent residence permit intends to temporarily stay in another place in Montenegro for longer than three days, he or she has to file the application for registration of residence. He or she has to file the application for registration of residence also in the event when he or she intends to stay in another place in Montenegro for longer than twenty-four

223. Article 6 of the Rulebook on the Method of Issuing and the Form of Permanent Residence Permit.
224. Article 90 of the Law on Foreign Nationals.
225. Article 91 of the Law on Foreign Nationals.

hours. He or she has to file to the police the application for the previous registration, within twenty-four hours from his or her arrival to the place of residence. Also, he or she is obliged to file to the police the application for deregistration of residence, on a prescribed form, within twenty-four hours prior to leaving the place of residence. For a child, the registration and deregistration of the previous mentioned residence shall be filed by a parent, adoptive parent, guardian, foster parent or the persons to whom the child is entrusted for care, raising, upbringing and education.[226]

§3. Legal Position of Long-Term Residents

165. In principle, long-term resident shall enjoy the same rights that the Montenegrin nationals are entitled to, except so-called rights reserved exclusively for domestic citizens like, for instance, voting or running for political office, holding certain jobs that have a high-level security clearance requirement, possessing Montenegrin travel documents, etc.

166. A foreign national holding a permanent residence permit has the right to:

- work, work placement, and the rights during unemployment;
- education and professional development;
- recognition of diplomas and certificates;
- social assistance, health and pension insurance;
- tax reliefs in accordance with the law;
- access to the goods and services market;
- freedom of association, connection and membership in organizations which represent the interests of workers or employers.

The above-listed rights shall be exercised in accordance with the laws governing the manner of exercising such rights.[227]

167. Rights to social security (pension and disability insurance, social protection and financial support to families and children) are regulated in accordance with bilateral agreements on social security with other countries. These agreements cover the basic principles and rules, such as: the principle of aggregation of insurance and residence periods necessary for establishing the right to social security benefits, equal treatment of citizens of the contracting states, the principle of preservation of the acquired rights, and the principle of payment of pensions within the territory of another contracting state. Foreign nationals are provided with equal access to the judicial system, without discrimination in relation to Montenegrin citizens. The Constitution of Montenegro and ratified international agreements provide equal protection of all persons in a general way, regardless of whether they are foreign or

226. Article 96 of the Law on Foreign Nationals.
227. Article 93 of the Law on Foreign Nationals.

Montenegrin citizens. Everyone has the right to equal legal protection, without discrimination, and to use maternal language in the proceedings before the court and other state bodies or institutions.

168. According to the Law on Social and Child Protection, the rights in the area of social and child protection established by this Law and international treaty may be exercised by a foreigner with granted permanent residence in the state, in accordance with a special law. Material benefits from social care are the following: material securing, personal disability benefit, allowance for care and assistance, funeral costs, single monetary assistance, allowance for a parent or guardian beneficiary of personal disability benefit.

169. Material benefits from child protection are as follows: allowance for newborn child, child allowance, nutrition costs in preschool institutions, assistance for upbringing and education of children and youth with special educational needs, reimbursement of salary compensation and salary compensation for maternity, i.e., parental leave, compensation based on childbirth, reimbursement of salary and salary compensation for work with half of full-time.

170. Primary education is obligatory for all children from the age of 6 to 15 and it lasts nine years. For the acquisition of general secondary education (high school) and vocational secondary education in an institution financed by the Budget of Montenegro, if a foreign national is a full-time student, he does not pay tuition fees. If he is a part-time student, he pays the appropriate tuition fees. Recognition of the certificate of acquired or commenced education (primary school, secondary vocational or secondary general school or higher education), in order to continue education, is carried out in the appropriate educational institution in which you wish to continue your education. The same is relevant for the higher education that has been commenced; i.e., the recognition is given by the institution of higher education where the education is to be continued.

171. According to the Law on Health Care, a foreign national is entitled to healthcare in accordance with this Law and international treaty. The healthcare institution and healthcare professionals are obliged to provide a foreign national with urgent medical assistance. A foreign national shall bear the costs of the emergency medical care or other healthcare provided, according to the price list of the health institution, unless otherwise regulated by an international treaty.

172. According to the Law on Health Insurance, the insured persons, for the purposes of this Law, are: a foreigner national who works in Montenegro with domestic legal entities, or individuals, on the basis of special agreements and agreements on international technical cooperation; a foreign national employed in Montenegro by international organizations and institutions and other foreign legal and natural persons, unless otherwise stipulated by an international treaty or insured under the regulations of another country; a foreign national with permanent residence who receive a pension or other benefit exclusively from a foreign insurance carrier, unless otherwise stipulated by an international agreement.

173. Also, according to the Law on Health Insurance, nationals of countries with which an international social security treaty has been concluded shall receive healthcare to the extent specified in that treaty. Persons who do not have the status of insured persons under any of the legal grounds, who have a residence, that is, the status of a person with permanent residence in Montenegro and do not have the status of an insured person in another country with which an international social insurance contract is concluded, may acquire the status of insured person provided that they have paid a contribution, in accordance with a separate law.

174. Also, after sometime in the status of permanent residence, a foreign national can apply for Montenegrin citizenship, according to conditions established by Law on Montenegrin Citizenship.[228]

§4. Position of Family Members of Long-Term Residents

175. A foreign national residing in Montenegro under a permanent residence permit has the right to family reunification with his/her close family members or as defined in the Law on Foreign Nationals – 'immediate family members'. According to the Law, as immediate family members are considered spouses, their minor children born in or out of wedlock, underage adopted children or underage stepchildren, parents or adoptive parents of minor children. Exceptionally, another relative may also be considered as an immediate family member if there are distinct, personal or humanitarian reasons for family reunification in Montenegro. In the case of a polygamous marriage, family reunification is to be allowed only to one spouse. Temporary residence permit may be extended until the conditions for obtaining the permanent residence permit are met.

176. The application procedure for obtaining permanent residence for family member is the same as the application procedure for every other foreign national with temporary residence applying for permanent residence. The applicant has to submit evidence on possession of permanent, regular and sufficient funds to support himself/herself; evidence on possession of health insurance and evidence on accommodation provided.

228. *Zakon o crnogorskom državljanstvu*, 'Official Gazette of Montenegro', Nos 13/2008, 40/2010, 28/2011, 46/2011, 20/2014, 54/2016.

Part III. Right of Residence for Specific Categories of Persons

Chapter 1. Nationals with Preferential Treatment

§1. EU CITIZENS

I. Entry of an EU Citizen and His/Her Family Member Who Is a Third-Country National

177. According to the Law on Foreign Nationals,[229] a national of an EU Member State may enter Montenegro if:

- he or she has a valid foreign travel document or personal identity card issued by the competent authority of such state;
- he or she is not banned from entering and staying in Montenegro;
- there are no grounds in relation to national, i.e., internal security or public health.

178. A national of an EU Member State may enter Montenegro without a visa or granted temporary residence. If a national of an EU Member State does not have the above-mentioned documents, the Police shall provide him or her with the opportunity to acquire necessary documents or otherwise prove that he or she is a national of the EU Member State. A national of an EU Member State with the valid travel document or personal identity card issued by the competent authority of such state has the right to leave Montenegro for the purpose of travelling to another Member State.[230]

179. A family member of an EU Member State national, who is a third-country national, may enter Montenegro for family reunification with a national of an EU Member State if:

- he or she has a valid travel document and issued visa, if visa is required, unless otherwise provided for by an international treaty;

229. Provisions of the Law on Foreign Nationals relating to EU Member State nationals with preferential treatment shall be applied from the date of accession of Montenegro to the European Union and relate to the nationals of Iceland, the Principality of Liechtenstein, the Kingdom of Norway, and the Swiss Confederation.

230. Article 150 of the Law on Foreign Nationals.

– he or she is not banned from entering and staying in Montenegro;
– the reasons of national, i.e., internal security or public health do not exist.

180. If a family member of an EU Member State national who is a third-country national does not have the documents referred above listed, the Police shall enable him or her to acquire the necessary document or otherwise prove that he or she is entitled to the freedom of movement and stay in the EU as a family member of the national of the EU Member State. To the third-country national, who is a family member of the EU Member State national, the police may issue a visa at the border crossing point, provided that the reasons of national, i.e., internal security or public health do not exist. A third-country national, who is a family member of an EU Member State national, is exempted from payment of the fee for visa issuing, in accordance with the law governing administrative fees. The family member of the EU Member State national, who is a third-country national with granted temporary residence in Montenegro, can enter Montenegro without visa. A family member of an EU Member State national, who is a third-country national with a valid foreign travel document issued by the competent authority of the third country, can leave Montenegro for the purpose of travel to another EU Member State.[231]

II. Short Stay of an EU Citizen and His/Her Family Member Who Is a Third-Country National

181. The national of an EU Member State has the right to stay in Montenegro for up to ninety days from the date of entry into Montenegro, provided that he or she has a valid travel document or a personal identity card issued by a competent authority of such state.[232]

182. A third-country national, who is a family member of an EU Member State national, has the right to stay in Montenegro for up to ninety days from the date of entry in Montenegro, provided that he or she holds a valid foreign travel document issued by the competent authority of the third country.[233]

III. Stay of an EU Citizen and His/Her Family Member Who Is a Third-Country National Longer than Ninety Days

183. A national of an EU Member State may stay in Montenegro for longer than ninety days for work or entrepreneurial activity; for studying or professional training; if he or she has enough funds to support himself or herself or his or her family

231. Article 161 of the Law on Foreign Nationals.
232. Article 151 of the Law on Foreign Nationals.
233. Article 162 of the Law on Foreign Nationals.

members during his or her stay in Montenegro and has social insurance in Montenegro, regardless of the purpose of stay; if he or she is a family member of a national of an EU Member State.[234]

184. A national of an EU Member State personally applies for residence registration for the purpose of work or entrepreneurial activity, in the place of residence. In addition, he or she is obliged to submit:

- a valid travel document or personal identity card issued by the competent authority of such state;
- employment contract concluded with the employer or the evidence that he or she has been registered as an entrepreneur, in accordance with the law governing the forms of carrying out entrepreneurial activities and their registration. The Ministry of Interior is in charge of the issuing of certificate of residence registration.[235]

185. A national of an EU Member State, whose employment has been terminated or who no longer carries out entrepreneurial activity, may continue to stay in Montenegro under the certificate of residence registration if:

- he or she is temporarily incapable of work due to illness or any kind of accident;
- the need for his or her work has ceased to exist through no fault of his or hers, and he or she has worked in Montenegro for a minimum of one year and was registered with the competent authority as an unemployed person;
- he or she becomes involved in the professional training programme which relates to the previous employment.

186. A national of an EU Member State, whose fixed-term employment contract concluded for a term shorter than twelve months has terminated, and who is registered with the competent authority as an unemployed person, or if in the first twelve months of work in Montenegro under permanent employment contract he or she lost their job through no fault of his or hers and is registered as an unemployed person, shall continue to stay in Montenegro under the certificate of residence registration, up to six months after the employment termination.[236]

187. A national of an EU Member State personally applies for residence registration for the purpose of studying or professional training, in the place of residence. In addition, he or she is obliged to submit:

- a valid foreign travel document or personal identity card issued by a competent authority of such state;
- evidence of possessing the means to support himself or herself and his or her family members (the amount of funds may not be lower than the amount of funds

234. Article 152 of the Law on Foreign Nationals.
235. Article 153 of the Law on Foreign Nationals.
236. Article 154 of the Law on Foreign Nationals.

provided for social welfare received by a Montenegrin national, in accordance with the regulations governing social welfare);
- evidence that he or she has health insurance;
- certificate issued by the institution of higher education confirming that he or she studies in Montenegro. The Ministry of Interior is issuing certificate of residence registration.[237]

188. In the case of a national of an EU Member State has enough funds to support himself or herself or his or her family members during his or her stay in Montenegro and has social insurance in Montenegro, regardless of the purpose of stay and he or she wants to reside in Montenegro, he or she personally applies for residence registration, in the place of residence. In addition, he or she is obliged to submit:

- a valid foreign travel document or a personal identity card issued by a competent authority of such state;
- evidence that he or she has taken out health insurance for himself or herself and for his or her family members;
- evidence of possessing sufficient means to support himself or herself and his or her family members while residing in Montenegro (the amount of funds may not be lower than the amount of funds provided for social welfare received by a Montenegrin national, in accordance with the regulations governing social welfare). The Ministry of Interior is issuing certificate of residence registration.[238]

189. A family member of a national of an EU Member State personally applies for residence registration, in the place of residence. The following persons are considered as family members:

- spouses;
- children of up to and including 21 years of age or dependents, as well as children of spouses or partners;
- relatives in a direct line who are dependents, as well as relatives in a direct line of spouses or partners;
- a person who in the country from which he or she came from is a dependent, or a household member of an EU Member State national, or when severe medical reasons strictly require an EU Member State national to personally care for a family member.

190. In addition, he or she is obliged to submit:

- a valid foreign travel document or personal identity card issued by the competent authority of such state;
- evidence of possessing means to support himself or herself and his or her family members;

237. Article 155 of the Law on Foreign Nationals.
238. Article 156 of the Law on Foreign Nationals.

– evidence that he or she, who has applied for the residence in Montenegro, is a family member of the national of the EU Member State.

Exceptionally, the evidence of possessing means to support himself or herself and his or her family members shall not be submitted by the family member of a national of an EU Member State who stays in Montenegro for the purpose of work or entrepreneurial activity. The Ministry of Interior is issuing certificate of residence registration.[239]

191. The certificate of residence registration in above-mentioned cases shall be issued within ten days from the date of application filing and upon the previously obtained opinion of the Agency for National Security and the Police on the existence of any obstacles for the reasons of national, i.e., internal security.[240]

192. The certificate of residence registration of a national of an EU Member State and of a member of his or her family shall cease to be valid if:

– he or she is banned from entering and staying in Montenegro;
– he or she was issued the certificate based on the untrue data or concealment of the actual objective and circumstances which were decisive for the issuing of the certificate;
– the reasons on the grounds of which the certificate was issued have ceased to exist;
– he or she deregisters his or her stay in Montenegro.

When deciding on the termination of validity of the certificate of residence, the duration of stay, as well as personal, family, economic and other circumstances shall be particularly taken into account.[241]

193. A third-country national, who is a family member of an EU Member State national, may be granted temporary residence if he or she has entered together with the EU Member State national or is joining the EU Member State national who temporarily stays in Montenegro. A third-country national, who is a family member of an EU Member State national, personally applies for the issuing of a temporary residence permit, in the place of residence. In addition, he or she is obliged to submit:

– a valid travel document;
– evidence of possessing the means to support himself or herself and his or her family members;
– evidence that he or she is a family member of the EU Member State national.

194. Exceptionally, the evidence of possessing the means to support himself or herself and his or her family members shall not be submitted if he or she is a family

239. Article 157 of the Law on Foreign Nationals.
240. Article 158 of the Law on Foreign Nationals.
241. Article 159 of the Law on Foreign Nationals.

member of the EU Member State national who holds the certificate of residence registration for the purpose of work or entrepreneurial activity.[242]

195. A temporary residence permit in the above-mentioned cases shall be issued within twenty days from the date of application filing and upon the previously obtained opinion of the Agency for National Security and the Police on the existence of any obstacles for the reasons of national, i.e., internal security and with the validity period of five years or for a shorter period, if the foreign national who has been issued the permit intends to stay in Montenegro for a period shorter than five years.[243]

196. In the case of death of the EU Member State national whose residence was registered in accordance with the Law on Foreign Nationals, or in the case of his or her departure from Montenegro, his or her family member, who is an EU Member State national, shall keep the right to temporary residence if he or she proves that he or she is employed in Montenegro or carries on entrepreneurial activity and has funds for support and health insurance for himself or herself or his or her family members, or if he or she is studying or attends professional training and submits evidence that he or she has funds for support and health insurance for himself or herself and his or her family members.

197. Also, in the case of death of an EU Member State national whose residence was registered in accordance with the Law on Foreign Nationals, his or her family member, who is a third-country national, shall keep the right to temporary residence if he or she stayed in Montenegro with the EU Member State national for at least one year and proves that he or she is employed in Montenegro or carries on entrepreneurial activity or has funds for support and health insurance for himself or herself and his or her family members.

198. In the case that an EU Member State national dies or leaves Montenegro, his or her children and the other parent taking care of such children shall keep the right to temporary residence, regardless of their citizenship, if the children stay in Montenegro and are enrolled in an educational institution, until the completion of their schooling. In the case of a divorce or marriage annulment, the spouse of an EU Member State national, who is an EU Member State national, shall keep the right to temporary residence if he or she is employed in Montenegro or carries out entrepreneurial activity and has funds for support and health insurance for himself or herself and his or her family members, or if he or she is studying or attends professional training and submits the evidence that he or she has funds for support and health insurance for himself or herself and his or her family members.

199. In the case of a divorce or marriage annulment, the spouse of the EU Member State national, who is a third-country national, and who is employed in Montenegro or carries out entrepreneurial activity, and submits evidence that has funds

242. Article 163 of the Law on Foreign Nationals.
243. Article 164 of the Law on Foreign Nationals.

for support and health insurance for himself or herself or his or her family members, can keep the right to temporary residence:

- if the marriage lasted at least three years, where the spouses spent a minimum of one year in Montenegro;
- in the case of enforcement of a parental right over the children of the EU Member State national who were entrusted to his or her custody by the agreement between spouses or under the court decision;
- in the case of enforcement of a parental right over the minor children who stay in Montenegro and who are entrusted for care and custody to another parent by the agreement of the spouses or under the court decision;
- due to extremely difficult circumstances such as domestic violence.[244]

200. A temporary residence permit of a family member of the EU Member State national, who is a third-country national, shall cease to be valid if:

- he or she is banned from entering and staying in Montenegro;
- he or she is granted temporary residence based on the untrue data or concealment of the actual objective and circumstances which were decisive for granting permanent residence;
- the reasons for which he or she was issued a temporary residence permit have ceased to exist;
- he or she deregisters his or her stay in Montenegro;
- he or she has stayed outside Montenegro during the period of temporary residence for longer than six months per year;
- during the validity period of temporary residence he or she has stayed outside Montenegro for longer than one year, uninterruptedly, unless he or she was absent for justifiable reasons such as pregnancy, birth of children, critical illness, studying, professional training, posting for work to another country or military service.[245]

IV. Permanent Residence of an EU Citizen and His/Her Family Member Who Is a Third-Country National

201. A permanent residence permit may be issued to an EU Member State national who until the date of the submission of application for the issuing of the permit has legally resided in Montenegro, for five years uninterruptedly, under the certificate of residence registration. The EU Member State national shall be considered to have uninterruptedly resided in Montenegro even when in the period of five years, he or she was absent from Montenegro more than once in the total duration of up to one year, or for six months during one year, or was absent from Montenegro due to the military service.

244. Article 165 of the Law on Foreign Nationals.
245. Article 166 of the Law on Foreign Nationals.

202. Exceptionally, a permanent residence permit may be issued to the EU Member State national if:

- he or she has temporarily stayed in Montenegro for work or entrepreneurial activity and has stopped working due to the fact that the conditions have been met for his or her old-age pension in Montenegro, and has been previously employed in Montenegro for a minimum of one year and has uninterruptedly resided in Montenegro for longer than three years;
- he or she is temporarily retired and has been previously employed in Montenegro for a minimum of one year and has uninterruptedly resided in Montenegro for longer than three years;
- he or she has temporarily stayed in Montenegro for work or entrepreneurial activity and has stopped working due to permanent work incapacity, and has uninterruptedly resided in Montenegro for longer than two years;
- he or she has temporarily stayed in Montenegro for work or entrepreneurial activity and has stopped working due to permanent work incapacity which is a consequence of a work-related injury or occupational disease based on which he or she has acquired disability pension in Montenegro, irrespective of the duration of his or her stay in Montenegro;
- he or she has temporarily stayed in Montenegro for work or entrepreneurial activity and after three years of uninterrupted work and residence in Montenegro became employed in another EU Member State, kept the temporary residence in Montenegro, and returns to Montenegro at least once a week.

203. An uninterrupted stay in Montenegro shall also be considered the period of residence for work or entrepreneurial activity of an EU Member State national who has worked in another EU Member State and has kept his or her residence in Montenegro. The unemployment period recorded with the competent employment authority which has occurred through no fault of the EU Member State national, and the period of incapacity for work due to illness or injury, shall be included in the employment period. An EU Member State national whose spouse, with whom he or she jointly stays in Montenegro, has Montenegrin citizenship or his or her Montenegrin citizenship was terminated upon the solemnization of marriage shall be granted permanent residence regardless of the duration of stay and employment in Montenegro.[246]

204. A permanent residence permit may be issued to a third-country national who is a family member of the EU Member State national if until the date of filing the application for the issuing of permit he or she has legally resided in Montenegro with the EU Member State national, for five years uninterruptedly, based on the granted temporary residence. A third-country national who is a family member of the EU Member State national shall be considered to have uninterruptedly resided in Montenegro even when in the period of five years, he or she was absent from Montenegro more than once in the total duration of up to one year or for six months

246. Article 167 of the Law on Foreign Nationals.

during one year, or was absent from Montenegro due to the military service. Exceptionally, a permanent residence permit may be issued to a third-country national who is a family member of the EU Member State national, if:

- the national of the EU Member State with whom he or she has resided in Montenegro died during the temporary residence, for the purpose of work which has lasted for two uninterrupted years prior to death or for a shorter period if death occurred as a consequence of a work-related injury or occupational disease;
- he or she has lost Montenegrin citizenship after marriage with the EU Member State national who is employed or carries on entrepreneurial activity;
- until the date of the submission of application for the issuing of the permit has legally resided in Montenegro, for five years uninterruptedly, under the certificate of residence registration. A third-country national family member who resides in Montenegro with an EU Member State national who has legally resided in Montenegro for five years uninterruptedly under the certificate of residence registration and has a permanent residence permit shall have the right to permanent residence, regardless of the duration of temporary residence in Montenegro.[247]

205. An EU Member State national and a third-country national who is a family member of an EU Member State national personally applies for the issuing of a permanent residence permit, in the place of residence. The Ministry of Interior is in charge to decide on the application for the issuing of a permanent residence permit to the EU Member State national, as soon as possible, not later than within three months from the date when the application was duly filed. On the application for the issuing of a permanent residence permit to a third-country national who is a family member of an EU Member State national, the Ministry of Interior is obliged to decide within six months from the date when the application was duly filed. The Ministry of Interior shall issue a permanent residence permit, with the prior opinion of the existence of obstacles for the reasons of national, i.e., internal security obtained from the Agency for National Security and the Police. A permanent residence permit validity period is ten years.[248]

206. Permanent residence shall be terminated for an EU Member State national and a third-country national who is a family member of an EU Member State national, if his or her entry and stay in Montenegro is banned and if it is established that he or she has uninterruptedly resided outside Montenegro for more than two years.[249]

247. Article 168 of the Law on Foreign Nationals.
248. Articles 169, 170, 171 and 172 of the Law on Foreign Nationals.
249. Article 173 of the Law on Foreign Nationals.

V. Purpose of Documents Issued to EU Member State Nationals and Members of Their Family

207. Certificate of residence registration, temporary residence permit and permanent residence permit issued to an EU Member State national, a family member of an EU Member State national, who is the national of the EU Member State, and to a third-country national who is a family member of an EU Member State national, shall be considered as public documents with which the foreign national proves that he or she has been granted residence in Montenegro.[250]

VI. Rights of an EU Member State National and Their Family Members

208. The rights of an EU Member State national as well as his or her family member, who has the right to reside in Montenegro, regardless of whether he or she is an EU Member State national or not, shall be equal to the rights of the Montenegrin nationals, in accordance with the Treaty on the Functioning of the EU. When issuing the documents on residence they shall be exempted from the payment of the fee.

209. The following members are considered as family:

- spouses;
- children of up to and including 21 years of age or dependents, as well as children of spouses or partners;
- relatives in a direct line who are dependents, as well as relatives in a direct line of spouses or partners;
- a person who in the country from which he or she came from is a dependent, or a household member of an EU Member State national, or when severe medical reasons strictly require an EU Member State national to personally care for a family member.[251]

250. Article 176 of the Law on Foreign Nationals.
251. Article 178 of the Law on Foreign Nationals.

Chapter 2. Students

210. A foreign national coming to Montenegro for participation in international pupil and student exchange programmes or in other youth programmes may be issued a temporary residence permit if he/she meets the following requirements:[252]

– he/she holds either a valid foreign travel document or identity card;
– he/she has not been imposed an entry and stay ban in Montenegro;
– in Montenegro he/she has not been pronounced a final judgment sentencing him/her to an effective imprisonment longer than six months, for a criminal offence that is pursued ex officio, or a judgment legal effects ceased (does not apply to a foreign national under the age of 16);
– in his/her country of origin he/she has not been pronounced a final judgment sentencing him/her to an effective imprisonment longer than six months, for a criminal offence that is pursued ex officio, or a judgment legal effects ceased (does not apply to a foreign national under the age of 16);
– national and/or internal security or public health-related restrictions do not exist;
– he/she has submitted evidence justifying his/her permit application (certificate of the state administration authority responsible for the implementation of international treaties on pupil or student exchange programmes, corroborating the participation of the foreign national in the international exchange programme and certificate of a competent authority or institution of financing the costs of schooling or study, support, accommodation and health insurance as well as the costs of return of the foreign national back to the country whose citizen he/she is. This Certificate is considered to be evidence of financial assets for support, provided accommodation and health insurance accompanying application for temporary residence permit).

211. In order to have the permit issued to a minor foreign national, a parental or guardian or legal representative consent is required. A student who has been issued the permit may work in Montenegro, but no longer than fifteen hours a week. After the completion of studies, a foreign national who meets the previously mentioned requirements may be issued a temporary residence permit in Montenegro for a validity period of nine months in order to seek employment.[253]

212. A temporary residence permit for specialization, professional training or practical training may be issued to a foreign national who has acquired a higher education qualification, for the purpose of professional training of interns, or to a foreign national who studies in another country for the purpose of practical training necessary to acquire a higher education qualification and who fulfils the following requirements:

– he/she possesses sufficient funds to support himself/herself;
– he/she has provided accommodation;

252. Article 48 of the Law on Foreign Nationals.
253. *Ibid.*

- he/she holds health insurance;
- he/she holds either a valid foreign travel document or identity card;
- he/she has not been imposed an entry and stay ban in Montenegro;
- in Montenegro he/she has not been pronounced a final judgment sentencing him/her to an effective imprisonment longer than six months, for a criminal offence that is pursued ex officio, or a judgment legal effects ceased (does not apply to a foreign national under the age of 16);
- in his/her country of origin he/she has not been pronounced a final judgment sentencing him/her to an effective imprisonment longer than six months, for a criminal offence that is pursued ex officio, or a judgment legal effects ceased (does not apply to a foreign national under the age of 16);
- national and/or internal security or public health-related restrictions do not exist;
- he/she has submitted evidence justifying his/her permit application (certificate of the competent authority, institution, or other legal entity in Montenegro that his/her specialization, professional training or practical course was approved, as well as the curriculum of the specialization, professional training or practical training also defining the duration thereof, and evidence of education level and qualifications acquired two years prior to filing the application, i.e., the evidence of the obligation to attend practical training for the purpose of acquiring a higher education qualification).[254]

213. Professional training, i.e., the practical training, shall be conducted in accordance with the curriculum containing:

- description of the curriculum for professional training of interns, i.e., for the practical training of students, and training, i.e., education objectives and phases;
- length of internship, i.e., of practical training;
- number of hours of professional training of interns, i.e., the hours of practical training;
- method of conducting and supervising the professional training of interns, i.e., the practical training;
- rights and obligations between interns, i.e., the students attending the professional training, and the employer.[255]

254. Article 49 of the Law on Foreign Nationals.
255. *Ibid.*

Chapter 3. Researchers

214. A temporary residence permit for scientific and research work may be issued to a foreign researcher who fulfils the following conditions:

- he/she possesses sufficient funds to support himself/herself;
- he/she has provided accommodation;
- he/she holds either a valid foreign travel document or identity card;
- he/she has not been imposed an entry and stay ban in Montenegro;
- in Montenegro he/she has not been pronounced a final judgment sentencing him/her to an effective imprisonment longer than six months, for a criminal offence that is pursued ex officio, or a judgment legal effects ceased;
- in his/her country of origin he has not been pronounced a final judgment sentencing him/her to an effective imprisonment longer than six months, for a criminal offence that is pursued ex officio, or a judgment legal effects ceased;
- national and/or internal security or public health-related restrictions do not exist;
- he/she has submitted evidence justifying his/her permit application (the contract concluded with a scientific or research institution or institution of higher education or with another legal entity or natural person).[256]

215. The certificate issued by a scientific research institution or higher education institution or another legal and natural person with whom the foreign researcher has concluded a contract is considered to be evidence on possessing means of subsistence and evidence on secured accommodation presented with the application, this certificate obliging the institution to bear the costs of subsistence, stay, accommodation and return of a foreign researcher. The researcher is a foreign national who has acquired an academic title of the Doctor of Philosophy or an appropriate higher education qualification which enables him or her the access to doctoral programmers, and who has been elected by a scientific and research institution or institution of higher education or other legal entity or natural person in Montenegro to carry out scientific and research activities for which such qualification is normally required. The contract concluded with a scientific or research institution or institution of higher education have to include:

- title or purpose of scientific and research activity or the research area;
- commencement date and completion date or the assessed duration of the scientific and research activity;
- obligation of a foreign researcher that he shall complete a scientific and research activity within the agreed period;
- obligation of a scientific and research institution or institution of higher education or other legal entity or natural person with whom the foreign researcher has concluded the contract that they shall create the conditions for such a foreign national to complete scientific and research activities;

256. Article 50 of the Law on Foreign Nationals.

– information of conducting scientific and research activity in one or more EU Member States if such information is known at the moment of the conclusion of the contract.

216. Temporary residence permit for scientific and research work validity period is up to one year. The foreign researcher may work as a lecturer or professor, however, no longer than fifteen hours a week. After the completion of the research, the foreign researcher, who meets the legal conditions, may be issued a temporary residence permit in Montenegro with a validity period of nine months, for the purpose of seeking employment.

217. A foreign researcher, who has concluded the contract with a scientific and research institution in an EU Member State and under such contract his or her stay in such country is approved, may work in Montenegro for the purpose of research without temporary residence and work permit or work registration certificate, up to three months, provided that he or she possesses sufficient funds to support himself or herself and that there are no obstacles in terms of national, i.e., internal security or public health. A foreign researcher, who has concluded the contract with the scientific and research institution in an EU Member State, and under such contract his stay in such country is approved, must have a temporary residence permit if he wishes to work in Montenegro for longer than three months for the purpose of conducting a research. A scientific and research institution, an institution of higher education, other legal entity or natural person who has concluded the contract with a foreign researcher who has been issued the temporary residence permit is obliged to inform the Ministry of Interior of any circumstances which may prevent the enforcement of the contract.[257]

257. *Ibid.*

Chapter 4. Labour and Economic Migration

§1. Labour Employment

218. A temporary residence may be granted to a foreign national intending to stay in Montenegro for longer than ninety days for the purposes of work. In that case, a temporary residence and work permit as one unique document shall be issued. Generally, a foreign national may work in Montenegro under a temporary residence and work permit or work registration certificate and only on jobs for which the temporary residence and work permit or work registration certificate was issued to him or her, and only for an employer who employs him or her. The employer may assign a foreign national only to the jobs for which a temporary residence and work permit or work registration certificate was issued to such a foreign national. The employer is obliged to inform the Ministry of Interior of the termination of foreign national's employment prior to the expiry of the residence and work permit validity.[258]

219. A temporary residence and work permit, according to its purpose, may be issued for employment of a foreign national, seasonal work of a foreign national and work of a posted worker. A posted worker is a foreign national who, for a limited period of time, works in Montenegro which is not the country in which he or she usually works and, in this case, the permit relates to provision of the agreed services or movement of person within a foreign company.[259]

§2. Seasonal Workers and Temporary Workers

220. A temporary residence and work permit for employment and for seasonal employment can be issued to a foreign national who fulfils the following conditions:

- he/she possesses sufficient funds to support himself/herself;
- he/she has provided accommodation;
- he/she holds health insurance;
- he/she holds either a valid foreign travel document or identity card;
- he/she has not been imposed an entry and stay ban in Montenegro;
- in Montenegro he/she has not been pronounced a final judgment sentencing him/her to an effective imprisonment longer than six months, for a criminal offence that is pursued ex officio, or a judgment legal effects ceased;
- in his/her country of origin he/she has not been pronounced a final judgment sentencing him/her to an effective imprisonment longer than six months, for a criminal offence that is pursued ex officio, or a judgment legal effects ceased;
- national and/or internal security or public health-related restrictions do not exist;

258. Articles 38 and 66 of the Law on Foreign Nationals.
259. Article 68 of the Law on Foreign Nationals.

- he/she has submitted evidence justifying his/her permit application (written offer of an employer for the employment of a foreign national at a particular job position; evidence of the acquired level of education and qualifications; evidence of medical fitness; excerpt from the document on job description of the employer).

221. There is no obligation for entrepreneurs and executive directors of business entities where they are the only owners or where they own more than 51% of equity to submit a written offer of an employer for their employment at a particular job position, whereby they shall be obliged to submit, in addition to the application, the evidence of ownership and registration of the entrepreneur or a business entity.

222. A temporary residence and work permit for seasonal employment shall not be issued to a foreign national in the following cases:

- if the employer from whom he or she has received the offer has been punished due to illegal employment or failure to register the work of foreign national;
- if the bankruptcy procedure of the company which sent him or her the offer is pending or such company has been in bankruptcy;
- if the employer from whom he or she has received the offer does not carry out the business activity; or
- if the employer from which he or she has received the offer has been punished because it failed to meet the liabilities for taxes and contributions for its employees.[260]

223. Validity period of a temporary residence and work permit for employment of a foreign national is up to one year and may be extended for a maximum of up to two years. A temporary residence and work permit for entrepreneurs and executive directors in business entities where they are the only owners or where they own more than 51% of equity may be extended as long as they fulfil the conditions prescribed by the Law on Foreign Nationals. The employer is obliged to conclude an employment contract with a foreign national, within eight days from the date of issuing of the temporary residence and work permit for employment, and he is obliged to register such foreign national for compulsory social insurance, in accordance with the labour regulations. If a foreign national does not start working within this period, the employer is obliged to inform the Ministry of Interior thereof, for the purpose of annulment of the residence and work permit, within no later than three days.[261]

224. Seasonal employment of a foreign national means a temporary employment for the purpose of seasonal works in the business activities of a seasonal character. The temporary residence and work permit for seasonal employment shall be issued within the time period of one year, and shall have a validity period of up to six months. Exceptionally, if the performance of seasonal work so requires, the permit may be extended for two more months, for work for the same or another

260. Article 69 of the Law on Foreign Nationals.
261. Article 70 of the Law on Foreign Nationals.

employer, whereby the permit validity period may not exceed eight months within a time period of one year. The employer is obliged to conclude an employment contract with a foreign national, within eight days from the date of issuing of the temporary residence and work permit for seasonal employment, and he is obliged to register such a foreign national for compulsory social insurance, in accordance with the labour regulations. If the employer fails to conclude the employment contract with the foreign national within the period of eight days, he is obliged to notify the Ministry of Interior thereof, for the purpose of annulment of the residence and work permit, within no later than three days.[262]

225. A foreign national may provide the services agreed under the contract concluded between a foreign company and a legal entity with the seat in Montenegro to which the services are rendered. The agreed services may be provided by a foreign national who is registered for carrying out business or other activities in another country, under the contract concluded with a legal entity which has a seat in Montenegro – so-called independent expert. A temporary residence and work permit for the provision of agreed services can be issued to a foreign national who fulfils the following conditions:

- he/she possesses sufficient funds to support himself/herself;
- he/she has provided accommodation;
- he/she holds health insurance;
- he/she holds either a valid foreign travel document or identity card;
- he/she has not been imposed an entry and stay ban in Montenegro;
- in Montenegro he/she has not been pronounced a final judgment sentencing him/her to an effective imprisonment longer than six months, for a criminal offence that is pursued ex officio, or a judgment legal effects ceased;
- in his/her country of origin he/she has not been pronounced a final judgment sentencing him/her to an effective imprisonment longer than six months, for a criminal offence that is pursued ex officio, or a judgment legal effects ceased;
- national and/or internal security or public health-related restrictions do not exist;
- he/she has submitted evidence justifying his/her permit application (contract on the provision of agreed services; evidence that he or she is employed by a foreign company (does not apply for the 'independent expert'); evidence that he or she has at least two years of work experience in a particular area which is the subject matter of the service contract; evidence that he or she possesses professional qualifications in the events when this is necessary for the provision of services in accordance with the law governing the provision of services in Montenegro; evidence on social insurance issued by the competent authority).

Validity period of a temporary residence and work permit for the provision of agreed services is up to one year and may be extended until the completion of the agreed services, that is, for no longer than two years.[263]

262. Article 71 of the Law on Foreign Nationals.
263. Articles 72 and 73 of the Law on Foreign Nationals.

226. A foreign company may temporarily post its employee for work to a part of a foreign company or to a foreign company which it has founded and which is registered in Montenegro, provided that such an employee has at least worked for one year on a job position of a manager or a specialist or worked for three months in the capacity of an intern with university education who is posted to such company for professional training and during such time receives wage allowances. A manager is a person who performs the managerial activities, or is a member of the management of a foreign company, or manages or runs an organizational unit under the decisions and the instructions of the management or shareholders of the company, or performs the activities of monitoring and control of the professional or managerial staff, and has authority to employ, dismiss and other competencies in connection with the organization of the work of employees. A specialist is a person who possesses professional knowledge necessary for the operations of a foreign company, including the possession of a high level of professional development, appropriate professional experience, and possible membership in an authorized professional association.

227. A temporary residence and work permit for movement of persons within a foreign company can be issued to a foreign national who fulfils the following conditions:

- he/she possesses sufficient funds to support himself/herself;
- he/she has provided accommodation;
- he/she holds health insurance;
- he/she holds either a valid foreign travel document or identity card;
- he/she has not been imposed an entry and stay ban in Montenegro;
- in Montenegro he/she has not been pronounced a final judgment sentencing him/her to an effective imprisonment longer than six months, for a criminal offence that is pursued ex officio, or a judgment legal effects ceased;
- in his/her country of origin he/she has not been pronounced a final judgment sentencing him/her to an effective imprisonment longer than six months, for a criminal offence that is pursued ex officio, or a judgment legal effects ceased;
- national and/or internal security or public health-related restrictions do not exist;
- he/she has submitted evidence justifying his/her permit application (evidence of temporary posting; evidence of social insurance issued by the competent authority; agreement on training of interns, which contains the duration and manner of training the intern, and the manner of supervision over the training of interns, as well as the intern training curriculum; evidence that a foreign company is a founder of a company in Montenegro or part of a foreign company to which he or she is posted; evidence that upon the expiry of the temporary posting a foreign national shall be returned for work to the foreign company from which he was temporary posted).

Validity period of a temporary residence and work permit is up to one year, and may be extended until the completion of business activities, that is, for a maximum of up to two years.[264]

228. The application for issuing of temporary residence and work permit has to be submitted to the Ministry of Interior, personally, in the place of residence. Exceptionally, the application for the issuing of temporary residence and work permit may also be filed by an employer in the place of the intended residence of a foreign national. A foreign national who has been issued visa for a longer stay (visa D) for the purpose of work is obliged to file the application for the issuing of a temporary residence and work permit, within ten days from the date of visa issuing. The Ministry of Interior shall issue a certificate of the acceptance of the application for issuing of temporary residence and work permit, and such certificate contains the determined deadline within which the applicant may take over the permit. Decision on the application for the issuing of a temporary residence and work permit shall be made within twenty days from the date when the application was duly filed and upon previously obtained opinion of the Agency for National Security and the Police on the existence of any obstacles for the reasons of national, i.e., internal security. Exceptionally, decision on the application for the issuing of a temporary residence and work permit for seasonal employment to a foreign national to whom the permit for seasonal employment has been issued at least two times in the past five years shall be made within ten days. If the applicant for the issuing of temporary residence and work permit fails to take over such permit not later than within five days upon the expiry of the period indicated in the certificate of the acceptance of the application, the applicant shall be considered to have waived the application.

229. A foreign national who intends to work in Montenegro on seasonal jobs have to file the application for the issuing of temporary residence and work permit for seasonal employment to the Ministry of Interior, through diplomatic or consular mission in the country of origin. He is obliged to submit the evidence of the fulfilment of the following conditions:

- he/she possesses sufficient funds to support himself/herself;
- he/she has provided accommodation;
- he/she holds health insurance;
- he/she holds either a valid foreign travel document or identity card;
- in his/her country of origin he/she has not been pronounced a final judgment sentencing him/her to an effective imprisonment longer than six months, for a criminal offence that is pursued ex officio, or a judgment legal effects ceased;
- he/she has submitted evidence justifying his/her permit application (written offer of an employer for the employment of a foreign national at a particular job position; evidence of medical fitness; excerpt from the document on job description of the employer).

264. Articles 74 and 75 of the Law on Foreign Nationals.

The diplomatic or consular mission shall issue to a foreign national the certificate of the receipt of application for issuing of temporary residence and work permit which contains a defined period within which the applicant may take over the permit. The temporary residence and work permit shall be delivered to a foreign national through a diplomatic or consular mission.[265]

230. A foreign national or an employer has to file the application for extension of temporary residence and work permit to the Ministry of Interior, in the place of residence of a foreign national, in the seat of the employer in Montenegro, or in the place of work of a foreign national, not later than within thirty days prior to the expiry of the validity period of the temporary residence and work permit. In addition, a valid travel document or personal identity card of a foreign national and the evidence of the grounds of application for the issuing of a permit have to be submitted. The evidence that the liabilities for taxes and contributions during the validity period of the temporary residence and work permit have been met have to be also submitted.[266]

§3. Independent Economic Activities

231. Conditions for independent economic activities of foreign nationals in Montenegro are regulated mostly within the same legal framework for employment and residence regime of all foreign nationals in general. Foreign nationals can set up companies in Montenegro in which they can become executive directors. If they want to be Chief Executive Officers, they are required to obtain a temporary residence and work permit, in accordance with the Law on Foreign Nationals. Also, in order to carry out any independent economic activities, a foreign national must obtain a temporary residence and work permit.

232. General rule is that, every year, the Government determines an annual number of temporary residence and work permits for foreign nationals – 'annual quota', in accordance with the migration policy, status and movements on the labour market in Montenegro. The annual quota also determines the business activities where the foreign nationals may be employed. A temporary residence and work permit beyond the annual quota may be issued to an executive director of a company and an entrepreneur who is registered in Montenegro in accordance with the law governing the form of carrying out business activities and their registration.

§4. Investment Activities

233. A temporary residence permit for use and disposal of the right to real estate possessed by a foreign national in Montenegro may be issued to a foreign national who fulfils the following conditions:

265. Article 81 of the Law on Foreign Nationals.
266. Article 82 of the Law on Foreign Nationals.

– he possesses sufficient funds to support himself/herself;
– he has provided accommodation;
– he holds health insurance;
– he holds either a valid foreign travel document or identity card;
– he has not been imposed an entry and stay ban in Montenegro;
– in Montenegro he has not been pronounced a final judgment sentencing him to an effective imprisonment longer than six months, for a criminal offence that is pursued ex officio, or a judgment legal effects ceased;
– in his country of origin he has not been pronounced a final judgment sentencing him to an effective imprisonment longer than six months, for a criminal offence that is pursued ex officio, or a judgment legal effects ceased;
– national and/or internal security or public health-related restrictions do not exist;
– he has submitted evidence justifying his permit application (a real estate folio in the land register or other evidence confirming the ownership of such real estate, in accordance with the law governing the real estate cadastre).

Real estate are considered family houses, country cottages, villas, apartments, hospitality industry facilities, residential and office buildings, and business premises.[267]

234. In January 2019, the Government of Montenegro launched the *Program for the acquisition of Montenegrin citizenship through investments*, which will last for three years, starting on 1 January 2019, and during that period, a maximum of two thousand applications for the acquisition of Montenegrin citizenship may be accepted. It is foreseen by the Decision on the Manner and Procedure for Selecting Persons Who May Acquire Montenegrin Citizenship by Admission for the Implementation of the Special Investment Program of Special Importance for the Economic Interest of Montenegro.[268]

235. According to the Government decision from December 2021, the Programme was extended for another year, until the end of 2022.

236. An applicant submits a request for the realization of a Special programme, i.e., the acquisition of Montenegrin citizenship through a mediating agent, and the check is carried out by an international eligibility assessment agent, who must be licensed. Also, certain checks, in accordance with the Law, are the responsibility of the Ministry of Interior of Montenegro.

237. An applicant may acquire Montenegrin citizenship under a Special programme if:

267. Article 56 of the Law on Foreign Nationals.
268. Government Decision on the criteria, manner and procedure for selection of persons who can acquire Montenegrin citizenship by admission for the purpose of implementation of a special investment programme of special importance for the business and economic interest of Montenegro.

(1) for the purpose of the costs of the proceedings, he made a payment in the amount of:
EUR 15,000.00 for the applicant;
EUR 10,000.00 individually per family member, up to a maximum of four family members;
EUR 50,000.00 for each additional family member.
(2) he deposited EUR 100,000.00 into the special account for the development of less developed municipalities;
(3) he has deposited at least EUR 450,000.00 into a special account for the purpose of investing in one of the development projects in the Capital City of Podgorica or the coastal region of Montenegro, or the amount of at least EUR 250,000.00, for the purposes of investing in one of the development projects in the north or the central region of Montenegro, except the capital Podgorica;
(4) in Montenegro or another State, he has not been the subject of a final sentence of unconditional imprisonment for a term exceeding one year for a criminal offence prosecuted ex officio or the legal consequences of a conviction for such a crime have ceased;
(5) the International Eligibility Assessment Agent has given a positive opinion, including proof of origin of the money intended for payment and investment.

238. Development project means the construction of hotels/mixed complex:

- five stars in the coastal region or the capital Podgorica or at least four stars in the northern or central region, except the capital Podgorica;
- which requires a minimum investment of EUR 15 million in the coastal region or the capital Podgorica or a minimum investment of EUR 5 million in the northern or central region, except the capital Podgorica;
- which will employ at least eighty employees in the coastal region or the Capital City of Podgorica or at least twenty-five employees in the northern or central region, except the capital Podgorica;
- which will have at least sixty accommodation units in the coastal region or the Capital City of Podgorica or at least thirty-five accommodation units in the northern or central region, except the capital Podgorica.

239. The list of development projects is established by the Government. Development projects are also projects in the field of agriculture that meet the requirements set by the Ministry of Agriculture and projects in the field of processing industry, which meet the requirements set by the Ministry of Economy.

240. The application for the acquisition of Montenegrin citizenship by admission under a Special programme is submitted by the applicant through the mediating agent to the competent authority for himself and his family members. Family members are considered to be: spouse; the children of the applicant who have attained the age of 18, who are being supported by the applicant; the children of the applicant under the age of 18 years.

241. Family members must satisfy the requirement that the International Eligibility Agent gives a positive opinion for them, including proof of origin of money intended for payment and investment, and the spouse and children of the applicant, who is 18 years of age, must also meet the requirement that in Montenegro or another states have not been convicted of an unconditional sentence of imprisonment for a term exceeding one year for a criminal offence prosecuted ex officio or the legal consequences of a conviction for such a crime have ceased to exist.

242. In addition to the application for the acquisition of Montenegrin citizenship, the applicant submits for himself and his family members the following documents:

- certified copies of passports and identity cards;
- birth certificates;
- excerpts from the register of weddings;
- insurance policies in force in Montenegro that cover health insurance;
- certificates that they do not suffer from infectious diseases, issued in accordance with the regulations of the country in which the applicant is a national.

Chapter 5. Humanitarian Reasons

§1. Humanitarian Grounds

243. A foreign national whom Montenegro is under an obligation to admit pursuant to an international treaty and where it is required for humanitarian, or internal security or public health reasons may enter Montenegro without a valid foreign travel document. Also, the visa validity period of the short-stay visa (C visa) may be extended only where an applicant presents evidence of humanitarian or force majeure reasons, or serious personal reasons existing.[269]

244. A temporary residence permit for humanitarian reasons may be issued to a foreign national for particularly justified reasons of humanitarian nature (events of force majeure, severe illness, permanent disability and other justified cases whose circumstances indicate their humanitarian character). In order to obtain a residence permit, a foreign national does not have to fulfil the conditions regarding sufficient funds to support himself/herself, provided accommodation and health insurance. A temporary residence permit can be issued based on the appropriate evidence produced by an international organization, NGO, or state administration authority who provides assistance and protection to a foreign national. Validity period of a temporary residence permit is up to one year and may be extended as long as the reasons for approving a permit exist. A foreign national who has been issued a temporary residence permit for humanitarian reasons has the right to accommodation, healthcare, education, work, and financial assistance. A foreign national who has been issued a temporary residence permit cannot be subject to forced removal due to an illegal entry or stay in Montenegro.[270]

§2. Unaccompanied Minor Children

245. A temporary residence permit for humanitarian reasons may be issued to a foreign minor, who has been abandoned or is a victim of organized crime, or is without parental care for other reasons, or is unaccompanied, or according to the employment regulations is illegally employed. In order to obtain a residence permit, a foreign national does not have to fulfil the conditions regarding sufficient funds to support himself/herself, provided accommodation and health insurance. A temporary residence permit shall be issued based on the appropriate evidence produced by an international organization, NGO, or state administration authority who provides assistance and protection to a foreign minor. A minor foreign national, for whom it has been established to have been the victim of a crime of trafficking in human beings, shall not be returned to any state if, after the evaluation of the threat and his or her security, there are circumstances which indicate that such return would not be in his or her best interest. Validity period of a temporary residence permit is up to one year and may be extended as long as the reasons for approving a

269. Articles 9 and 28 of the Law on Foreign Nationals.
270. Articles 52, 53 and 55 of the Law on Foreign Nationals.

permit exist. A foreign minor who has been issued a temporary residence permit has the right to accommodation, healthcare, education, work, and financial assistance. A foreign national who has been issued a temporary residence permit cannot be subject to forced removal due to an illegal entry or stay in Montenegro.[271]

§3. Victims of Trafficking in Human Beings

246. A temporary residence permit for humanitarian reasons may be issued to a foreign national presumed to have been the victim of a crime of trafficking in human beings or of a crime of domestic violence. A foreign national whom the police determine to be the victim of the crime of human being trafficking shall have the right to decide, within ninety days, whether he or she will cooperate in the criminal procedure or whether he or she will either join criminal prosecution or become a witness in such a procedure (reflection period). In order to obtain a residence permit, a foreign national does not have to fulfil the conditions regarding sufficient funds to support himself/herself, provided accommodation and health insurance. A temporary residence permit can be issued based on the appropriate evidence produced by an international organization, NGO, or state administration authority who provides assistance and protection to a foreign national, or evidence produced by a competent state authority confirming that a foreign national collaborates in the investigation of criminal offences. In cooperation with authorities, non-governmental and other organizations that are in charge or that deal with the prevention, education, reporting, and prosecution of the perpetrators and protection of the victims of trafficking in human beings and, in regard to a minor foreign national, in cooperation with the Centre for Social Work, the police shall establish if the foreign national is a victim of a crime of trafficking in human beings. A foreign national who has been issued a temporary residence permit cannot be subject to forced removal due to an illegal entry or stay in Montenegro. A foreign national for whom there is a reasonable concern that by giving a statement in a criminal procedure he or she could be exposed to the threat for his or her life, health, physical integrity or freedom shall be provided with protection and the exercise of rights in accordance with the law governing witness protection.[272]

271. *Ibid.*
272. Articles 52, 53, 54 and 55 of the Law on Foreign Nationals.

Chapter 6. Asylum

§1. General Remarks

247. Asylum is the protection provided by the state to an individual at his request, either on its territory or on certain facilities that do not constitute its territory, but are under the jurisdiction of its authorities.[273] The asylum system in Montenegro was established in 2007. The Law on Asylum[274] was enacted on 17 July 2006, and entered into force on 25 July 2006, and its enforcement started on 25 January 2007. In June 2007, following the establishment of the Asylum Office within Ministry of Interior, the United Nations High Commissioner for Refugees (UNHCR) Office in Podgorica and the Ministry of Interior signed the Memorandum on Cooperation and interim assistance in enforcing the Asylum Law in order to establish cooperation in administering the procedure for evaluating asylum applications, and providing for asylum seekers, refugees and persons who are granted additional protection. The Memorandum stipulated the responsibilities of the UNHCR to implement the procedure and interview asylum seekers until the end of 2007, and the responsibility of the Ministry, or the Asylum Office to make decisions based on written recommendations of the UNHCR. As of 1 January 2008, the Ministry of Interior, i.e., the Asylum Office, assumed from the UNHCR the administration of the procedure and deciding upon asylum applications. Montenegro is also bound by the SAA with the EU and their Member States. In SAA Montenegro is committed to harmonize her legislation in the relevant sectors to that of the EU law, and to implement it. In the last Progress Report of European Commission for Montenegro it was said:

> With the adoption of the secondary legislation for the Law on asylum, Montenegro is now equipped with a largely EU-compliant legal framework. The Decree on financial assistance to people under international protection provides for monthly payments of financial assistance to refugees and a single payment to asylum seekers. The role of the Ministry of Interior has been strengthened, including a coordinating role for the integration of people under international protection, and the provision of financial assistance. A database of people granted international protection is being developed with the aim of tracing the public services delivered.
>
> Efforts should be continued to further enhance reception and operational capacities. Modernizing the data collection tools would prevent double registration of migrants in the asylum system following secondary movements, as

273. Milenko Kreća, *Međunarodno javno pravo,* Pravni fakultet Univerzitet u Beogradu (Belgrade 2016).
274. *Zakon o azilu,* 'Official Gazette of the Republic of Montenegro', No. 45/06.

re-entry, subsequent applications or further representations have to be correctly registered in line with the relevant EU asylum rules. Better inter-ministerial coordination and more involvement of the social ministries in the integration phase are necessary for the country's asylum policy to reach its full potential.[275]

248. Due to its position on the so-called the Balkan route, Montenegro has been hit by increased mixed migration flows since 2011, which is also reflected by an increasing trend in the number of asylum applications: 46 applications were submitted in 2006–2010; 235 in 2011; 1,531 in 2012; 3,554 in 2013; 2,312 in 2014, etc. The main route used by migrants who appear and seek protection in Montenegro includes Turkey, Greece, Albania and, to a lesser extent, Kosovo. Montenegro is considered a transit country; that is, asylum seekers perceive Montenegro only as a transit country where they do not stay long and continue on their way to Western Europe. For this reason, foreigners seeking international protection rarely attend interviews conducted by the Ministry of the Interior's Asylum Office, and so the vast majority of decisions (over 90%) relate to suspending proceedings because foreigners seeking international protection have left Montenegro. Thus, in the last three years, more than four thousand foreigners have sought asylum in Montenegro, only twenty-one persons have been granted permanent refugee status, and seven have received additional protection (temporary residence).[276] The question arises as to where several thousand foreigners who did not receive a positive response to their asylum application end up.[277] The SOCTA (Serious and Organized Crime Threat Assessment) Report entails the term 'fake asylum seekers' who abuse asylum procedures, with the help of organized groups of smugglers[278] (*see* more in Part V Chapter 2).

249. In Montenegro, the right to asylum is a constitutional category. Namely, the Constitution of Montenegro stipulates:

> 'A foreign national who has a well-founded fear of persecution because of his race, language, religion or affiliation with a nation or group, or because of his political convictions may seek asylum in Montenegro' (Article 44, paragraph 1).

---

275. European Commission, *Montenegro Progress Report* (Brussels, 29 May 2019).
276. Press release of the Center for Investigative Reporting (CIN-CG), source: Directorate of Asylum – Ministry of Interior, *see* more on the website http://www.cin-cg.me/azilanti-crna-gora-tranzitna-zona-za-izbjeglice-hiljade-traze-azil-pa-se-svercuju-ka-eu/.
277. *Ibid.*
278. Out of the 9,192 asylum applications submitted in the period from 2007 to May 2015, protection was granted to only 14 persons. For other persons, the asylum procedure is to the greatest extent suspended, because asylum seekers do not respond to the summon for giving a statement on the circumstances of leaving the country of origin, since they leave the territory of Montenegro after few days, *see* more in the Serious and organized crime threat assessment in Montenegro (SOCTA).

'A foreign national may not be expelled from Montenegro where, on account of race, religion, language or nationality, he would be threatened with a sentence of death, torture, inhuman humiliation, persecution or serious violation of the rights guaranteed by this Constitution' (Article 44, Paragraph 2).
'A foreign national may be expelled from Montenegro only on the basis of a decision of the competent authority and in the procedure prescribed by law' (Article 44, paragraph 3).

250. Law on International and Temporary Protection of Foreigners[279] implements international humanitarian law and human rights standards in the development and implementation of admission policies and the need to create a safe and dignified environment for foreigners seeking international protection, discouraging any form of abuse in the asylum system:

(1) recognizes the need to establish and implement fair and expeditious asylum procedures in order to identify, in a timely manner, those in need of international protection and those who are not, thus avoiding long periods of uncertainty for foreigners seeking international protection, discouraging abuse of the system asylum and facilitating overall requirements in the admission system;
(2) recommends that the reception of foreigners seeking international protection should be guided *inter alia* by the following general principles:
  - respect for human dignity and applicable international and human rights standards;
  - access to relevant governmental and non-governmental entities, when they need assistance to meet their basic support needs, including food, clothing, housing and healthcare, as well as respect for their privacy;
  - gender sensitivity and sensitivity to the age of foreigners seeking international protection – especially educational, psychological, recreational and other special needs of children, especially unaccompanied and separated children, as well as victims of sexual abuse and exploitation, trauma and torture, including other vulnerable groups;
  - facilitating family unity, especially in the context of stay in reception centres;
  - in order to protect foreigners seeking international protection from return to the countries of origin, they should be registered and issued with appropriate documentation reflecting their status, which should remain in force until the final decision on the asylum application is made;
  - creating public opinion for the benefit of foreigners seeking international protection and creating confidence in the asylum system.

251. The Law on International and Temporary Protection of Foreigners defines the following institutes of European legislation:

279. Law on international and temporary protection of foreigners, 'Official Gazette of Montenegro', Nos 2/2017, 3/2019.

- special procedural guarantees;
- acts of persecution;
- persecutors;
- reasons for exclusion;
- safe countries of origin;
- safe third countries;
- the European safe third country;
- procedure at the border;
- judicial protection.

252. The Law on International and Temporary Protection of Foreigners makes a clear distinction between the category of a foreigner seeking international protection and persons with granted international protection (asylum or subsidiary protection). Persons with granted protection enjoy almost all rights as Montenegrin citizens (social protection, healthcare, right to education, right to recognize diplomas and in cases where there is no material evidence – prior learning). Persons with granted protection are under the full responsibility of the Ministry of Labor and Social Welfare, which is obliged to provide them with accommodation for two years and to establish and implement an Integration Plan that ensures persons full inclusion in Montenegrin society. With the entry into force of the Law on International and Temporary Protection of Foreigners (1 January 2018), the Law on Asylum ceased to be valid.

253. Law on International and Temporary Protection of Foreigners transposes the following EU directives and regulations:

- Council Directive 2001/55/EC of 20 July 2001 on minimum standards for giving temporary protection in the event of a mass influx of DPs and on measures promoting a balance of efforts between Member States in receiving such persons and bearing the consequences thereof (OJ L 212, 7.8.2001).
- Council Directive 2003/86/EC of 22 September 2003 on the right to family reunification (OJ L 251, 3.10.2003).
- Directive 2011/95/EU of the European Parliament and of the Council of 13 December 2011 on standards for the qualification of third-country nationals or stateless persons as beneficiaries of international protection, for a uniform status for refugees or for persons eligible for subsidiary protection, and for the content of the protection granted (revised) (OJ L 337, 20.12.2011).
- Directive 2013/32/EU of the European Parliament and of the Council of 26 June 2013 on common procedures for granting and withdrawing international protection (recast) (OJ L 180, 29.6.2013).
- Directive 2013/33/EU of the European Parliament and of the Council of 26 June 2013 laying down standards for the reception of foreigners seeking international protection (revised) (OJ L 180/96, 29.6.2013).

– Commission Regulation (EC) No. 1560/2003 of 2 September 2003 laying down detailed rules for the application of Council Regulation (EC) No. 343/2003 establishing the criteria and mechanisms for determining the Member State responsible for examining an asylum application lodged in one of the Member States by a third-country national (OJ L 222, 5.9.2003).
– Regulation (EU) No. 603/2013 of the European Parliament and of the Council of 26 June 2013 on the establishment of 'Eurodac' for the comparison of fingerprints for the effective application of Regulation (EU) No 604/2013 establishing the criteria and mechanisms for determining the Member State responsible for examining an application for international protection lodged in one of the Member States by a third-country national or a stateless person and on requests for the comparison with Eurodac data by Member States' law enforcement authorities and Europol for law enforcement purposes, and amending Regulation (EU) No. 1077/2011 establishing a European Agency for the operational management of large-scale IT systems in the area of freedom, security and justice (OJ L 180, 29.6.2013).
– Regulation (EU) No. 604/2013 of the European Parliament and of the Council of 26 June 2013 establishing the criteria and mechanisms for determining the Member State responsible for examining an application for international protection lodged in one of the Member States by a third-country national or a stateless person (OJ L 180, 6.29.2013).
– Commission Implementing Regulation (EU) No. 118/2014 of 30 January 2014 amending Regulation (EC) No. 1560/2003 laying down detailed rules for the application of Council Regulation (EC) No. 343/2003 establishing the criteria and mechanisms for determining the Member State responsible for examining an asylum application lodged in one of the Member States by a third-country national (OJ L 222, 5.9.2003).

254. According to the Law on International and Temporary Protection of Foreigners, the international protection of a foreigner seeking international protection includes asylum and subsidiary protection. Asylum can be granted to a foreigner seeking international protection, who is outside the country of his origin, and owing to a well-founded fear of being persecuted for reasons of race, religion, nationality, membership of a particular social group or political opinion is unable or, owing to such fear, is unwilling to avail himself of the protection of that country. Subsidiary protection can be granted to a foreigner seeking international protection, who does not qualify for asylum, if substantial grounds have been shown for believing that, if returned to the country of origin, he would face a real risk of suffering serious harm, and who is unable, or, owing to such risk, unwilling to avail himself of the protection of that country. A foreigner seeking international protection, or an applicant who has lodged an application for international protection, means a third-country national or a stateless person who has stated his intention to lodge an application for international protection.[280]

280. Articles 2, 3, 4 and 6 of the Law on International and Temporary Protection of Foreigners.

255. Temporary protection can be granted to a third-country national and a stateless person in the event of a mass influx or imminent mass influx of persons from third countries who are unable to return to their country of origin, in particular if there is a risk that the system for granting international protection cannot be efficient due to this mass influx, in the interests of the persons concerned and other persons requesting international protection.[281]

§2. CONDITIONS

I. Refugee and Subsidiary Protection Status

256. The conditions relating to the grounds, the acts and the actors of persecution, or serious harm, as well as in relation to the existence of protection against persecution or serious harm in their country of origin, are examined in the procedure upon an application for international protection.[282]

257. The grounds for persecution may include:

- race, which implies skin colour, origin and belonging to a particular ethnic group;
- faith, which implies theistic, non-theistic and atheistic beliefs, participation or nonparticipation in public or private formal religious rites, individually or in community with others, other religious ceremonies or practice of the faith, or forms of personal or communal conduct based on religious belief or resulting therefrom;
- nationality, which implies belonging to a group which is determined by its cultural, ethnic, or linguistic identity, common geographical or political origins or its relationship with the population of another country, which may also include a citizenship;
- political opinion, which implies an opinion, attitude or belief about issues related to possible actors of persecution, and their policies or methods, whether or not the foreigner seeking international protection acted on this opinion, attitude or belief;
- a particular social group that includes members who have common inborn traits or common background that cannot be changed, or characteristics or beliefs, to the extent relevant for their identity or conscience that those persons should not be forced to give up, and such a group has a distinct identity in the relevant country because the society that surrounds it considers it to be distinct.

258. Depending on the circumstances in the country of origin, a particular social group can denote a group which has the common characteristics of sexual orientation, whereas acts criminalized in the legislation of Montenegro may not be regarded as sexual orientation. The features related to gender identity, including sex,

281. Article 5 of the Law on International and Temporary Protection of Foreigners.
282. Article 22 of the Law on International and Temporary Protection of Foreigners.

shall be taken into account when examining membership to a particular social group, or to determine the characteristics of such groups.[283]

259. The acts serious enough in their nature or repeated to constitute serious violation of fundamental human rights or a set of different measures which constitute violation of human rights shall be deemed as persecution. These acts may include:

– physical or psychological violence, including sexual violence;
– legal, administrative, police and/or judicial measures that are discriminatory or are implemented in a discriminatory manner;
– prosecution or punishment which is disproportionate or discriminatory;
– the denial of rights in judicial proceedings that may occur due to the disproportionate or discriminatory punishment;
– prosecution or punishment for refusal of military service during the conflict, if the performance of military service meant execution of the following offences or actions: a crime against peace, a war crime or a crime against humanity, a serious non-political crime prior to his/her arrival to Montenegro, if committed with an allegedly political objective, particularly cruel actions, if committed with an allegedly political objective, acts contrary to the purpose and principles of the UN;
– the acts of persecution specifically related to sex or children.

260. The existence of persecution shall be determined by a connection of the acts of persecution and/or lack of protection against such acts and the grounds for persecution from paragraph number 260. When assessing whether an applicant had a well-founded fear of persecution, it is irrelevant whether the applicant actually has racial, religious, national, social or political features which cause persecution, provided this feature is attributed to the applicant by the actors of persecution.[284]

261. Serious harm consists of the threat of death penalty or execution, or torture or inhuman or degrading treatment or punishment or serious and individual threat to a civilian's life or person by reason of indiscriminate violence in situations of international or internal armed conflict. The activities and actions taken by the following actors shall be deemed to be persecution and serious harm:

– state authorities;
– parties, national or international organizations controlling the state or a substantial part of the territory of the state;
– non-state actors, if it can be determined that state authorities or parties or national or international organizations controlling the state or a substantial part of the territory of the state are unable or unwilling to provide protection against persecution or serious harm.[285]

283. Article 23 of the Law on International and Temporary Protection of Foreigners.
284. Article 24 of the Law on International and Temporary Protection of Foreigners.
285. Articles 25 and 26 of the Law on International and Temporary Protection of Foreigners.

262. Protection against persecution and serious harm in the country of origin can only be provided by state authorities or parties, national or international organizations controlling the state or a substantial part of the territory of the state if they are able and willing to do so. When assessing whether parties, national or international organizations control the state or a substantial part of the territory of the state, the data from official acts and guidance of the EU shall be taken into account. Protection implies the existence of an effective legal system for the detection, prosecution and punishment of actors of the acts constituting persecution or serious harm, as well as the possibility of exercising such protection by taking justified measures to prevent persecution or suffering serious harm on the account of which a foreigner seeks international protection.[286]

263. International protection cannot be granted if it is determined that a foreigner seeking international protection has the possibility of travelling to a part of the country of origin:

- where there is no well-founded fear of persecution or suffering serious harm;
- where there is access to protection against persecution or serious harm;
- if he/she can safely and legally travel to that part of the country;
- where he/she can gain admittance; and
- if he/she can reasonably be expected to settle there.[287]

264. Asylum cannot be granted to a foreigner seeking international protection if:

(1) he/she enjoys protection or receives assistance from organs or agencies of the UN other than the UNHCR;
(2) he/she has approved residence in the country which recognizes, based on such residence, the same rights and obligations which are attached to the possession of the nationality of that country;
(3) there are serious reasons for considering that he/she committed, incited or otherwise participated in the commission of:
  - a crime against peace, a war crime or a crime against humanity as defined in the international instruments;
  - a serious non-political crime prior to his arrival to Montenegro, if committed with an allegedly political objective;
  - particularly cruel actions, if committed with an allegedly political objective;
  - acts contrary to the purpose and principles of the UN.

265. In case the protection or assistance should cease from whatever reason beyond the influence of the foreigner seeking international protection, and where his/her status has not been finally resolved in accordance with the United Nations General Assembly instruments, asylum shall be granted.[288]

286. Article 27 of the Law on International and Temporary Protection of Foreigners.
287. Article 28 of the Law on International and Temporary Protection of Foreigners.
288. Article 29 of the Law on International and Temporary Protection of Foreigners.

266. Subsidiary protection cannot be granted to a foreigner seeking international protection if:

(1) there are serious reasons for considering that he/she committed, incited or otherwise participated in the commission of:
   - a crime against peace, a war crime or a crime against humanity as defined in the international instruments;
   - a serious crime (a crime punishable in Montenegro by imprisonment of five or more years);
   - acts contrary to the purpose and principles of the UN.

(2) he/she, prior to arrival to Montenegro, has committed a crime punishable in Montenegro by imprisonment, and if he/she left his/her country of origin solely in order to avoid sanctions stipulated in that country;

(3) he/she constitutes a danger for national security and public order in Montenegro.[289]

II. Temporary Protection

267. In the event of a mass influx or imminent mass influx of persons from third countries who are unable to return to their country of origin, if there is a risk that the international protection system will be unable to process this influx efficiently, in the interests of the persons concerned, temporary protection for such persons may be granted. The foreigners are third-country nationals and stateless persons who have had to leave their country or region of origin, or have been evacuated, and are unable to return in safe conditions because of the situation prevailing in that country, in particular, if they have fled areas of armed conflict or endemic violence or they are at serious risk of, or who have been the victims of, systemic or generalized violations of their human rights. The mass influx referred to refers to a large number of persons who come from a specific country or geographical area, whether their arrival was spontaneous or organized. The decision to grant temporary protection is made by the Government, at the proposal of the Ministry of Interior.[290] The decision may be adopted by the Government even in the cases when the European Council establishes the existence of a mass influx.[291]

268. The duration of temporary protection is one year. Upon the expiry, temporary protection may be extended by six monthly periods for a maximum of one year. Temporary protection may be extended by the decision of the European Council by up to one year. Temporary protection shall end by the expiry of the time frame for which it was introduced, or by the decision of the European Council.[292]

289. Article 30 of the Law on International and Temporary Protection of Foreigners.
290. Article 93 of the Law on International and Temporary Protection of Foreigners.
291. This provision of the Law on International and Temporary Protection of Foreigners shall be applied from the date of accession of Montenegro to the European Union.
292. Article 93 of the Law on International and Temporary Protection of Foreigners (shall be applied from the date of accession of Montenegro to the European Union).

269. Temporary protection cannot be granted to a third-country national and a stateless person if there are serious reasons for considering that:

(1) he/she has committed, incited or otherwise participated in the commission of:
   - a crime against peace, a war crime or a crime against humanity, as defined in the international instruments;
   - a serious crime (a crime punishable in Montenegro by imprisonment of five or more years);
   - acts contrary to the purposes and principles of the UN.

(2) he/she, prior to arrival to Montenegro, has committed a crime punishable in Montenegro by imprisonment, and if he/she left his/her country of origin solely in order to avoid sanctions stipulated in that country;

(3) he/she constitutes a danger to national security and public order in Montenegro, or

(4) he/she was convicted of a serious crime which is punishable in Montenegro by imprisonment of five or more years.[293]

270. At the request of a foreigner granted temporary protection or a person whose temporary protection ceased, the Ministry of Interior is obliged to take appropriate measures to facilitate the voluntary return to their country of origin, taking due account of human dignity. In the case of enforced return of such person, the Ministry of Interior has to consider the relevant reports on the situation in the country of origin and take into account serious humanitarian reasons which would make the return of the individuals temporarily impossible or unreasonable, and notify the foreigner granted temporary protection thereof.[294]

III. International Protection of Citizens of EU Member States

271. A national of a Member State of the EU is not entitled to apply for international protection, except when the conditions set out in Protocol 24 of the Treaty of Lisbon on Amendments to the Treaty on EU and the Treaty Establishing the European Community are met. If the conditions are fulfilled, such person can be subject to the provisions of the Law on International and Temporary Protection of Foreigners relating to the general principles, conditions and procedures for granting international protection, cessation, termination and withdrawal of international protection, as well as the rights and obligations of a foreigner seeking international protection, an asylee and a foreigner granted subsidiary protection.[295]

293. Article 94 of the Law on International and Temporary Protection of Foreigners.
294. Article 95 of the Law on International and Temporary Protection of Foreigners.
295. Article 91 of the Law on International and Temporary Protection of Foreigners.

§3. Procedures

I. General Framework

272. The public is excluded from the process of granting international protection. The interview may be attended by a representative of the UNHCR or other organizations dealing with the protection of human rights and the rights of refugees, or asylees, if the foreigner seeking international protection does not object to that.[296]

273. The procedure of examining the application for international protection is conducted in Montenegrin language. When a foreigner seeking international protection does not understand Montenegrin language, he/she shall be provided with an interpreter for the language he/she is reasonably assumed to understand and in which he/she can communicate. A foreigner seeking international protection shall be provided with an interpreter, ex officio or at his/her request, if feasible of the same sex, when this is necessary in order to fully explain the application for international protection or for other legitimate reasons.

274. A foreigner seeking international protection is obliged to communicate the reasons for seeking international protection through an interpreter, unless the participation of a particular interpreter might lead to an incomplete and inaccurate presentation of these reasons. If an applicant considers that the participation of a particular interpreter could lead to an incomplete and incorrect presentation of his/her reasons for seeking international protection, he/she is obliged to present the legitimate reasons thereof. The legitimacy of reasons shall be decided by the Ministry of Interior and if it estimates that the participation of a particular interpreter could lead to an incomplete and inaccurate presentation of the reasons for international protection, a foreigner seeking international protection shall be provided another interpreter.

275. A foreigner seeking international protection may hire at his/her own expense an interpreter who meets legal requirements, within the deadline set by the Ministry of Interior. In case an applicant should unjustifiably refuse to provide during the procedure the reasons for seeking international protection through an interpreter provided by the Ministry of Interior, and fail to hire an interpreter who meets legal requirements, he/she shall be deemed unwilling to state the reasons to be examined in deciding whether he/she meets the requirements for granting international protection. A foreigner seeking international protection is obliged to submit a certified translation of a foreign document he/she refers to, i.e., by which he/she is proving his/her allegations. If a foreigner seeking international protection does not have his own financial means for the translation of the foreign documentation, the

296. Article 17 of the Law on International and Temporary Protection of Foreigners.

translation of the foreign documentation shall be provided by the Ministry of Interior, if it is determined that the documentation is relevant for the examination of the application for international protection.[297]

276. An interpreter may be a person who in addition to proficiency in Montenegrin, or English or French, has the knowledge of the language for the interpretation of which he/she is engaged and has not been sentenced to an unconditional custodial sentence or no criminal proceedings are pending against him/her in Montenegro. In the procedure for examining the application for international protection, the interpreter is obliged to interpret truthfully, accurately and impartially. The interpreter is obliged to safeguard the information disclosed to him/her during the process of examining the application for international protection. If for objective reasons it is not possible to provide an interpreter for a specific language, the Ministry of Interior may request the assistance of another state. In the procedure of examining an application for international protection, interpretation may be provided via telecommunication or electronic audiovisual devices.[298]

277. A foreigner seeking international protection who, due to personal features and circumstances (age, sex, sexual orientation, gender identity, severe illness, mental health or consequences of torture, rape or other severe forms of psychological, physical or gender-based violence), is not fully able to pursue own rights and perform duties without adequate assistance is entitled to special procedural safeguards. Appropriate support to applicants for the purpose of pursuing rights and executing duties is considered as special procedural safeguard. In the procedure from the moment of expressing intent to lodge an application for international protection until taking decision upon the application for international protection, trained police officers and authorized officials of the Ministry of Interior and other competent authorities are determining the above-mentioned features and circumstances. The provisions of general procedures for granting international protection prescribed by the Law on International and Temporary Protection of Foreigners shall not apply to the procedure upon the application for international protection of an applicant in need of special procedural safeguards, in particular at the request of a victim of torture, rape and other serious forms of psychological, physical or gender-based violence, unless appropriate support is provided.[299]

278. A well-founded fear of being persecuted or a real risk of suffering serious harm may be based on *(the Principle of 'sur place')*:

- events which have taken place since the foreigner seeking international protection has left the country of origin;
- activities which the foreigner seeking international protection has engaged in since he/she left the country of origin, in particular where it is established that

297. Article 18 of the Law on International and Temporary Protection of Foreigners.
298. Article 19 of the Law on International and Temporary Protection of Foreigners.
299. Article 20 of the Law on International and Temporary Protection of Foreigners.

the activities relied upon constitute the expression and continuation of convictions or orientations held in the country of origin.

279. In case an applicant seeking international protection files a subsequent application for international protection, the well-founded fear of being persecuted or a real risk of suffering serious harm may not be based on circumstances which the applicant has created purely in order to meet the requirements for being granted international protection.[300]

II. Asylum Procedure

A. Procedure for Granting International Protection

280. A third-country national or a stateless person can express his/her intention to apply for international protection during the checks at the border crossing point. The intention to apply for international protection is an oral or written statement of intention of a third-country national or a stateless person to apply for international protection in Montenegro. If a third-country national or stateless person is already within the territory of Montenegro, the intention is expressing in the competent organizational unit of the border police in the place where he/she is found or at the Reception Centre for the irregular migrants. On the occasion of expressing the intention, police officers or Reception Centre staff are obliged to collect the data concerning the identity of the foreigner who has expressed the intention to submit an application for international protection, the route taken from the country of origin to Montenegro, as well as personal features and circumstances why he/she left the country of origin, so as to assess whether it is necessary to provide special procedural safeguards.

281. In order to determine the identity of a foreigner who expresses the intention to apply for international protection, fingerprints of all fingers and a photo are taken. Should it not temporarily be possible to take fingerprints of the foreigner who expresses the intention to apply for international protection, due to medical or other reasons that he/she did not deliberately cause, he/she is obliged to enable fingerprints being taken immediately after the reasons have ceased to exist. A foreigner who states the intention to apply for international protection without a justified reason, but fails to provide the data concerning the identity, the route taken from the country of origin to Montenegro, personal features and circumstances why he/she left the country of origin referred shall be deemed to be illegally staying in Montenegro.[301]

282. A foreigner seeking international protection is obliged to submit an application for international protection to the Ministry of Interior as soon as possible, and not later than fifteen days from the statement of intention, in the stipulated form, or

300. Article 21 of the Law on International and Temporary Protection of Foreigners.
301. Article 34 of the Law on International and Temporary Protection of Foreigners.

verbally on the record, which marks the commencement of the procedure for granting international protection. A foreigner seeking international protection who is placed in a healthcare institution shall be given the opportunity to apply for international protection in the healthcare institution in which he is situated.[302]

283. The Ministry of Interior shall verify whether the fingerprints are already in the fingerprint database of the country responsible for examining the application for international protection.[303]

284. A person stating his/her intention to apply for international protection at the border crossing point or in the transit area of an airport or seaport, who does not meet the requirements for legal entry into Montenegro, or comes from a safe country of origin, a safe third country, as well as in the event of a subsequent application for international protection, may be detained at the border crossing point or in the transit area of an airport or seaport, where it would be made possible for him to lodge an application for international protection.[304]

285. In the case when a person states his/her intention to apply for international protection at the border crossing point or in the transit area of an airport or seaport, the procedure upon the application for international protection shall be conducted at the border crossing point or in the transit area if a foreigner does not meet the requirements for granting an asylum and subsidiary protection, or presents only the data that are of no relevance for the assessment of qualifications for granting international protection, or if his application may be rejected according to the Law on International and Temporary Protection of Foreigners. In this case, the decision upon the application for international protection shall be made as soon as possible, and no later than twenty-eight days after the day when the application was lodged. If the decision is not made within twenty-eight days from the day of the application, a foreigner seeking international protection shall be granted entry into Montenegro in order to conduct the procedure of granting international protection, on which the Ministry of Interior shall issue a decision. A foreigner shall also be granted entry into Montenegro in the case where it is determined that there exist conditions for granting international protection. The administrative dispute can be initiated before the Administrative Court within five days following the receipt of the decision. The proceedings before the Administrative Court shall be urgent.[305]

286. Upon the application for international protection, the Ministry of Interior, as soon as feasible, is obliged to conduct the examination procedure and allow the foreigner seeking international protection to be heard in person regarding all the

302. Article 35 of the Law on International and Temporary Protection of Foreigners.
303. This provision of the Law on International and Temporary Protection of Foreigners shall be applied from the date of accession of Montenegro to the European Union.
304. Article 36 of the Law on International and Temporary Protection of Foreigners.
305. Article 37 of the Law on International and Temporary Protection of Foreigners.

facts and circumstances relevant to the procedure for granting international protection. A foreigner seeking international protection is obliged to personally attend and participate in the interview regardless of whether he/she has a legal representative, a guardian and/or an attorney.

287. The interview with a foreigner seeking international protection who has an attorney may be conducted in the absence of the attorney and he/she is obliged to present during the interview credible and convincing reasons on which he grounded his application for international protection and to submit all the evidence which he/she has at disposal or is able to obtain, and which support his/her application, as well as to respond truthfully to all questions addressed to him/her.

288. The Ministry of Interior shall, if possible and justified, and if so requested by the foreigner seeking international protection, ensure that the procedure upon the application for international protection is conducted by an authorized official of the same sex as the applicant's. In order to determine the facts of the case, a foreigner seeking international protection may be interviewed several times. The interview may be omitted if:

- the decision granting international protection can be taken based on the evidence submitted by the foreigner seeking international protection;
- the foreigner seeking international protection is not capable or able to be interviewed because of personal features and circumstances he has no influence over;
- a subsequent application is inadmissible.[306]

289. The statement of a foreigner seeking international protection shall be deemed credible where a particular fact or circumstance is not supported by evidence if:

- the plausibility of his/her statement as regards the general and specific information about the country of origin and the place he/she claims to have come from had been established;
- he/she has made genuine efforts to substantiate his/her application for international protection;
- he/she has submitted evidence he/she had on disposal, and for other evidence not in his/her possession, he/she has given a satisfactory explanation;
- it was ascertained that his/her statement was consistent and credible, and that it was not inconsistent with the available general and specific information relevant for examining the application for international protection; and
- he/she applied for international protection as soon as feasible, or gave justified reasons for not doing so.[307]

290. A foreigner seeking international protection is obliged to cooperate with the Ministry of Interior, to submit all the documentation at his/her disposal and

306. Article 42 of the Law on International and Temporary Protection of Foreigners.
307. Article 43 of the Law on International and Temporary Protection of Foreigners.

present true and accurate information concerning his/her identity, age, nationality, family, countries of previous residence, previous applications for international protection, travel routes, the documents that can be used for determining his/her identity and the reasons for seeking international protection. When deciding on the merits of an application for international protection, the Ministry of Interior is collecting and examining all relevant facts and circumstances, in particular:

- the statements and evidence that the foreigner seeking international protection has given, in particular such information as to whether he/she was or may be subjected to persecution or risk of suffering serious harm;
- current facts on the country of origin and, if necessary, on the countries through which he/she travelled, the laws and regulations of those countries and the manner in which they are enforced, based on various reports and other documents by the UNHCR and the EASO and other human rights organizations;
- whether the personal features and circumstances of the foreigner seeking international protection, in particular gender and age, and the position in society, were the cause of actions or acts of persecution or suffering serious harm which he/she had been or may be subjected to;
- on the activities of the foreigner seeking international protection, after leaving the country of origin, which are aimed at creating the conditions necessary for granting international protection, where it shall be assessed whether these activities may expose the foreigner to persecution or risk of suffering serious harm if he/she returns to that country;
- whether the foreigner seeking international protection could get protection from the country whose nationality he/she could prove; and
- whether the foreigner seeking international protection has applied for such protection within a reasonable time after his/her arrival in Montenegro, and if not, whether he/she stated reasonable grounds therefor.

291. If ascertained that a foreigner seeking international protection was subjected to persecution or risk of suffering serious harm, or threat of such persecution or harm, it shall be considered that there is a well-founded fear of persecution or suffering serious harm, unless there are reasonable grounds to believe that such persecution or serious harm will not be repeated.[308]

292. For the purpose of conducting a procedure upon an application for international protection, the Ministry of Interior collects personal and other data from the applicant. These data may also be collected from state authorities, state administration authorities, local self-government authorities and legal entities and natural persons in Montenegro, if it is in the interests of the foreigner seeking international protection, permitted by the law or other regulations, or necessary to verify the information on the foreigner seeking international protection. The previously mentioned authorities and persons that possess the data relating to a foreigner seeking international protection are obliged, at the request of the Ministry of Interior, to provide the requested information within fifteen days.

308. Article 44 of the Law on International and Temporary Protection of Foreigners.

293. The Ministry of Interior shall not collect the data on the foreigner seeking international protection from the country of his/her origin if the collection of such data could pose a danger and/or harm to the physical integrity of the applicant and his/her family members who have applied for international protection with him/her, or to the liberty and safety of family members who live in the country of origin. Personal and other data collected during the procedure upon the application for international protection, in particular the fact that the application has been lodged, constitute confidential information and may not be disclosed to the country of origin of a foreigner seeking international protection, an asylee or a foreigner granted subsidiary protection and to the state authorities, state administration authorities, local self-government authorities and legal entities and natural persons in Montenegro not being part of the procedure. The data on the first and family name, date of birth, sex, nationality, family members, documents issued by the country of origin and the last address in the country of origin, fingerprints and photos may be provided to the country of origin or a third country for a third-country national or a stateless person whose application for international protection was rejected by a final decision, provided such country accepts him/her and to the authorities of a third country that has ratified and applies the 1951 Convention relating to the Status of Refugees. The collection and the use of personal data shall be done in accordance with the regulations governing personal data protection.[309]

294. The data on a foreigner seeking international protection may be shared with the Member States of the EU with the view of implementing Regulation (EU) No. 604/2013 and Regulation (EU) No. 603/2013 of the European Parliament and the Council of 26 June 2013 on the establishment of 'Eurodac' for the comparison of fingerprints for the effective application of Regulation (EU) No. 604/2013 establishing the criteria and mechanisms for determining the Member State responsible for examining an application for international protection lodged in one of the Member States by a third-country national or a stateless person and on requests for the comparison with Eurodac data by the Member States' law enforcement authorities and Europol for law enforcement purposes, and amending Regulation (EU) No. 1077/2011 establishing a European Agency for the operational management of large-scale IT systems in the area of freedom, security and justice.[310]

295. The procedure for granting international protection may be terminated if the foreigner seeking international protection:

- abandons the application;
- avoids being served the summons for a personal interview;
- fails to appear when summoned for the interview, and fails to justify the nonappearance within fifteen days of the scheduled interview;

309. Article 45 of the Law on International and Temporary Protection of Foreigners.

310. This provision of the Law on International and Temporary Protection of Foreigners shall be applied from the date of accession of Montenegro to the European Union.

- leaves the place of residence for more than three days without notifying the Reception Centre thereof or fails to obtain the approval of the Reception Centre or the Ministry of Interior, except in cases of force majeure.

296. The decision to terminate the procedure is made by the Ministry of Interior. In this case, the Ministry of Interior shall reject an application for international protection if, based on determined facts and circumstances, it can be deemed that the conditions for granting international protection were not satisfied. In case a third-country national or a stateless person expresses his/her intention to apply for international protection after the final decision to terminate previously initiated procedure upon his/her application, such person shall not be obliged to relodge the application for international protection, and the terminated procedure shall be continued. Administrative dispute may be initiated before the Administrative Court against the decision to terminate the procedure within fifteen days after the receipt of the decision.[311]

297. Upon examining an application for international protection, the Ministry of Interior can:

- grant asylum if the foreigner seeking international protection meets the legal requirements for granting asylum;
- grant subsidiary protection if the foreigner seeking international protection meets the legal requirements for granting subsidiary protection;
- reject the application for international protection if the foreigner seeking international protection does not meet the legal requirements for asylum or subsidiary protection;
- reject the application for international protection in the following cases (if applicant enjoys protection or receives support of an organ or agencies of the UN, except for the UNHCR; if applicant already has a residence permit in the country which grants the same rights and obligations as those of the nationals of that country; if applicant had committed, incited or otherwise participated in the commission of crime against peace, war crime and crime against humanity defined by international instruments, serious crime of no political character, before arrival in Montenegro, and if committed for alleged political objectives, acts constituting cruel treatment, and if committed for alleged political objectives, acts that are contrary to the purposes and principles of the UN; if applicant has committed a criminal offence before entering Montenegro, which is punishable by imprisonment in Montenegro, while the reason for leaving the country of origin being only to avoid punishment prescribed in that country; if applicant represents a danger to national security and public order of Montenegro);
- grant or reject the application for international protection in the expedited procedure.

298. The applications for international protection, which can be granted based on the available evidence, may be processed as a matter of priority. Administrative

311. Article 46 of the Law on International and Temporary Protection of Foreigners.

dispute may be initiated before the Administrative Court against the previously mentioned decisions within fifteen days from receipt of the decision.[312]

299. A subsequent application for international protection may be submitted by a third-country national or a stateless person, within two years from the previous final decision rejecting his/her application or terminating the procedure. The subsequent application for international protection shall be submitted to the Ministry of Interior directly, verbally on the record. The admissibility of a subsequent application shall be decided upon by the Ministry of Interior not later than fifteen days after its receipt. Subsequent application for international protection is admissible if it contains facts and evidence that have arisen after the final decision was taken upon the earlier application, or facts and evidence that the foreigner seeking international protection, for justified reasons, has not stated in the earlier procedure and where those facts and evidence are of importance for determining whether the requirements for granting international protection are fulfilled. The admissibility of a subsequent application for international protection is estimated on the basis of facts and evidence contained in the application, in conjunction with the facts and evidence already set out in the previous procedure without interviewing the foreigner seeking international protection. When the subsequent application for international protection is found admissible, the application is going to be re-examined. When the subsequent application for international protection is found inadmissible, the application shall be rejected. Subsequent application for international protection of a foreigner in transfer shall be rejected by the Ministry of Interior as inadmissible.[313]

300. Ministry of Interior is obliged to decide on the application for international protection within six months from the day of lodging the application for international protection, or the day of the decision on the admissibility of a subsequent application for international protection. In the case when under Regulation (EU) 604/2013 Montenegro is designated as the responsible state for examining the application for international protection, the deadline shall start from the day of such designation or the day of taking over the applicant.[314] The deadline may be extended for additional nine months if:

- the application for international protection involves identifying complex factual circumstances or clarifying a complex legal matter;
- a large number of third-country nationals or stateless persons lodge applications for international protection at the same time;
- a foreigner seeking international protection fails to act in accordance with his legal obligations.

312. Article 48 of the Law on International and Temporary Protection of Foreigners.
313. Article 49 of the Law on International and Temporary Protection of Foreigners.
314. This provision of the Law on International and Temporary Protection of Foreigners shall be applied from the date of accession of Montenegro to the European Union.

301. Also, the deadline may be extended for additional three months in order to fully examine the application for international protection. Where it is reasonable to expect that a decision cannot be made within the previously mentioned period, the foreigner seeking international protection shall be notified thereof in writing and, upon his/her request, he/she shall be informed of the reasons for which it is not possible to take the decision within this time frame and the deadline within which a decision can be expected. Where it is reasonable to expect that a decision on the application for international protection cannot be made within the previously mentioned period, for the reasons of temporarily unsafe conditions in the country of origin, the Ministry of Interior shall review the situation in the country of origin every six months and inform the foreigner seeking international protection and the EC within a reasonable period about the reasons for not taking the decision. The final decision shall be adopted not later than within twenty-one months from the day the application for international protection was lodged.[315]

302. The Ministry of Interior can take the decision upon an application for international protection in an expedited procedure within two months from the day of lodging the application if in examination of the application it is determined that:

- the foreigner seeking international protection presented only the data which are irrelevant for examining the application;
- the foreigner seeking international protection gave false information, or made available or attached documents that were not authentic or failed to provide relevant data or concealed the documents which could adversely affect the outcome of the procedure, having thus mislead or could have mislead the authorized officer;
- the foreigner seeking international protection has destroyed the documents establishing his/her identity or nationality, and there is a possibility that it has been done with an intention to give false information about the identity or nationality;
- the foreigner seeking international protection made inconsistent, contradictory, clearly false or improbable representations which contradict sufficiently verified country-of-origin information, thus making his/her application for international protection clearly unconvincing;
- the foreigner seeking international protection already stayed in Montenegro for a while failing without any justified reason to state his/her intention to lodge an application earlier;
- the foreigner seeking international protection is making an application for international protection merely in order to delay or frustrate the enforcement of an earlier or imminent decision which would result in his/her removal from Montenegro;
- the foreigner seeking international protection constitutes a danger to the national security or the public order of Montenegro; or
- the foreigner seeking international protection comes from a safe country of origin.

---

315. Article 50 of the Law on International and Temporary Protection of Foreigners.

303. The applicant shall be informed that his/her application for international protection shall be processed in an expedited procedure. When a decision cannot be taken within the two months deadline, the application for international protection shall be processed within the regular deadline (max twenty-one months). In the case when under Regulation (EU) 604/2013 Montenegro is designated as the state responsible for examining the application, the deadline shall start from the day of such designation.[316] Administrative dispute may be initiated before the Administrative Court against the previously mentioned decision within fifteen days from receipt of the decision.[317]

304. When the application for international protection or the subsequent application was rejected by a final decision, or the procedure upon his/her application has been terminated, or the decision was made to terminate asylum or subsidiary protection, he/she shall be considered to be residing illegally in Montenegro and the measures for his/her return shall be taken in accordance with the Law on Foreign Nationals, with preference given to voluntary return.[318]

B. Cessation, Termination and Withdrawal of International Protection

305. Asylum shall cease if:

- the asylee voluntarily accepts the protection of the country of his nationality;
- the asylee acquires the nationality of a country whose protection he may enjoy;
- the asylee voluntarily returns and settles in the country which he had left or outside of which he had stayed because of fear of persecution;
- the circumstances in the asylee's country of origin on the basis of which he was granted international protection cease to exist; or
- the asylee voluntarily reacquires the nationality of the country of origin, which he had previously lost.[319]

306. Subsidiary protection shall cease if the circumstances under which subsidiary protection was granted cease or transform to such an extent that further protection is no longer necessary. When the Ministry of Interior determines that there is a permanent cessation or permanent and significant change of circumstances in the country of origin, it shall inform the asylee or foreigner granted subsidiary protection, and enable them to make a statement thereon verbally on the record. The decision on cessation of asylum or subsidiary protection shall be taken by the Ministry of Interior. Administrative dispute may be initiated before the Administrative

316. This provision of the Law on International and Temporary Protection of Foreigners shall be applied from the date of accession of Montenegro to the European Union.
317. Article 51 of the Law on International and Temporary Protection of Foreigners.
318. Article 53 of the Law on International and Temporary Protection of Foreigners.
319. Article 54 of the Law on International and Temporary Protection of Foreigners.

Court against the decision on cessation of asylum or subsidiary protection within fifteen days from receipt of the decision.[320]

307. Asylum and subsidiary protection shall terminate by operation of law when the asylee or foreigner granted subsidiary protection has been granted permanent residence in Montenegro or has acquired Montenegrin citizenship and upon the death of the asylee or the foreigner granted subsidiary protection. The decision on termination of asylum or subsidiary protection in such cases shall be taken by the Ministry of Interior.[321]

308. Asylum or subsidiary protection shall be withdrawn pursuant to an annulment of the decision thereon if:

- the existence of reasons for exclusion of the right to asylum and subsidiary protection is discovered subsequently;
- it is discovered that international protection had been granted on the basis of misrepresentation of facts or due to concealing facts relevant for the decision-making;
- if the beneficiary of international protection constitutes a danger for national security and public order of Montenegro, determined by a final decision of the competent authority.

309. In the event of determining such circumstances, the asylee or the foreigner granted subsidiary protection shall be notified thereof and given the opportunity to make a statement on these circumstances verbally on the record. The annulment decision shall be issued by the Ministry of Interior. Administrative dispute may be initiated before the Administrative Court against the decision within fifteen days from receipt of the decision. When the Ministry of Interior has adopted the annulment decision whose enforcement has not been postponed at the request of foreigner, such foreigner shall be considered to be illegally residing in Montenegro, and measures for his return shall be taken, in accordance with the Law on Foreign Nationals.[322]

III. Review of the Decision Rejecting the Application for Asylum

310. An application for international protection shall be rejected if:

- the foreigner seeking international protection has been granted international protection in a Member State of the EU;
- the foreigner seeking international protection has been granted international protection in a third country whose rights he still enjoys, which respects the principle of *non-refoulement*, and such country will accept him again;

320. *Ibid.*
321. Article 55 of the Law on International and Temporary Protection of Foreigners.
322. Articles 56 and 57 of the Law on International and Temporary Protection of Foreigners.

- there is a possibility that a foreigner seeking international protection is granted international protection by a safe third country;
- there is a possibility that a foreigner seeking international protection is granted international protection by a European safe third country;
- the state responsible for examining the given application has been determined;
- the foreigner seeking international protection is a national of a Member State of the EU.

311. Administrative dispute may be initiated before the Administrative Court against the decision to reject the procedure within fifteen days after the receipt of the decision.[323]

IV. Unaccompanied Minor Asylum Claimants

312. In the procedures conducted under the Law on International and Temporary Protection of Foreigners, due consideration shall be given to the best interests of a minor, taking into account:

- the minor's well-being and social development and his/her origin;
- the minor's safety and security, in particular where there is a risk of the minor being a victim of human trafficking;
- the views of the minor, in accordance with his/her age and maturity, and
- family reunification possibilities.

313. In pursuing the best interests of an unaccompanied minor, the minor's guardian shall undertake all the necessary actions, including contacts and interactions with state authorities, state administration bodies, foreign bodies, international and non-governmental organizations, in order to reunite the minor with his family, if that is in the best interest of the minor.[324]

314. For a minor, the intention to lodge an application for international protection shall be stated or the application for international protection lodged by his/her legal representative. A minor above 16 years of age, who is married, can autonomously state the intention and lodge an application. A minor and his/her legal representative are obliged to take part in the procedure upon the application for international protection. A minor may participate in the procedure without his/her legal representative if it is deemed to be in his/her best interests, in accordance with the regulations governing the protection of children's rights.[325]

315. The Centre for social work shall assign to an unaccompanied minor, who states an intention to apply for international protection, a guardian trained to work with minors seeking international protection, and whose interests are not contrary

323. Article 47 of the Law on International and Temporary Protection of Foreigners.
324. Article 15 of the Law on International and Temporary Protection of Foreigners.
325. Article 39 of the Law on International and Temporary Protection of Foreigners.

to the interests of the minor. An unaccompanied minor shall immediately be informed of the appointment of a guardian. An unaccompanied minor above 16 years of age and married shall not be assigned a guardian. An unaccompanied minor shall lodge the application for international protection personally in the presence of the guardian. Also, the application for international protection may be lodged by the guardian on behalf of the unaccompanied minor if, in the process of return, or enforced return to their country of origin, it is considered that he/she is in need of international protection with regard to his/her personal features and circumstances. The procedure for granting international protection to an unaccompanied minor shall be carried out by an authorized official who conducts the administrative procedure and issues an administrative act trained to work with minors seeking international protection. The guardian is obliged to promptly prepare the unaccompanied minor for the interview and provide him/her with information on the meaning and consequences of the personal interview. An unaccompanied minor is required to personally appear at the interview in the presence of a guardian. The decision upon the application for international protection of an unaccompanied minor shall be taken urgently, while an expedited procedure may be adopted only in cases if it contains facts and evidence that the applicant for international protection, due to legitimate reasons, has not stated in the earlier proceeding and where those facts and evidence are of importance for determining whether the requirements for granting an international protection are fulfilled and if in the procedure upon the application for international protection it was identified that an applicant for international protection is a danger to national security or public order of Montenegro or an applicant for international protection was coming from a safe country of origin. An unaccompanied minor may not be detained at a border crossing point or in the transit area.[326]

316. In case of a doubt as to the age of the minor in the procedure for granting international protection, the process of age assessment shall be conducted. Age assessment shall be conducted on the basis of available data on the minor, the expert opinion of the officials of the Reception Centre involved in the work with the minor, as well as on the opinion of the minor's guardian. If, on the basis of available data and mentioned opinions, it is not possible to determine the age of the minor, a medical examination shall be conducted with the prior written consent of the minor and the guardian. The medical examination shall be conducted by means of a physical examination, X-rays of teeth and/or of a hand, with full respect for the dignity of the minor. A minor and his guardian must be informed in a language he/she is reasonably assumed to understand and in which he/she can communicate, on the method of examination and its possible effects on the health, possible consequences of the results of such medical examination on the assessment of the application for international protection, as well as the consequences of denial of consent of the minor and the guardian. During the medical examination, if necessary, the minor shall be provided with an interpreter for the language he/she is reasonably assumed to understand and in which he/she is able to communicate. The costs of the medical examination shall be borne by the Ministry of Interior. In the case of unjustified

326. Article 40 of the Law on International and Temporary Protection of Foreigners.

denial of previously mentioned consent, the minor shall be deemed to be an adult applicant for international protection. An application for international protection may not be rejected solely on the ground of the denial of consent to conduct a medical examination. If, even following the results and the report on the medical examination undertaken, there is still a doubt as to the age of the minor, the concept of the benefit of the doubt shall be applied.[327]

V. Safe Country of Origin and Safe Third Country

317. A country is considered as a safe country of origin where, on the basis of the legal situation, the application of the law within a democratic system and the general political circumstances, it can be shown that there is no persecution and no risk of suffering serious harm, as determined based on the information on:

- the relevant laws and regulations of the country and the manner in which they are applied;
- observance of the rights and freedoms laid down in the European Convention for the Protection of Human Rights and Fundamental Freedoms, the International Covenant on Civil and Political Rights, as well as the United Nations Convention against Torture and Other Cruel, Inhuman or Degrading Treatment or Punishment;
- respect for the prohibition of expulsion or return (*non-refoulement*) in accordance with the 1951 Convention on the Status of Refugees;
- provision for a system of effective legal remedy.

318. The above-mentioned information could be collected from the reports and other valid sources, particularly from the Member States to the EU, the EASO, the UNHCR, the Council of Europe and other relevant international organizations. Based on this information, the Ministry of Interior, with prior opinion obtained from the Ministry of Foreign Affairs, shall establish a list of safe countries of origin and inform the EC thereof.[328] In examining the application for international protection, the Ministry of Interior, on a case-by-case basis, determines whether the applicant comes from a safe country of origin. Any country from the list of safe countries of origin shall be considered as a safe country of origin if a foreigner seeking international protection is a national of that country or had the last residence as a stateless person in that country, and if he/she failed to plausibly explain why that country of origin cannot be regarded as a safe country of origin in his/her particular case. Ministry of Interior is obliged to inform a foreigner seeking international protection that the country from which he/she comes is included in the list of safe countries of origin and that he/she may submit reasons why, in his/her case, that country should not be considered as a safe country of origin. In the case where, in the procedure

327. Article 41 of the Law on International and Temporary Protection of Foreigners.

328. This provision of the Law on International and Temporary Protection of Foreigners shall be applied from the date of accession of Montenegro to the European Union.

upon the application for international protection, it is established that it involves a safe country of origin, the application shall be rejected.[329]

319. According to Rulebook on Determining the List of Safe Countries of Origin of Foreigners Seeking International Protection,[330] the following countries are considered safe countries of origin: the Republic of Albania, Bosnia and Herzegovina, the Republic of North Macedonia, the Republic of Kosovo, the Republic of Serbia, the Republic of Turkey.

320. A safe third country is a country in which a foreigner seeking international protection is safe from persecution or risk of suffering serious harm, which respects the prohibition of expulsion or return (*non-refoulement*) and in which the possibility exists to receive international protection. In examining the application for international protection, the Ministry of Interior, on a case-by-case basis, determines whether it constitutes a safe third country, as well as whether there exists a connection between that country and the foreigner seeking international protection on the basis of which it would be reasonable for that person to go to that country and seek international protection, taking into account all the facts and circumstances of his/her application. Ministry of Interior is obliged to inform an applicant for international protection that in his/her case there is a safe third country and that he/she may state his/her reasons why this country may not be regarded as a safe third country considering his/her personal features and circumstances. In case when it is established in the process of assessing an application for international protection that there exists a safe third county, the application will be rejected, and the applicant shall be issued a certificate as confirmation that the merits of his/her application for international protection have not been examined in the procedure. In the event that the safe third country should refuse to accept a foreigner whose application was rejected, his/her application for international protection shall be re-examined.[331] The Ministry of Interior shall inform the EC regularly of the countries established to be safe third countries.[332]

321. According to the Law on International and Temporary Protection of Foreigners, a European safe third country is a country that has ratified and observes the provisions of the 1951 Convention relating to the Status of Refugees, without geographic limitations, and the European Convention for the Protection of Human Rights and Fundamental Freedoms. In examining the application for international protection, the Ministry of Interior, on a case-by-case basis, determines whether it constitutes a European safe third country. An applicant seeking international protection shall be duly informed that, in his/her case, there is a European safe third country and that he/she can submit reasons why, in his/her case, that country cannot be

329. Article 31 of the Law on International and Temporary Protection of Foreigners.

330. *Pravilnik o utvrđivanju liste sigurnih zemalja porijekla stranaca koji traže međunarodnu zaštitu*, 'Official Gazette of Montenegro', No. 69/2019.

331. Article 32 of the Law on International and Temporary Protection of Foreigners.

332. This provision of the Law on International and Temporary Protection of Foreigners on informing the European Commission shall be applied from the date of accession of Montenegro to the European Union.

considered a European safe country of origin, given the specificity of his/her personal features and circumstances. An application for international protection of foreigner who has illegally entered the territory of Montenegro from a European safe third country shall be rejected if such country adheres to the prohibition of expulsion or return (*non-refoulement*), unless there are special circumstances of humanitarian or political nature. In that case, the foreigner seeking international protection shall be issued a confirmation that the merits of his/her application for international protection have not been examined in the procedure. In the event that the European safe third country should refuse to accept a foreigner whose application was rejected, his/her application for international protection shall be re-examined.[333] The Ministry of Interior shall regularly inform the EC about the countries which have been designated as European safe third countries.[334]

§4. Legal Position

I. Rights and Duties of a Foreigner Seeking International Protection

322. A foreigner seeking international protection is entitled to: residence in Montenegro; freedom of movement within Montenegro; reception; healthcare; primary and secondary education; information necessary for their residence and legal counselling in reference to the procedure upon the application for international protection and free legal assistance; free legal assistance; work; documents in accordance with the Law on International and Temporary Protection of Foreigners; family unity. In the enjoyment of these rights, due consideration shall be given to the needs of a foreigner seeking international protection who needs special procedural safeguards. These rights shall not pertain to a foreigner seeking international protection retained at a border crossing point or in a transit area.[335]

323. A foreigner seeking international protection is obliged to:

- observe the Constitution and laws of Montenegro;
- cooperate with the state authorities and act upon their orders and instructions;
- provide the information necessary for establishing the identity and facilitate taking of photographs and fingerprints, as well as other checks needed to determine his identity;
- undergo a medical examination;
- comply with the rules of stay and the house rules of the Reception Centre;
- lodge an application for international protection within the set time frame;
- respond to the invitation of the Ministry of Interior for a personal interview and cooperate in the procedure of granting international protection;

333. Article 33 of the Law on International and Temporary Protection of Foreigners.
334. This provision of the Law on International and Temporary Protection of Foreigners on informing the European Commission shall be applied from the date of accession of Montenegro to the European Union.
335. Article 58 of the Law on International and Temporary Protection of Foreigners.

- remain within the territory of Montenegro for the duration of the procedure upon the application for international protection;
- notify the Ministry of Interior of any change of address within three days;
- comply with the Ministry's orders and measures on restriction of freedom of movement.

A foreigner seeking international protection may enjoy his/her rights and exercise his/her duties pending the final decision upon his/her application.[336]

324. A foreigner seeking international protection has the right of residence in Montenegro from the day of stating the intention to apply for international protection until the decision rejecting his/her application has become final. Family members of a foreigner seeking international protection, who came along with him/her, also have a right of residence. When a foreigner seeking international protection lodges a subsequent application, and when such application is found inadmissible, he/she shall have the right of residence until the receipt of the decision rejecting the subsequent application. If a foreigner whose subsequent application for international protection was rejected lodges a new subsequent application, he/she shall have no right of residence in Montenegro. A foreigner seeking international protection who is in the process of surrender or extradition shall have no right of residence in Montenegro.[337]

325. The procedure of granting international protection does not prevent the extradition or surrender of an applicant for international protection for whom a European arrest warrant has been issued or a decision on extradition or surrender to a Member State of the EU or the International Criminal Court had been passed, also to a third country of an applicant for international protection, for whom an international arrest warrant had been issued, unless the decision on extradition violates the principle of non-refoulement or return.

326. Pursuant to the Law on Asylum which was applicable until 1 January 2018, the asylum seekers were placed in the Centre for reception and accommodation of asylum seekers (so-called Asylum Centre)[338] and located therein until the end of asylum procedure. An asylum seeker was also entitled to use other accommodation options (renting an apartment or hotel accommodation, etc.), at his/her own expense. Once the asylum procedure was finished and the negative decision became final, that person moved from the umbrella of the asylum system under the umbrella of the Law on Foreign Nationals. The Law on International and Temporary Protection of Foreigners, which began with the implementation on 1 January 2018, brings one novelty, namely the possibility of the asylum seeker to be restricted of his/her freedom of movement.

---

336. Articles 59 and 60 of the Law on International and Temporary Protection of Foreigners.
337. Article 61 of the Law on International and Temporary Protection of Foreigners.
338. The Centre for the reception of asylum seekers was opened on 3 Feb. 2014 and put into operation on 20 Feb. 2014. It is located in Spuž (Municipality Danilovgrad) and has the capacity for accommodation of eighty persons, of which sixty-five places are permanent, while fifteen are additional. From 1 Jan. 2018 it is called Reception Centre.

327. A foreigner seeking international protection can enjoy the freedom of movement in Montenegro, which implies the choice of the place of residence, while being under the obligation to notify the Ministry of Interior of such place and address within three days after making the choice or changing the place of residence and address. A foreigner seeking international protection may have limited freedom of movement if, based on the facts and circumstances of his/her case, it is considered necessary for the following:

- determining facts and circumstances on which the application for international protection is based, and which cannot be established without limitation of movement, especially if it is deemed that there is a risk of absconding based on previous wilful attempts of leaving Montenegro, earlier refusal of checks to establish his/her identity, concealing or providing false information on identity or nationality, a serious violation of the rules of stay and house rules of the Reception Centre, as well as the results obtained through the Eurodac fingerprint database under Regulation (EU) 603/2013;[339]
- establishing and verifying the identity or nationality;
- protection of national security and public order of Montenegro;
- preventing misuse of the procedure when there is reasonable suspicion that he/she expressed the intention to apply for international protection during the procedure in order to prevent enforced return.[340,341]

328. The following measures may be imposed on a foreigner seeking international protection for the purpose of limiting the freedom of movement:

- prohibition of movement outside the Reception Centre;
- prohibition of movement outside a specified area;
- prohibition of leaving accommodation at a specific address that he has reported;
- mandatory stay at the Reception Centre;
- temporary seizure of travel and other documents;
- placement in the Detention Centre.

329. In the event of seizure of a travel or other document, such travel or other document shall be kept during the period of existence of grounds for their keeping, and a receipt shall be issued. Placement in the Detention Centre may be imposed only if the personality assessment of the foreigner seeking international protection has established that other measures would not achieve the purpose of limitation of the freedom of movement. A foreigner placed in the Detention Centre, and who expresses an intention to apply for international protection, or lodges an application for international protection, may not leave the Detention Centre pending the decision upon his/her application. The placement in the Detention Centre may be imposed on a foreigner who was afforded special procedural safeguards by way of

339. This provision of the Law on International and Temporary Protection of Foreigners shall be applied from the date of accession of Montenegro to the European Union.
340. *Ibid.*
341. Article 62 of the Law on International and Temporary Protection of Foreigners.

an exception only when his/her personal features and circumstances, or needs, in particular his/her health condition, allow so. The measures for the purpose of limiting the freedom of movement imposed on a foreigner seeking international protection may last as long as there are reasons for it, and not longer than three months. These measures may be extended for another three months, when there are justifiable reasons therefor. Placement of an unaccompanied minor in the Detention Centre may be imposed for a period of up to thirty days. An unaccompanied minor placed in the Detention Centre must be accommodated separately from adults. The decision on imposing these measures and the duration of such measures shall be taken by the Ministry of Interior. Administrative dispute may be initiated before the Administrative Court against the decision within three days of receipt of such decision.[342]

330. A foreigner seeking international protection is entitled to reception, which includes accommodation in the Reception Centre, food and clothing, public transportation allowance if transportation is required to participate in the procedure upon the application for international protection or enjoyment of other rights in accordance with the Law on International and Temporary Protection of Foreigners, as well as financial support. In accordance with the Government Regulation on the amount of money granted to applicants and to persons under international protection,[343] an applicant may be granted one-off financial assistance of EUR 5,000. The type of accommodation at the Reception Centre shall be determined by the Ministry of Interior with regard to personal features and circumstances, or the needs of the applicant. Financial support to a foreigner seeking international protections shall be granted by the Centre for Social Work.

331. The right to reception of a foreigner may be restricted or denied if he/she:

- fails to stay at the Reception Centre he/she has been assigned to;
- leaves the Reception Centre for more than twenty-four hours without permission;
- has the means to afford an adequate standard of living;
- violates the rules of stay and house rules at the Reception Centre.

332. The decision on the restriction or deprivation of the right to reception in previous cases shall be issued by the Ministry of Interior, on the basis of individual assessment of a foreigner seeking international protection, taking into account a living standard which ensures his/her dignity and is proportionate to the purpose pursued by the restriction or denial of the right to reception. Administrative dispute may be initiated before the Administrative Court against the decision on the restriction or deprivation of the right to reception within eight days from the receipt of the decision. In the cases when foreigner has the means to afford an adequate standard of living and violates the rules of stay and house rules at the Reception Centre, the

---

342. Article 63 of the Law on International and Temporary Protection of Foreigners.
343. *Uredba o visini novčane pomoći strancu koji traži međunarodnu zaštitu i azilantu i strancu pod subsdijarnom Zaštitom*, 'Official Gazette of Montenegro', No. 28/2018.

Ministry of Interior shall be entitled to require from a foreigner seeking international protection who is exercising the right to reception the reimbursement of the costs of reception, as well as the compensation for material damages caused.[344]

333. Accommodation, food and clothing, reimbursement of public transportation costs if transportation is required to participate in the procedure upon the application for international protection or enjoyment of other rights shall be provided by the Reception Centre. A foreigner accommodated at the Reception Centre shall be provided with basic hygienic products and mandatory medical examination. When accommodating a foreigner seeking international protection in the Reception Centre, due consideration shall be given to gender, age, vulnerability, health condition and disability, as well as family unity. Other forms of assistance, through special assistance programmes delivered at the Reception Centre, may be provided by the Red Cross and other organizations dealing with the protection of rights of refugees or asylees, or with humanitarian work, with prior approval by the Ministry of Interior. A foreigner seeking international protection may leave the Reception Centre for more than twenty-four hours with the prior approval of the authorized officer of the Reception Centre. The protection of persons and property in the Reception Centre is provided by plainclothes police officers specially trained to work with foreigners seeking international protection.[345]

334. Healthcare afforded to a foreigner seeking international protection includes emergency medical assistance, necessary treatment of diseases and serious mental disorders (diagnosis, treatment at all healthcare levels in Montenegro, and pharmaceuticals from the list of drugs that are prescribed and issued at the expense of the Health Insurance Fund of Montenegro). Foreigners seeking international protection in need of special procedural safeguards, in particular victims of torture, rape or other serious forms of psychological, physical or sexual violence, are entitled to the healthcare services appropriate to their specific state or consequences caused by such torture and other serious forms of violence. The mandatory medical examination and healthcare are provided by a healthcare institution with which the Health Insurance Fund of Montenegro has entered into an agreement. The costs of healthcare shall be borne by the Health Insurance Fund of Montenegro.[346]

335. The right to primary and secondary education is provided for a minor foreigner seeking international protection under the same conditions as for Montenegrin nationals, in accordance with the regulations governing primary and secondary education. A minor foreigner seeking international protection, who began exercising the right to secondary education, shall be allowed to continue such education even after becoming of age, under the same conditions as a Montenegrin national. The exercise of the right to education shall be granted to a minor foreigner seeking international protection within three months from the day of application for international protection until the enforcement of the decision on return. When a minor

344. Article 64 of the Law on International and Temporary Protection of Foreigners.
345. Article 65 of the Law on International and Temporary Protection of Foreigners.
346. Article 66 of the Law on International and Temporary Protection of Foreigners.

foreigner seeking international protection does not know Montenegrin language enough for attending school, he/she shall be provided preparatory and remedial teaching, including Montenegrin language classes, in order to exercise the right to education, in accordance with the regulations governing education.[347]

336. At the Reception Centre, upon the request of the foreigner seeking international protection, he/she shall be provided with information relevant for his/her residence, counselling regarding the procedure upon his/her application for international protection, as well as free legal assistance, in a language he/she is reasonably assumed to understand and in which he/she can communicate.[348]

337. A foreigner seeking international protection is entitled to free legal assistance in an administrative dispute concerning the application for international protection, at personal request, provided that he/she does not have money or valuables, and that the complaint is not manifestly unfounded. Free legal assistance includes assistance in making the complaint, representation before the Administrative Court, exemption from the payment of costs of the administrative dispute. The decision on granting free legal assistance shall be taken by the Ministry of Interior and furnished to the Administrative Court. A foreigner may initiate administrative dispute before the Administrative Court against the Ministry's decision rejecting an application for free legal assistance within eight days. Based on the decision on granting free legal assistance, the Ministry of Interior is obliged to appoint a lawyer by order from the list of lawyers which the Bar Association of Montenegro submits to the Ministry of Interior. For the provision of free legal assistance, a lawyer is entitled to compensation determined in accordance with the law governing legal aid. The costs of free legal assistance are covered by the Ministry of Interior. A foreigner seeking international protection can be provided free legal assistance during the application procedure for international protection before the Ministry of Interior by NGOs providing legal aid to foreigners seeking international protection.[349]

338. A foreigner seeking international protection acquires the right to work nine months after the day of lodging the application for international protection, which is still pending before the Ministry of Interior. Such foreigner seeking international protection may work without a residence and work permit or work registration certificate until the finality of the decision upon his/her application for international protection.[350]

339. The Ministry of Interior is obliged, within three days from receiving an application for international protection, to issue to the foreigner seeking international protection a certificate proving that he/she lodged an application for international protection. This certificate serves him/her as a residence document in

347. Article 67 of the Law on International and Temporary Protection of Foreigners.
348. Article 68 of the Law on International and Temporary Protection of Foreigners.
349. Article 69 of the Law on International and Temporary Protection of Foreigners.
350. Article 70 of the Law on International and Temporary Protection of Foreigners.

Montenegro pending the final decision on the application for international protection. This certificate is not a proof of identity of the applicant to whom the document was issued. The residence document shall not be issued to a foreigner seeking international protection who has applied for international protection at a border crossing point or in a transit area. An applicant who has been issued a document is obliged to return the document to the Ministry for its cancellation, upon termination of the right of residence.[351]

340. At the request of the UNHCR, third-country nationals and stateless persons seeking international protection and in need of such protection may be resettled in Montenegro. A third-country national or a stateless person who is resettled is entitled to international protection in accordance with the provisions of the Law on International and Temporary Protection of Foreigners. These persons shall also enjoy the rights and exercise the duties in accordance with the Law on International and Temporary Protection of Foreigners. The decision and the resettlement programme of persons shall be made by the Government at the proposal of the Ministry of Interior and the Ministry of Foreign Affairs.[352]

341. In order to share responsibilities based on the principle of solidarity within the EU, and in accordance with the Treaty on the Functioning of the EU, Montenegro is obliged to accept a certain number of third-country nationals and stateless persons, determined to be in need of or already benefitting from some form of international protection.[353]

342. A third-country national or a stateless person relocated in accordance with the previous paragraph is also entitled to international protection in accordance with the Law on International and Temporary Protection of Foreigners. These persons shall also enjoy the rights and exercise the duties in accordance with the Law on International and Temporary Protection of Foreigners. The relocation of a certain number of persons shall be ensured by the Government through its competent authorities.[354]

II. Rights and Duties of Asylees and Foreigners Granted Subsidiary Protection

343. An asylee and a foreigner granted subsidiary protection are entitled to: residence in Montenegro; accommodation and financial support; work; healthcare; education; free legal assistance; social protection; family reunification; assistance with

351. Article 71 of the Law on International and Temporary Protection of Foreigners.
352. Article 73 of the Law on International and Temporary Protection of Foreigners.
353. This provision of the Law on International and Temporary Protection of Foreigners shall be applied from the date of accession of Montenegro to the European Union.
354. Article 74 of the Law on International and Temporary Protection of Foreigners.

integration; learning the Montenegrin language, history and culture; property; documents; acquisition of Montenegrin nationality.[355]

344. An asylee and a foreigner granted subsidiary protection are obliged to:

- observe the Constitution and the laws of Montenegro;
- report his residence address within fifteen days from receiving the decision granting international protection;
- have an ID with him and show it to an authorized official at his request.

General information about the rights and duties is provided to an asylee or foreigner granted subsidiary protection by the Ministry of Interior.[356]

345. An asylee and a foreigner granted subsidiary protection are entitled to residence in Montenegro from the date of granting international protection. If an asylee or a foreigner granted subsidiary protection moves from Montenegro or continuously resides in another country for more than six months, without having previously informed the Ministry of Interior, the decision granting protection shall be revoked in the part relating to the right of residence in Montenegro. In the event that an asylee or a foreigner granted subsidiary protection returns to Montenegro, the Ministry of Interior shall issue a new decision approving the right of residence in Montenegro.[357]

346. An asylee and a foreigner granted subsidiary protection are entitled to suitable accommodation and financial support for no longer than two years since the delivery of the decision granting international protection. Accommodation shall be provided to these persons in a facility of state property, or a facility owned by a legal or natural person with whom the Ministry of Labor and Social Welfare has signed a contract on provision of accommodation services. For a pregnant woman, a single parent with a child up to the age of 3, a disabled person, an elderly and severely ill person who is in dire need of help and the care of another person, a person who is dependent on alcohol and narcotic substances, an unaccompanied minor, a minor with a behavioural disorder, accommodation can be provided in an appropriate institution. Also, for these categories of people, the accommodation and financial support can be extended until the personal features and circumstances are changed to the extent that those persons can reasonably be expected to take care of themselves. The right to financial support shall cease before the expiry of the period of two years if the asylee or foreigner granted subsidiary protection gets a job. The Ministry of Labor and Social Welfare provides accommodation and financial support. If an asylee or a foreigner granted subsidiary protection refuses provided accommodation without a justified reason, he/she shall lose the right to accommodation at the expense of the state of Montenegro.[358]

---

355. Article 75 of the Law on International and Temporary Protection of Foreigners.
356. *Ibid.*
357. Article 76 of the Law on International and Temporary Protection of Foreigners.
358. Article 77 of the Law on International and Temporary Protection of Foreigners.

347. In accordance with the Government Regulation on the Amount of Money Granted to Applicants and to Persons under International Protection,[359] the amount of the monthly monetary assistance is:

- for an individual, EUR 6,668;
- for a family with two members, EUR 8,008;
- for a family with three members, EUR 9,611;
- for a family with four members, EUR 11,347;
- for a family with five and more members, EUR 12,677.

348. An asylee and a foreigner granted subsidiary protection are permitted to work in Montenegro without a residence and work permit or work registration certificate within the meaning of the Law on Foreign Nationals. Also, they are entitled to adult education in relation to employment, professional development and gaining practical work experience under the same conditions as Montenegrin nationals.[360]

349. An asylee and a foreigner granted subsidiary protection can register in the records of unemployed persons of the Employment Agency of Montenegro – Labor Bureau – if they are between 15 and 67 years of age, capable or partially able to work, if they are actively seeking employment and available for work. As unemployed persons, they are entitled to the following possibilities:

- informing about the possibilities and conditions for employment;
- counselling in order to increase employability and employment;
- professional orientation;
- mediation in employment;
- exercising the right to monetary compensation during unemployment in accordance with the law;
- exercising the right to monetary assistance and reimbursement of transportation costs during education and training and inclusion in other measures aimed at increasing employment, i.e., reducing unemployment, in accordance with the law and the act of the state administration body competent for labour affairs.

350. An asylee and a foreigner granted subsidiary protection have the status of an insured person in accordance with the regulations governing healthcare and health insurance under the same conditions as Montenegrin nationals. They exercise healthcare through the healthcare system in Montenegro which is organized in three levels:

(1) PRIMARY – Primary healthcare centre.
(2) SECONDARY – Hospitals (general and specialized).
(3) TERTIARY – Clinical Centre and Public Health Institute.

359. *Uredba o visini novčane pomoći strancu koji traži međunarodnu zaštitu i azilantu i strancu pod subsdijarnom Zaštitom*, 'Official Gazette of Montenegro', No. 28/2018.
360. Article 78 of the Law on International and Temporary Protection of Foreigners.

351. They are entitled to healthcare on the basis of a health booklet, which is issued by the Health Insurance Fund of Montenegro after they have been registered in the database of insured persons. Within the right to primary healthcare, they have the right to select the following doctor:

– general practitioner for adults;
– paediatrician for children of up to 18 years of age;
– gynaecologist for female persons;
– dentist for children of up to 18 years of age and persons older than 65 years of age.

352. When exercising the right to primary healthcare they have the right to the following:

– on the basis of a prescription issued by a doctor in primary healthcare, collect the prescribed medication in pharmacies with which the Fund has concluded a contract on issuing medication;
– protection from and treatment of infectious diseases (right to voluntary and confidential counselling and testing for HIV/AIDS, as well as testing for syphilis);
– be informed by doctors in primary healthcare of the need and possibilities for the protection and treatment of infectious diseases, as well as the importance of carrying out the compulsory immunization programme;
– to healthcare in centres and support units on the proposal and on the instructions of primary healthcare doctors.

353. If the selected doctor deems that an asylee or a foreigner granted subsidiary protection is in need of a specialist examination, hospital treatment or other type of healthcare, this doctor shall refer them to the secondary and tertiary level of healthcare. If they are dissatisfied with the healthcare services provided or have been denied treatment, they have the right to file a complaint (verbally or in writing). The complaint is submitted to the Protector of patient's rights at the healthcare facility.

354. An asylee and a foreigner granted subsidiary protection exercise the right to primary, secondary and higher education under the same conditions as Montenegrin citizens. Primary education is obligatory for all children from the age of 6 to 15 and it lasts nine years. If the child is late in mastering the school curriculum, or is having difficulty mastering the materials envisaged, the school may organize additional classes, which are free of charge. Also, they are entitled to adult education under the same conditions as Montenegrin citizens and to the recognition of foreign educational documents.[361]

355. For the acquisition of general secondary education (high school) and vocational secondary education in an institution financed by the Budget of Montenegro, if they are a full-time student they do not pay tuition fees. If they are a part-time

361. Article 80 of the Law on International and Temporary Protection of Foreigners.

student, they pay the appropriate tuition fees. If they wish to obtain a professional qualification, they must submit an application to an education organizer of adults licensed by the Ministry of Education. Recognition of the certificate of acquired or commenced education (primary school, secondary vocational or secondary general school or higher education), in order to continue education, is carried out in the appropriate educational institution in which they wish to continue their education. The same is relevant for the higher education that has been commenced; i.e., the recognition is given by the institution of higher education where the education is to be continued.

356. An asylee and a foreigner granted subsidiary protection are entitled to free legal assistance equally to Montenegrin citizens, by submitting an application for granting free legal assistance to the service of the competent basic court, according to the place of residence. The service is obliged to give them information and advice on the possibilities and conditions for exercising the right to free legal assistance, and may also provide them with legal counselling as a form of free legal assistance. All forms of free legal assistance are provided by lawyers. A foreigner seeking international protection shall be entitled to free legal assistance in an administrative dispute concerning an application for international protection, at his/her personal request, if he/she does not possess any monetary assets or things of greater value and if the claim is not manifestly unfounded. Legal assistance, in the sense of the previous sentence, includes assistance in the preparation of a claim, representation before the Administrative Court, exemption from payment of administrative fees.

357. An asylee and a foreigner granted subsidiary protection are entitled to social protection in accordance with the law governing social protection, and the entitlements enjoyed on this ground may not be lesser in contents and scope than the ones accorded to Montenegrin citizens.[362]

358. Within social and child care they have the right, under the certain requirements, to material benefits and services. Material benefits from social care are the following:

- material securing;
- personal disability benefit;
- allowance for care and assistance;
- funeral costs;
- single monetary assistance;
- allowance for a parent or guardian beneficiary of personal disability benefit.

359. As the beneficiaries of any of the material benefits, they are entitled to exercising healthcare at the expense of the Health Insurance Fund of Montenegro. Material benefits from child protection are as follows:

- allowance for newborn child;

362. Article 82 of the Law on International and Temporary Protection of Foreigners.

- child allowance;
- nutrition costs in preschool institutions;
- assistance for upbringing and education of children and youth with special educational needs;
- reimbursement of salary compensation and salary compensation for maternity, i.e., parental leave;
- compensation based on childbirth;
- reimbursement of salary and salary compensation for work with half of full-time.

360. The services of social and child care are: support for life in community, counselling and therapy and social and educational service, accommodation and urgent intervention. For no longer than three years from the date of delivery of the decision granting international protection, an asylee and a foreigner granted subsidiary protection are entitled to assistance during integration into Montenegrin society. Assistance during integration includes developing the integration plan for an asylee or a foreigner granted subsidiary protection, in respect to their individual needs, knowledge, abilities and skills, assisting them in implementing the Integration Plan and monitoring the Integration Plan implementation. The Ministry of Labor and Social Welfare provides assistance during integration. This assistance could also be provided by other public administration bodies and non-governmental organizations.[363]

361. An asylee and a foreigner granted subsidiary protection are entitled with the possibility to learn Montenegrin language, history and culture for the purpose of better integration. The Ministry of Education is in charge to provide the teaching of Montenegrin language, history and culture. An asylee and a foreigner granted subsidiary protection are obliged to attend the course or other form of delivery for the Montenegrin language, history and culture provided. Attendance and learning of the Montenegrin language, history and culture are free of charge. In case of unjustified failure to attend the course or other form of delivery for the Montenegrin language, history and culture provided, they are obliged to reimburse the costs.[364]

362. An asylee and a foreigner granted subsidiary protection are entitled to property, in accordance with special regulations, in the same way as a foreigner with permanent residence in Montenegro.[365] This right includes the purchasing/ownership of a residential facility. There are various restrictions regarding the ownership of land on which there is no residential facility.

363. An asylee is entitled to the following documents:

- personal ID for an asylee, issued for the period of five years;
- travel document for an asylee, issued for the period of five years.

363. Article 84 of the Law on International and Temporary Protection of Foreigners.
364. Article 85 of the Law on International and Temporary Protection of Foreigners.
365. Article 86 of the Law on International and Temporary Protection of Foreigners.

364. A foreigner under subsidiary protection is entitled to the following documents:

- personal ID for a foreigner under subsidiary protection, issued for the period of three years;
- travel document for a foreigner under subsidiary protection, issued for the period of three years.

365. ID and travel documents shall not be issued in the following cases:

- an asylee or the foreigner granted subsidiary protection is attempting to escape the enforcement of a criminal judgment;
- if they avoid the payment of claims stemming from marital relationship or the relationships between parents and children, a tax liability or other material liability for which there is an enforcement document in place;
- this is required for reasons of national security or public order in Montenegro.

A travel document shall be also withdrawn if the existence of previous reasons is established.[366]

366. An asylee and a foreigner granted subsidiary protection may acquire Montenegrin citizenship in accordance with the law governing Montenegrin citizenship (after a certain time of residence in Montenegro or if they enter marriage with a Montenegrin citizen).

III. Rights and Duties of a Foreigner Granted Temporary Protection

367. A foreigner granted temporary protection is entitled to residence in Montenegro; suitable accommodation, necessary assistance and means of subsistence; healthcare; primary and secondary education; information about rights and duties; work; family reunification; the document; the right to apply for international protection.[367]

368. A foreigner granted temporary protection have the following duties:

- observe the Constitution and laws of Montenegro;
- cooperate with the state authorities and act upon their orders and instructions;
- provide the information necessary for establishing the identity and facilitate taking of photographs and fingerprints, as well as other checks needed to determine his/her identity;
- undergo a medical examination;
- comply with the rules of stay and the house rules of the Reception Centre;
- lodge an application for international protection within the set time frame;

366. Articles 87, 88 and 89 of the Law on International and Temporary Protection of Foreigners.
367. Article 96 of the Law on International and Temporary Protection of Foreigners.

- respond to the invitation of the Ministry of Interior for a personal interview and to be cooperative;
- remain within the territory of Montenegro;
- notify the Ministry of Interior of any change of address within three days;
- comply with the Ministry's orders and measures on restriction of freedom of movement.

369. A foreigner granted temporary protection who, during the temporary protection, applies for international protection may not exercise the rights of a foreigner seeking international protection as long as the temporary protection lasts.[368]

370. A foreigner granted temporary protection shall, at his/her request, be provided the information necessary for residence and enjoyment of rights and exercise of duties in a language he/she is reasonably assumed to understand and in which he/she is able to communicate.[369]

371. A foreigner granted temporary protection has the right to reside in Montenegro for the duration of temporary protection. For the duration of temporary protection, a foreigner granted temporary protection is entitled to suitable accommodation and means of subsistence (food, clothing, hygiene, etc.) if he/she does not have any personal means. Suitable accommodation, necessary assistance and means of subsistence shall also be provided to a person whose temporary protection has ceased if he does not have any personal means, while his/her return to the country of origin is not feasible due to serious health reasons. The healthcare of a foreigner granted temporary protection includes emergency medical assistance, necessary treatment of diseases and serious mental disorders (diagnosis, treatment at all healthcare levels in Montenegro and pharmaceuticals from the list of drugs that are prescribed and issued at the expense of the Health Insurance Fond). A foreigner granted temporary protection is entitled to primary and secondary education, and retraining and further training under the same conditions as a Montenegrin national.[370]

372. A foreigner granted temporary protection may work in Montenegro without a residence and work permit or work registration certificate, within the meaning of the Law on Foreign Nationals. A foreigner granted temporary protection is entitled to adult education related to employment, professional development and gaining practical work experience under the same conditions as a Montenegrin national.[371]

373. An application for family reunification shall be lodged by a foreigner granted temporary protection (in case of a minor) or a member of his family. A family member shall be granted temporary protection on that ground, which shall be

368. *Ibid.*
369. Article 101 of the Law on International and Temporary Protection of Foreigners.
370. Articles 97, 98, 99 and 100 of the Law on International and Temporary Protection of Foreigners.
371. Article 102 of the Law on International and Temporary Protection of Foreigners.

decided by the Ministry of Interior. In cases where family members enjoy temporary protection in different countries, their best interests shall be taken into account when deciding on family reunification.[372]

374. A foreigner granted temporary protection is entitled to a document for foreigners granted temporary protection, which is considered as a residence permit in Montenegro. Validity period of the issued document is one year and may be extended to six months, but not longer than one year. Also, the document may be extended based on the decision of the Council of the EU, for a maximum of one more year.[373] A foreigner granted temporary protection is obliged to return the document to the Ministry of Interior once temporary protection has ended.[374]

375. A foreigner granted temporary protection may lodge an application for international protection. The procedure upon applications shall be conducted in accordance with legal procedure and may be completed even after the temporary protection has ended.[375]

§5. Position of Family Members

376. A family member of a foreigner seeking international protection, an asylee, a foreigner granted subsidiary protection or a foreigner granted temporary protection is deemed to be:

- the spouse or the common-law spouse, under the laws of Montenegro, as well as the person considered to be the civil partner;
- the common minor child of spouses or common-law spouses, their common minor adoptive child, the minor child and the minor adoptive child of one of the spouses or common-law spouses or the civil partner who has custody over that child;
- the adult child of a foreigner seeking international protection, an asylee, a foreigner granted protection or a foreigner granted temporary protection, who is not married, and who due to his medical condition is unable to take care of himself/herself;
- the parent or other legal guardian of a minor a foreigner seeking international protection, an asylee, a foreigner granted subsidiary protection or a foreigner granted temporary protection;

372. Article 103 of the Law on International and Temporary Protection of Foreigners.
373. This provision of the Law on International and Temporary Protection of Foreigners shall be applied from the date of accession of Montenegro to the European Union.
374. Article 104 of the Law on International and Temporary Protection of Foreigners.
375. Article 105 of the Law on International and Temporary Protection of Foreigners.

– a first-degree relative in the direct ascending line who lived in the common household with a foreigner seeking international protection, an asylee, a foreigner granted subsidiary protection or a foreigner granted temporary protection if found to be dependent on the assistance of such person.[376]

377. A foreigner seeking international protection, an asylee, a foreigner granted subsidiary protection and a foreigner granted temporary protection are entitled to family unity. To ensure the enjoyment of family unity benefits, in the process of reunification of family members with an asylee, a foreigner granted subsidiary protection or a foreigner granted temporary protection, a diplomatic or consular mission of Montenegro abroad can, at the proposal of the Ministry of Interior, issue a visa to the family members of such person, and if no conditions are met for visa issuance, they can issue a travel document for foreigners.[377]

378. An asylee and a foreigner granted subsidiary protection are entitled to reunification with their family members. Family members of an asylee or a foreigner granted subsidiary protection are, on that ground, entitled to asylum or subsidiary protection, and the decision is taken by the Ministry of Interior. In the procedure of granting asylum or subsidiary protection, for a person who cannot obtain documentary evidence of the family relationship, the circumstances under which it is possible to assess whether there is such a relationship shall be taken into account. The decision to reject the application for family reunification may not be based solely on the fact that there is no documentary evidence of the family relationship. A family member of an asylee or a foreigner granted subsidiary protection lawfully residing in Montenegro shall enjoy the same rights as the asylee or the foreigner granted subsidiary protection.[378]

§6. STATISTICS[379]

379. Table 2 shows the number of asylum applications submitted, the number of granted protections and the countries of origin of persons granted protection, starting from 2007, when the asylum system in Montenegro was established. Also, Tables 3 and 4 show the number of international protection seekers in 2018 and 2019, with information regarding their countries of origin.

376. Article 7 of the Law on International and Temporary Protection of Foreigners.
377. Article 14 of the Law on International and Temporary Protection of Foreigners.
378. Article 83 of the Law on International and Temporary Protection of Foreigners.
379. Ministry of Interior work reports published on the website, www.mup.gov.me.

Table 2 Overview of the Number of Applications, Number of Protection Granted and Countries of Origin of Persons Granted Protection by Each Year

Year	*Number of Applications*	*Protection Granted*	*Countries of Origin of Persons Granted Protection*
2007	3	1 (asylum)	1 Macedonia
2008	7	1 (subsidiary protection)	1 Belarus
2009	20	–	–
2010	9	–	–
2011	239	3 (subsidiary protection)	1 Morocco, 1 Algeria, 1 Iraq
2012	1,529	1 (asylum) and 1 (subsidiary protection)	1 Yemen (A), 1 Iraq (SP)
2013	3,554	–	–
2014	2,312	2 (asylum) and 2 (subsidiary protection)	2 Nigeria (SP), 1 Syria (A), 1 Iran (A)
2015	1,611	14 (asylum) and 2 (subsidiary protection)	14 Syria (A), 2 Ukraine (SP)
2016	335	12 (asylum) and 11 (subsidiary protection)	7 Cuba (A), 5 Yemen (A), 8 Syria (SP), 1 Russia (SP), 2 Yemen (SP)
2017	849	1 (asylum) and 7 (subsidiary protection)	1 Lebanon (A), 1 Ghana (SP), 2 Yemen (SP), 2 Afghanistan (SP), 2 Belarus (SP)
2018	3,104	10 (asylum) and 4 (subsidiary protection)	5 Iran (A), 2 Syria (A), 1 Yemen (A),1 Cuba (A),1 Russia (A), 3 Ghana (SP), 1 Belarus (SP)
2019	1,921	5 (asylum) and 1 (subsidiary protection)	4 Syria (A), 1 Ethiopia (A), 1 Belarus (SP)
TOTAL	**15,493**	**78**	**78**

Table 3 Number of International Protection Seekers in 2018[380]

Country	*January*	*February*	*March*	*April*	*May*	*June*	*July*	*August*	*September*	*October*	*November*	*December*	*Total*
Afghanistan		4	13	6	6	6	3		2	3	4		47
Albania							1						1
Algeria		5	108	41	32	35	47	6	3	11	5	11	304
Bangladesh									3	2			5
Belarus								1					1
Cameroon								1					1
Cuba				4			3	1					8
Egypt		1	2	2		1	1		1				8
Eritrea						1	1						2
Ethiopia											1		1
Ghana	1											2	3
India				2			1			1			4
Iran	10			10	9	5	4	9	5		5	6	63
Iraq		1	2	56	49	38	15	18	8	30	21	7	245
Israel										1			1
Kazakhstan						1							1
Kuwait						1							1
Libya	2	1	9	29	42	11	9	6	4	8	6	4	131
Mauritania								1					1

380. *Ibid.*

Country	*January*	*February*	*March*	*April*	*May*	*June*	*July*	*August*	*September*	*October*	*November*	*December*	*Total*
Morocco	2	7	48	19	33	15	16	3	3	9	11	11	177
Nepal							4		7	9			20
Pakistan		8	65	48	84	146	121	43	80	38	9	17	659
Palestine			4	20	13	17	6	11	25	44	9	8	157
Russian Federation		1	2		1		1				3	1	9
Serbia												1	1
Somalia					1		1						2
Sweden			3										3
Syria	8	34	62	233	277	160	68	104	55	98	65	35	1199
Tunisia	1		9		3	1							14
Turkey				1								1	2
Ukraine												1	1
Uzbekistan											1		1
Western Sahara							1						1
Yemen			2	3	9	4	3	9					30
Grand Total	**24**	**62**	**329**	**474**	**559**	**442**	**306**	**213**	**196**	**254**	**140**	**105**	**3,104**

Table 4 Number of International Protection Seekers in 2019[381]

Country	*January*	*February*	*March*	*April*	*May*	*June*	*July*	*August*	*September*	*October*	*November*	*December*	*Total*
Afghanistan			3	9	3			4	4	20	52	10	105
Albania						1					1		2
Algeria	18	43	26	11	25	8	22	31	16	24	36	25	285
Cuba		1					2					4	7
Egypt		1	4		1			1	1		2	2	12
Ethiopia											1		1
India					1								1
Iran	5	2	5	15	8	11	2	7	4	3	14	1	77
Iraq	3	41	54	87	44	14	7	3	1	1			255
Libya	22	15	7	6	2	3			3	1	1		60
Morocco	23	37	35	24	12	17	24	51	59	92	152	132	658
Nepal						12							12
Pakistan		9	1	44	18	2	3	3	2	3	5	1	91
Palestine	2	23	2	3	3	1	1		8	5		1	49
Romania	1												1
Russia	1						3		1	1	5		11
Serbia		1					1				1	1	4
Syria	25	23	59	82	26	10	8	2	1	7	7		250
Turkey										2	6	2	10

381. *Ibid.*

Country	*January*	*February*	*March*	*April*	*May*	*June*	*July*	*August*	*September*	*October*	*November*	*December*	*Total*
Tunisia	2		1	1		1		4			1		10
Yemen					1					1			2
Eritrea					1								1
Somalia					2				2				4
Sudan						3							3
Belarus						1		1					2
Jordan								4					4
Myanmar/ Burma										1			1
Columbia												1	1
Ecuador												2	2
Grand Total	**102**	**196**	**197**	**282**	**147**	**84**	**73**	**111**	**102**	**161**	**284**	**182**	**1,921**

Chapter 7. Others Grounds

§1. Regulation of the Status of Displaced and Internally Displaced Persons in Montenegro

380. The wave of refugees arriving in Montenegro during the 1990s was triggered by armed conflicts in the territory of the republics of the former Yugoslavia and Kosovo. In 1992, as a reaction to the refugee crisis, the Government of Montenegro issued a 'Decree on the Care of Displaced Persons,' enabling the Ministry of Interior to grant 'DP' status to people from Croatia and Bosnia and Herzegovina. Later, when IDPs from Kosovo arrived in Montenegro in 1998 and 1999, the Montenegrin institutions registered them as IDP under an ad hoc administrative measure responding to the emergency situation. This status was also granted to refugees from Albania, who resided in Kosovo and fled to Montenegro together with others.[382]

381. Following the Decree on the Care of Displaced Persons,[383] during 1992 the decision on recognizing status of being displaced in the territory of Montenegro was made for 34,307 persons from Croatia and Bosnia and Herzegovina. Based upon the Rulebook on Identity Documents of Displaced Persons,[384] all persons with such status were issued identity cards of DPs. Following that, two registrations were carried out in 1996 and 2000, and although they did not represent legal and formal revisions of the status of DPs, they had impact over the register of such persons in Montenegro. In accordance with this, 28,338 DPs were registered in 1996, while 14,418 DPs were registered at the end of 2000. At the registration conducted in 2004, 8,474 persons in total were registered. Out of 8,474 persons, 6,105 are from Bosnia and Herzegovina, 2,343 are from Croatia, while twenty-six persons are from Slovenia.

382. Through a public call in March 2009 and repeated public calls in summer 2010, the Ministry of Interior, together with UNHCR, called DPs from Croatia and Bosnia and Herzegovina to approach the Ministry in order to reconfirm 'DPs' status in Montenegro. Re-registration was conducted in the period between 30 March and 31 July 2009, and resulted in some 5,500 persons re-registered in Ministry of Interior database as 'DPs'. This number represents a decrease of some 3,000 DPs in the period between the two re-registrations (2004–2009). For those who did not respond to the public call and did not approach the Ministry, the Ministry revoked their DP status by the Decision of June 2010.

383. At the end of 1999 when persons from Kosovo, not having crossed internationally recognized border, entered Montenegro, their number was 30,289. At the time of their arrival, the former Commissariat for Displaced Persons established the

382. Montenegro hosts a number of Albanian citizens who were granted refugee status under the federal laws of the former Yugoslavia. These are mostly ethnic Serbs and Montenegrins who arrived in Montenegro (then SFRY) in 1991, and have subsequently moved throughout Serbia and Montenegro (many residing in Kosovo until 1999 and then fleeing back to Montenegro). Their number is about 1,600 persons based on UNHCR 2010 survey.

383. *Uredba o zbrinjavanju raseljenih lica*, 'Official Gazette of RM', No. 37/92.

384. *Pravilnik o ličnim dokumentima raseljenih lica*, 'Official Gazette of RM', No. 41/92.

status of being internally displaced and issued adequate documents. It should be noted that all such persons until June 2006, i.e., until Montenegro gained independence, were able to regulate registration of residence and identity card in Montenegro if they wanted, which a number of them actually did. The majority of IDPs, in addition to the ID issued by the Commissariat, also possessed a Serbian identity card. With regards to 'internally displaced persons' from Kosovo, a re-registration was conducted between 14 September 2009 and 14 February 2010. The exercise resulted in the confirmation of the status of some eleven thousand persons. The re-registration resulted in a decrease of some five thousand IDPs between two re-registrations (2003–2009).

384. In order to address permanently and sustainably the issues of displaced persons from the Former Yugoslav Republics and internally displaced persons from Kosovo, in 2009 the Government of Montenegro, in cooperation with UNHCR and EU Delegation to Montenegro, adopted the Action Plan for Resolving the Status of Displaced Persons from Former Yugoslav Republics and Internally Displaced Persons from Kosovo residing in Montenegro. The Action Plan created a mechanism for DPs and IDPs to have privileged access to the status of foreigner with permanent residence. In accordance with the Action Plan, this change in status was made possible by the adoption of the Law on Amending the Law on Foreign Nationals in October 2009.

385. The Law on Foreign Nationals was updated by the Law on Amending the Law on Foreign Nationals, which entered into force on 7 November 2009. The Law on Amending the Law on Foreign Nationals specifically provides for the integration of 'DPs' and 'internally displaced persons' through privileged access to permanent residence in Montenegro. A Decree No. 03-6378 of 2010 on the Manner of Exercising the Rights by Displaced Persons from the Former Yugoslav Republics and Internally Displaced Persons from Kosovo Residing in Montenegro was adopted on 8 July 2010 to guarantee these persons full access to rights, until the acquisition of the new legal status of foreigner with permanent residence. This temporary measure foreseen the concerned persons to exercise their rights in the areas of healthcare, education, employment, pension and social and child protection as Montenegrin citizens until 7 January 2012. The deadline for applying for status regulation, prescribed by Law, was two years, i.e., until 7 November 2011. Subsequently, the deadline for applying for the status of these persons was extended three more times, until the end of 2014.

386. In accordance with legal provisions, these persons, unlike other foreign nationals in Montenegro, enjoy the right of permanent residence in Montenegro under privileged conditions. The privileged position of these persons is that, unlike other foreign nationals, they are exempt from the obligation to provide proof of the means of subsistence provided, accommodation and health insurance, which is a legal obligation for all other foreigners when applying for a permanent residence permit.

387. These persons were also given the legal possibility to obtain a temporary residence permit of up to three years if they did not hold a valid passport of the country of origin, which is at the same time a period within which, if they obtain a valid passport, they are entitled to a permanent residence permit.

388. As foreign nationals with a permanent residence permit, these persons enjoy the following rights: the right to work; the right to education and vocational training; the right to recognize diplomas and certificates; the right to social assistance, health and pension insurance; the right to tax benefits; the right of access to the market for goods and services; freedom of association and membership in organizations representing the interests of workers or employers. A whole range of laws and by-laws which defines criteria for enjoyment of rights attached to the status of foreigner were harmonized with the Law on Amending the Law on Foreign Nationals in order to enable full enjoyment of rights guaranteed by the Law.

389. Also, the resolution of the status of these persons in the previous period was also possible through the admission to Montenegrin citizenship, in accordance with the existing legal regulations, which a number of them used. From 7 November 2009 (date of entry into force of the Law on Amending the Law on Foreign Nationals), as of 31 December 2019, Displaced and Internally Displaced Persons submitted a total of 15,237 applications for permanent residence and temporary residence permits for up to three years. Out of this number, 15,050 requests have been resolved, while 187 requests are pending. Out of the 15,050 cases resolved, 12,366 persons were granted permanent or temporary residence for up to three years, 286 applications were rejected, while 2,398 cases were rejected/suspended (there were double or incomplete applications).[385]

§2. Stateless Person

390. Considering the importance of statelessness, as a global problem, as well as the fact that Article 15 of the Universal Declaration of Human Rights provides that: 'Everyone has the right to a nationality and no one shall be arbitrarily deprived of his or her nationality, nor should he or she be denied the right to change his or her nationality', Montenegro is a signatory to the following conventions: the 1954 Convention Relating the Status of Stateless Persons, the 1961 Convention on the Reduction of Statelessness, the 1997 European Convention on Nationality and the 2006 Council of Europe Convention on the Avoidance of Statelessness in relation to State Succession. By ratifying the previous mentioned Conventions, Montenegro has joined the circle of states which, by their legislation, seek to achieve the purpose of the conventions as much as possible.

391. Montenegro is a country that, after the war of the 1990s, has received 130,000 refugees, which it has accepted, with at least 30,000 remaining to live in

385. Government of Montenegro, *Report on the Implementation of the Action Plan for the Implementation of the Strategy for Integrated Migration Management for 2019* (Podgorica 2020).

Montenegro. Montenegro had a comprehensive legislative framework both as a member of Yugoslavia and as an independent state when it passed the Montenegrin Citizenship Law in 2008 which left no room for any person born on the territory of Montenegro to remain stateless. However, with the arrival of IDPs and DPs from the Former Yugoslav Republics, there were stateless among them, but not in large numbers.

392. The Law on Montenegrin Citizenship[386] respects the principles of the European Convention on Citizenship, namely:

- avoidance of statelessness;
- preventing the arbitrary deprivation of citizenship;
- preventing discrimination;
- the right to a nationality as well as Council of Europe Recommendations on the Prevention and Reduction of Statelessness, the Universal Declaration of Human Rights, the International Covenant on Civil and Political Rights, the Convention on the Rights of the Child and the Convention on the Elimination of All Forms of Discrimination against Women.

This Law defines the circle of persons who must be provided with an easier way of acquiring citizenship, not only by origin but also by naturalization, and prescribes a facilitated (privileged) way of acquiring Montenegrin citizenship by admission categories of persons. The Law on Montenegrin Citizenship, in particular, took into account the privileged way of acquiring Montenegrin citizenship of citizens of the republics of the former SFRY.

393. Conditions for the acquisition of Montenegrin citizenship prescribed by the Law on Montenegrin Citizenship apply without exception, to all applicants for the acquisition of Montenegrin citizenship on any of the prescribed grounds, excludes discrimination on any grounds (gender, religion, race, colour or national and ethnic origin), with the built-in principle that statelessness should be avoided. Also, this Law ensures equality among its citizens, regardless of whether they acquired Montenegrin citizenship by origin or admission.

394. Montenegro is one of the few countries to have established a procedure for determining the status of stateless persons through the adoption of the new Law on Foreign Nationals, which entered into force in March 2018. In addition to the Law on Foreign Nationals, the Law on Extra-Judicial Proceedings[387] was amended, and it simplified the procedure for registering persons born outside a healthcare facility. The law, prepared in collaboration with UNHCR and United Nations Children's Fund, prescribes a procedure for determining the time and place of birth, which

386. Law on Montenegrin Citizenship, 'Official Gazette of Montenegro', Nos 13/2008, 40/2010, 28/2011, 46/2011 and 54/2016.

387. *Zakon o vanparničnom postupku*, 'Official Gazette of Montenegro', Nos 20/2015, 75/2018, 67/2019.

regulates the status of persons not registered in birth registers and persons born outside healthcare institutions. Ongoing measures to raise awareness of the need to register births are constantly taken, especially when not done immediately after birth, to reduce the number of such cases, especially among the Roma population, and thus eliminate the root cause of statelessness.

395. According to the Law on Foreign Nationals, a stateless person may be issued a temporary residence permit if he or she fulfils the following conditions:

- he/she has provided accommodation;
- he/she holds health insurance;
- he/she holds either a valid foreign travel document or identity card issued to him/her by another country's competent authority or a stateless travel document;
- he/she has not been imposed an entry and stay ban in Montenegro;
- he/she submits the evidence that he or she has been actually residing in Montenegro for a minimum of three years prior to filing the application and that he or she intends to continue his or her stay in Montenegro. Prior to issuing a temporary residence permit, application for establishing whether the applicant is a stateless person should be filed to the Ministry of Interior personally, in the place of residence. In the procedure upon the application, the Ministry of Interior may obtain or exchange information with the state authorities, state administration authorities, authorities of other states, and international organizations and NGOs. Upon personal request, the Ministry of Interior shall issue to the person for whom is established stateless person status, a travel document for a stateless person, with a validity period of one year. A stateless person may stay in Montenegro based on a travel document for a stateless person or temporary residence permit.[388] Since the beginning of the implementation of the new Law on Foreign Nationals four travel documents have been issued for stateless persons, two temporary residence permits have been issued for stateless persons, while nine requests for determining stateless status are in procedure.[389]

§3. Stay and Work of Third-Country Nationals with Granted Permanent Residence in Another EU Member State and of Their Family Members

396. A third-country national with granted residence in another EU Member State may stay in Montenegro for up to ninety days from the day of entry into Montenegro, i.e., until the expiry of the period for which visa or residence permit has been issued to him or her by another EU Member State, if the validity period of visa

388. Articles 59 and 60 of the Law on Foreign Nationals.
389. Government of Montenegro, *Ministry of Interior Work Report*, Podgorica, 2020.

or residence permit is shorter than ninety days.[390] If he/she intends to stay in Montenegro for longer than ninety days, shall prior to the expiry of visa or residence permit validity period issued by another EU Member State file to the Ministry of Interior the application for the issuing of a temporary residence permit, in the place of residence. He/she is obliged to submit the evidence of the fulfilment of legal conditions for residence (he/she possesses sufficient funds to support himself/herself; he/she has provided accommodation; he/she holds health insurance; a valid foreign travel document or identity card or a stateless travel document; in his/her country of origin he/she has not been pronounced a final judgment sentencing him/her to an effective imprisonment longer than six months, for a criminal offence that is pursued ex officio, or a judgment legal effects ceased; he/she has submitted evidence justifying his/her permit application).[391]

397. A family member of a third-country national with permanent residence granted in another EU Member State can personally file to the Ministry of Interior the application for the issuing of a temporary residence permit, in the place of residence. He/she is obliged to submit the evidence of the fulfilment of legal conditions for residence (sufficient funds to support himself/herself; provided accommodation; health insurance; a valid foreign travel document or identity card or a stateless travel document; no criminal record in the country of origin or in Montenegro; he/she has submitted evidence justifying his/her permit application; as well as evidence that his/her temporary residence is granted in another EU Member State and evidence that he or she is a family member of a third-country national with granted permanent residence in another EU Member State). Of the issued temporary residence permit to a third-country national with permanent residence granted in another EU Member State and to his or her family member, of the extension of the temporary residence, and of the expulsion of such persons, the Ministry of Interior shall notify the competent authority of another EU Member State where permanent residence is granted to a third-country national.[392]

§4. Stay and Work of Third-Country Nationals with Higher Education Qualifications: EU Blue Card

398. A third-country national with higher education qualifications who possesses necessary, i.e., appropriate, expertise and a temporary residence and work permit may become employed in Montenegro in accordance with the regulations on employment.[393] Higher education qualification shall be considered a qualification

390. Provisions of the Law on Foreign Nationals relating to third-country nationals with granted permanent residence in another EU Member State and of their family members shall be applied from the date of accession of Montenegro to the European Union.
391. Articles 179 and 180 of the Law on Foreign Nationals.
392. Articles 181 and 183 of the Law on Foreign Nationals.
393. Provisions of the Law on Foreign Nationals relating to EU Blue Card shall be applied from the date of accession of Montenegro to the European Union and shall not relate to the persons referred to in Art. 3 para. 2 of Directive 2009/50/EC on the conditions of entry and residence of third-country nationals for the purposes of highly qualified employment.

acquired upon the completion of an appropriate study programme, in accordance with the regulations governing higher education. Temporary residence and work permit of a third-country national with higher education qualifications – so-called 'EU Blue Card' – can be issued to a foreign national who meets general legal conditions regarding accommodation, funds, health insurance, a valid foreign travel document or identity card, no criminal record; there are no obstacles of national, i.e., internal security. He/she is obliged to apply for issuing EU Blue Card personally, in the place of residence. In addition to evidence of the fulfilment of general legal conditions, he/she is obliged to submit employment contract concluded with the employer in Montenegro, for the term of minimum twelve months and evidence of higher education or of completed undergraduate or postgraduate studies. The employment contract has to indicate annual gross salary, the amount of which may not be lower than one and a half of average gross salary in Montenegro. The validity period of the EU Blue Card is up to two years and can be extended. If the employment contract has been concluded for the term shorter than two years, the EU Blue Card shall be issued for the term of the employment contract, increased by additional three months.[394]

399. The EU Blue Card holder may work in Montenegro only on the jobs for which the EU Blue Card has been issued to him or her, and only for the employer who employs him or her. The employer may assign an EU Blue Card holder only to such jobs for which the EU Blue Card was issued. The employer is obliged to keep a copy of the EU Blue Card in the business premises or at the place of work of the foreign national. Where the employment contract terminates and where other conditions based on which the EU Blue Card was issued cease to exist, the employer or the EU Blue Card holder are obliged to notify the Ministry of Interior thereof, not later than within eight days from the date when such circumstances have arisen. The EU Blue Card holder, who changes his employer within the first two years of stay in Montenegro, is obliged to submit to the Ministry of Interior an application for the issuing of a new EU Blue Card, within eight days from the date of termination of employment with the initial employer.[395]

400. The EU Blue Card holder in Montenegro is entitled to:

- work, work placement, and the rights during unemployment;
- education and professional development;
- recognition of diplomas and certificates;
- social assistance, health and pension insurance;
- tax reliefs in accordance with the law;
- access to the goods and services market;
- freedom of association, connection and membership in organizations which represent the interests of workers or employers.

394. Articles 184, 185 and 187 of the Law on Foreign Nationals.
395. Articles 189 and 191 of the Law on Foreign Nationals.

The above-mentioned rights shall be exercised in accordance with the laws governing the manner of exercising such rights.[396]

401. A family member of the EU Blue Card holder may be issued a temporary residence permit for family reunification. A temporary residence permit for family reunification shall be issued with the validity period until the expiry of the EU Blue Card validity. A family member of the EU Blue Card to whom temporary residence is granted for the purpose of family reunification may become employed in Montenegro.[397]

402. A permanent residence permit may also be issued to an EU Blue Card holder if until the date of submission of the application for the issuing of permit he or she has legally stayed in Montenegro pursuant to the EU Blue Card, for five uninterrupted years. Exceptionally, a permanent residence permit may be issued to a third-country national who has stayed in another EU Member State as an EU Blue Card holder for uninterrupted five years, of which he or she stayed in Montenegro as an EU Blue Card holder for a minimum of two years prior to filing the application for the issuing of a permanent residence permit. It shall be considered that the EU Blue Card holder has uninterruptedly stayed in Montenegro even in the event when he or she stayed outside the EU for up to one year, or more than once, up to eighteen months in total. Exceptionally, the EU Blue Card holder shall be considered to have uninterruptedly stayed in the area of the EU also in the event when he or she stayed outside the EU for uninterrupted twenty-four months, provided that he or she proves that he or she was absent for work or entrepreneurial activity, charity work, studying in the country of origin.[398]

403. EU Blue Card holder is obliged to apply for issuing a permanent residence permit personally, in the place of residence. In addition to the application, he/she is obliged to submit evidence of the fulfilment of the following conditions: valid travel document; permanent, regular and sufficient funds; health insurance; accommodation; knowledge of the Montenegrin language.[399]

404. A third-country national with the EU Blue Card issued in another EU Member State may file an application for the issuing of a temporary residence and work permit in Montenegro, after eighteen months from the date of the Blue Card issued. In addition to the application, a third-country national with the EU Blue Card issued in another EU Member State is obliged to submit the evidence that the EU Blue Card has been issued to him or her in another EU Member State for at least eighteen months. Family members of the EU Blue Card holder shall have the right to join him or her for family reunification if they have legally stayed with him or her in another EU Member State. They are in obligation to submit to the Ministry

396. Article 192 of the Law on Foreign Nationals.
397. Article 194 of the Law on Foreign Nationals.
398. Article 195 of the Law on Foreign Nationals.
399. Article 196 of the Law on Foreign Nationals.

of Interior the application for temporary residence for family reunification within thirty days from the date of entry into Montenegro. In addition, they are obliged to submit the following:

– a valid travel document, i.e., visa, if necessary;
– a permit evidencing that they have stayed in the EU Member State as family members;
– evidence of health insurance;
– evidence of means to support themselves.[400]

400. Articles 199 and 201 of the Law on Foreign Nationals.

Part IV. Loss of Right of Residence

Chapter 1. Conditions under Which the Right of Residence Might Be Lost

§1. Loss of Right to Short Stay

405. A stay of up to ninety days of a foreign national may be cancelled if:

- he/she does not meet entry and stay requirements in Montenegro as prescribed by the Law on Foreign Nationals;
- this is required by national or internal security reasons;
- he/she does not justify the purposes and circumstances of his/her entry and stay of up to ninety days;
- he/she has been returned to Montenegro pursuant to an international agreement (readmission), due to an illegal stay;
- there are grounds for suspicion that his/her stay is not for the purposes for which it was approved;
- he/she has not settled his/her financial and legal obligations that became due pursuant to a final judgment rendered by the court.[401]

§2. Loss of Right to Temporary Residence

406. A temporary residence permit shall cease to be valid:

- upon the expiry of the validity period;
- after the reasons for which the permit was issued have ceased to exist;
- if during his or her temporary residence, a foreign national stays outside Montenegro for more than thirty days (exceptionally, temporary residence permit shall not cease to be valid for a foreign national who, for justified reasons, stayed outside Montenegro for up to ninety days, provided that he or she has previously informed the police of the reasons for leaving Montenegro);
- if the existence of the reasons of refusal of entry is subsequently determined;

401. Article 35 of the Law on Foreign Nationals.

- if a foreign national has been imposed a protective measure of expulsion of foreign national from the country or a protective measure of expulsion of foreign national from the territory of Montenegro;
- if a foreign national does not use his/her residence in Montenegro for the purpose for which such residence was granted;
- in the event when a foreign national was granted a temporary residence permit for the purpose of family reunification, and it is subsequently determined that the marriage was arranged for convenience;
- when a foreign national acquires the right to permanent residence.[402]

§3. Loss of Right to Temporary Residence and Work Permit

407. A temporary residence and work permit shall cease to be valid:

- upon the expiry of the validity period;
- upon the termination of employment contract or the contract on the provision of the agreed services, or upon the termination of the decision on temporary posting;
- if a foreign national carries out business activities for which the temporary residence and work permit has not been issued to him/her;
- if the existence of the reasons of refusal of entry is subsequently determined;
- if a foreign national has been pronounced a protective measure of expulsion of foreign national from the country or a protective measure of expulsion of foreign national from the territory of Montenegro;
- if during temporary residence, a foreign national stays outside Montenegro for longer than thirty days (exceptionally, a temporary residence and work permit shall not cease to be valid for a foreign national who, for justified reasons, stayed outside Montenegro for up to ninety days, provided that he or she has previously informed the police of the reasons for leaving Montenegro);
- if the employer from whom he/she has received the offer has been punished due to illegal employment or failure to register the work of foreign national;
- if the bankruptcy procedure of the company which sent him/her the offer is pending or such a company has been in bankruptcy;
- if the employer from whom he/she has received the offer does not carry out the business activity;
- if the employer from which he/she has received the offer has been punished because it failed to meet the liabilities for taxes and contributions for its employees;
- if the main reason for founding a company or part of a foreign company in Montenegro is to facilitate the entry of a foreign national;
- when a foreign national acquires the right to a permanent residence.[403]

408. Temporary residence and work permit shall be annulled:

---

402. Article 65 of the Law on Foreign Nationals.
403. Article 83 of the Law on Foreign Nationals.

- if it has been issued based on the untrue information on a foreign national or employer;
- if a foreign national does not start working within the period of eight days from the date of issuing of the temporary residence and work permit for employment;
- if the employer fails to conclude the employment contract with the foreign national within the period of eight days from the date of issuing of the temporary residence and work permit for seasonal employment;
- if a foreign national does not use his residence in Montenegro for the purpose for which the residence was granted to him/her.[404]

§4. Loss of Right to Permanent Residence

409. Permanent residence shall terminate if:

- a foreign national has been convicted in Montenegro by a final judgment pronouncing non-suspended term of imprisonment exceeding six months, for a criminal offence prosecutable ex officio;
- that is required for the reasons of national, i.e., internal security;
- a foreign national has provided false information on identity, or the permanent residence permit has been issued based on the untrue information on the foreign national;
- a foreign national has been pronounced a protective measure of expulsion of foreign national from the country or a protective measure of expulsion of foreign national from the territory of Montenegro;
- it is established that a foreign national has moved from Montenegro or has uninterruptedly stayed in another country for longer than one year;
- a foreign national has abandoned permanent residence;
- a foreign national has acquired Montenegrin citizenship.[405]

§5. Loss of Right to EU Blue Card

410. The EU Blue Card shall cease to be valid:

- upon the expiry of its validity period;
- if the EU Blue Card holder has failed to notify the Ministry of Interior of the change of employer (exceptionally, the EU Blue Card shall not cease to be valid if the EU Blue Card holder, for the reasons beyond his or her control, has failed to inform the Ministry of Interior of the change of employer);
- if the EU Blue Card holder works for an employer for which he/she was not issued the EU Blue Card;

404. Article 84 of the Law on Foreign Nationals.
405. Article 94 of the Law on Foreign Nationals.

- if the EU Blue Card holder performs jobs for which the EU Blue Card was not issued, or performs other jobs for which he/she could not be issued the EU Blue Card;
- if the EU Blue Card holder does not have any means to support himself/herself and he/she has applied for social welfare;
- after the conditions for its issue have ceased to exist;
- in the event that the employment contract concluded with the employer in Montenegro, for the term of minimum twelve months, terminates;
- if during the validity of the EU Blue Card, the EU Blue Card holder was unemployed for more than three months without interruptions or became unemployed two or more times;
- if the EU Blue Card holder was pronounced a protective measure of removal, a security measure of expulsion of foreign national from the state or protective measure of expulsion of foreign national from the territory of Montenegro;
- when the EU Blue Card holder acquires the right to permanent residence.[406]

§6. Loss of Right to Permanent Residence of the EU Blue Card Holder

411. Permanent residence of a third-country national and former EU Blue Card holder shall terminate if:

- his or her entry and stay in Montenegro is banned;
- it is established that he or she has stayed outside Montenegro for longer than uninterrupted two years.[407]

406. Article 193 of the Law on Foreign Nationals.
407. Article 198 of the Law on Foreign Nationals.

Chapter 2. Legal and Administrative Procedures

412. The Police are in charge of issuing the Decision concerning a stay up to ninety days cancellation and entering such stay cancellation in a foreign travel document. The Decision shall set down the deadline within which the foreign national concerned must leave the territory of Montenegro, while the ban from entering Montenegro may be imposed as well. The entry ban period may range from thirty days to one year and it shall be counted as of the day of leaving Montenegro. The Ministry of Interior may be presented an appeal against the Decision concerning a stay up to ninety days cancellation, within eight days as of the day of receiving the Decision. The appeal shall not postpone the Decision enforcement.[408]

413. The Police are obliged to inform the Ministry of Interior of the reasons for termination of temporary residence permit validity. The Ministry of Interior is in charge of issuing the Decision on the termination of temporary residence permit validity. The Decision shall determine the period within which a foreign national must leave Montenegro, which may not be longer than thirty days, and an entry and stay ban in Montenegro may be pronounced for the period of one to five years. The period of entry and stay ban shall be counted from the date of leaving Montenegro. Against the Decision on the termination of temporary residence permit validity, an appeal may be lodged to the Ministry of Interior, within eight days from the date of receipt of the Decision.[409]

414. The labour inspection, employer, and other authorities, which, within their competence, may establish the existence of the reasons for termination of temporary residence and work permit validity are obliged to inform the Police thereof. The Ministry of Interior is in charge of issuing the Decision on the termination of the validity of temporary residence and work permit. The Decision shall determine the time limit within which a foreign national must leave Montenegro, which may not be longer than thirty days, and also an entry and stay ban in Montenegro may be pronounced for the period from one to five years. The period of the entry ban shall become effective from the date of leaving Montenegro. Against the Decision on the termination of the validity of temporary residence and work permit, an appeal may be lodged to the Ministry of Interior, within eight days from the date of receipt of the Decision.[410]

415. The Ministry of Interior is in charge of issuing the Decision on the annulment of the temporary residence and work permit. Against the Decision on the annulment of the temporary residence and work permit, an appeal may be lodged to the Ministry of Interior, within eight days from the date of receipt of the Decision. The appeal shall not postpone the execution of the Decision.[411]

---

408. Article 36 of the Law on Foreign Nationals.
409. Article 65 of the Law on Foreign Nationals.
410. Article 83 of the Law on Foreign Nationals.
411. Article 84 of the Law on Foreign Nationals.

416. The Ministry of Interior is in charge of issuing the Decision on the termination of permanent residence. Prior to issuing the Decision, the following shall be particularly taken into account:

- duration of stay in Montenegro;
- personal, family, economic and other circumstances;
- foreign national's age;
- consequences of termination of permanent residence on a foreign national and members of his or her family;
- connection with the country of residence or lack of connection with the country of origin.

417. The Decision shall determine the time limit within which a foreign national must leave Montenegro, and which may not exceed thirty days from the date of submission of the Decision, and an entry and stay ban in Montenegro may also be pronounced for the period from one to five years. The time of entry ban shall start running from the date of leaving Montenegro. Against the Decision on the termination of permanent residence, an administrative procedure may be initiated.[412]

418. The Ministry of Interior is in charge of issuing the Decision on the termination of validity of the EU Blue Card. Against the Decision, an appeal may be lodged to the Ministry of Interior within eight days from the date of receipt of the Decision.[413]

419. The Ministry of Interior is in charge of issuing the Decision on the termination of a permanent residence of the EU Blue Card holder. Prior to issuing the Decision, the following shall be particularly taken into account:

- duration of stay in Montenegro;
- personal, family, economic and other circumstances;
- foreign national's age;
- consequences of termination of permanent residence on a foreign national and members of his or her family;
- connection with the country of residence or lack of connection with the country of origin.

420. The Decision shall determine the time limit within which a foreign national must leave Montenegro, and which may not exceed thirty days from the date of submission of the Decision, and an entry and stay ban in Montenegro may also be pronounced for the period from one to five years. The time of entry ban shall start running from the date of leaving Montenegro. Against the Decision on the termination of a permanent residence of the EU Blue Card holder, an administrative procedure may be initiated.[414]

---

412. Article 94 of the Law on Foreign Nationals.
413. Article 193 of the Law on Foreign Nationals.
414. Article 198 of the Law on Foreign Nationals.

421. The reasons or obstacles in terms of national security shall exist if the person:

- carries out or has carried out the activities which could lead to the commission of criminal offences against humanity and other resources protected by the international law;
- carries out the activities which could lead to the commission of criminal offences against the constitutional system and security of Montenegro;
- belongs or has belonged to the organizations and groups advocating a violent change of the constitutional system or acting in the manner which threatens human rights and freedoms stipulated by the Constitution;
- publically advocates and disseminates ideas which incite national, religious or racial discrimination;
- belongs or has belonged to the organizations and organized criminal groups which prepare or commit criminal offences or supports such organizations and groups in any other way;
- has or has had connections or maintains connections with persons who unauthorizedly collect classified and other data, terrorists, saboteurs, members of organized criminal groups, or persons for whom there is a reasonable doubt that they belong to such groups;
- does not respect the state of Montenegro and its symbols, fails to execute decisions of courts, state administration authorities and other authorities, or circumstances point out that such person would not respect the legal system of Montenegro after being issued a temporary residence permit, temporary residence and work permit, and permanent residence permit;
- carries out other activities which may pose a threat to national and international security.

When based on the opinion of the Agency for National Security, the Ministry of Interior or the Police issue the decision which is based on reasons, i.e., obstacles in terms of national security; such reasons shall not be specified in the rationale of the decision.[415]

---

415. Article 95 of the Law on Foreign Nationals.

Part V. Sanction

§1. General Remarks

422. The adoption of the new Law on Courts in 2015[416] resulted in the establishment of misdemeanour courts as a part of the unified judicial system of Montenegro, which were entrusted with deciding on misdemeanours and imposing misdemeanour sanctions, which were previously under the jurisdiction of regional (administrative) misdemeanour authorities. A misdemeanour is an act that constitutes a violation of public order, and which is defined as a misdemeanour under the law or other piece of legislation and for which sanctions are provided.[417] Unlike criminal offences that can be prescribed only by the law, misdemeanours and misdemeanour sanctions can be prescribed not only by the law but also by a Decree of the Government of Montenegro and a decision of a local self-government unit. Thus, misdemeanours are not codified by a single code, as is the case with criminal offences codified by the Criminal Code. When it comes to misdemeanours in the field of migration law, they are prescribed by the umbrella laws such as the Law on Foreign Nationals, Law on Temporary and International Protection of Foreigners, Law on Border Control, etc. Misdemeanor sanctions are considered 'soft' sanctions, and their purpose is for the citizens to respect the legal system, to express public disapproval towards an offender from committing a misdemeanour and to influence him and all other persons to refrain from committing misdemeanours in the future.[418] Thus, misdemeanour sanctions are penalties, warning measures, protective measures and corrective measures. A legal entity and a responsible person may be sanctioned with a monetary fine for misdemeanour. A misdemeanour procedure cannot be conducted for persons under the age of 14 (a child), and therefore no misdemeanour sanction can be imposed. With regard to the sanctions, misdemeanour courts may impose sentence of imprisonment, a fine and community service.[419] A term of imprisonment may be imposed only for misdemeanours that if committed may pose a threat to public health and safety or cause a serious disturbance of the public peace and order, as well as domestic violence misdemeanours. Therefore, misdemeanours related to migrations are not subject to the prison sentence.[420] A fine may be imposed in the range or in a certain amount, for physical persons ranging from EUR 3,000 to EUR 2,000 and for legal entities from EUR 500

416. Law on Courts, 'Official Gazette of Montenegro', No. 011/15 of 12.3.2015.
417. Article 2 of the Law on Misdemeanors.
418. Article 6 of the Law on Misdemeanors.
419. Article 23 of the Law on Misdemeanors.
420. *Ibid.*

to EUR 20,000.[421] Instead of prison sentence or a fine, an offender may be sentenced to community service, whereas his consent is obligatory. The purpose of admonitions and suspended sentences, within the framework of the general purpose of misdemeanour sanctions, is to avoid application of penalties on offenders guilty of committing misdemeanour of a minor nature, when it is not necessary for protection from misdemeanours under law and when it can be expected that only a warning (admonition) or warning with threat of punishment (suspended sentence) will suffice to influence the offender to refrain from committing misdemeanours in the future.[422]

423. The misdemeanour courts may, in addition to the imposed penalty or admonition, impose one or more protective measures on the offender, the purpose of which is to remove situations or conditions that might influence an offender to commit misdemeanours in future.[423] One of the protective measures that can be imposed is the measure of expulsion of foreigners from the territory of Montenegro. The court may expel a foreigner who has committed a misdemeanour due to which his further stay in the country is undesirable from the territory of Montenegro for a period of up to one year.[424] In assessing whether to impose the measure, the court will take into account the nature and gravity of the offence, the motives from which the offence was committed, the manner of commission of the offence and other circumstances that indicate the undesirable stay of a foreigner in Montenegro cannot be imposed on a perpetrator who enjoys protection in accordance with ratified international treaties.[425]

424. The Montenegrin legal system does not recognize administrative sanctions for illegal crossing of the state border, but in addition to misdemeanour sanctions, a foreigner may be subject to criminal sanctions for criminal offences pertaining to illegal crossing of the state border, smuggling of persons and trafficking in human beings. The Criminal Code of Montenegro[426] lays down criminal sanctions: penalties, admonitions, security measures and corrective measures, the purpose of which is to suppress acts that violate or endanger the values protected by the criminal law. Thus, the perpetrator of a criminal offence may be sentenced to a long-term prison sentence (from thirty to forty years), short-term prison sentence, a fine or community work. Prison sentence may not be less than thirty days nor more than twenty years. Admonitions may be a suspended sentence and a judicial admonition, while the court may impose one or more security measures on the perpetrator of a criminal offence when there are legal grounds for thereof. A foreigner may be ordered to

421. Article 24 of the Law on Misdemeanors.
422. Article 33 of the Law on Misdemeanors.
423. Article 41 of the Law on Misdemeanors.
424. Article 48 of the Law on Misdemeanors.
425. *Ibid.*
426. *Krivični zakonik Crne Gore*, 'Official Gazette of the Republic of Montenegro', Nos 070/03 of 25.12.2003, 013/04 of 26.2.2004, 047/06 of 25.7.2006, 'Official Gazette of Montenegro', Nos 040/08 of 27.6.2008, 025/10 of 5.5.2010, 073/10 of 10.12.2010, 032/11 of 1.7.2011, 064/11 of 29.12.2011, 040/13 of 13.8.2013, 056/13 of 6.12.2013, 014/15 of 26.3.2015, 042/15 of 29.7.2015, 058/15 of 9.12.2015, 044/17 of 6.7.2017, 049/18 of 17.7.2018, 003/20 of 23.1.2020.

be expelled from the country, provided that he is a repeat perpetrator.[427] In deciding whether to impose the aforementioned measure, the court shall give due consideration to the nature and seriousness of the offence committed, the motives out of which the criminal offence was committed, the manner in which it was committed, and any other circumstances that indicate why the foreigner should not be allowed to stay in Montenegro.[428] Of course, the measure of expulsion of a foreigner from the country cannot be imposed on a perpetrator who could be subjected to torture or inhuman or degrading treatment in the country to which he would be expelled or who enjoys other protection in accordance with ratified international treaties. A foreigner may be expelled from the territory of Montenegro for a term from one to ten years, but he may be also expelled for good.

425. The adoption of the new Criminal Procedure Code, which application started off in 2011, in Montenegro has radically changed the criminal procedure normative environment, introducing a number of new institutes and criminal procedure mechanisms, such as a completely changed concept of investigation, now within the competence of the state prosecutor, replacement of the pre-criminal proceedings with the preliminary investigation led by the state prosecutor, introduction of a plea agreement, etc.[429] Thus, unlike the old Criminal Procedure Code, the role of the state prosecutor has been completely changed, who is now entrusted with the formal management of the preliminary investigation, but the state prosecutor is also responsible for conducting investigations, which is an expression of tendency that is a common feature of most continental European criminal procedures. Although the prosecutor is formally a party, he is basically not a typical party, but in conducting the procedure he must not be guided only by his narrow party interests, but vice versa, the state prosecutor as a state body must keep in mind the interest of the defence; i.e., he must examine and determine the facts which are exculpatory and inculpatory for the accused.[430]

426. The criminal legislation of Montenegro shall also apply to a foreigner who commits a criminal offence against Montenegro or its national outside the territory of Montenegro, provided that he is caught in the territory of Montenegro or gets extradited to Montenegro.[431] Furthermore, the criminal legislation of Montenegro shall also be applicable to a foreigner who commits a criminal offence abroad against a foreign country or a foreigner where such offence is punishable under the law of the country where it was committed by a prison term of five years or longer, provided that he is caught in the territory of Montenegro but not extradited to a foreign country. Unless otherwise provided by this Code, in such a case, a court may pronounce punishment which is more severe than the punishment provided for by the law of the country where the criminal offence was committed.[432]

---

427. Article 76 of the Criminal Code.
428. *Ibid.*
429. Milan Škulić, *Comments to the Criminal Procedure Code, OSCE Mission to Montenegro*, Podgorica, 2009, p. 27.
430. *Ibid.*, 30.
431. Article 137 of the Criminal Code.
432. *Ibid.*

Chapter 1. Sanctions

§1. Administrative Sanctions

427. There are no administrative sanctions for the violation of entry into, exit from, movement throughout, stay and work of foreign nationals in Montenegro and/or cross-border regime which are imposed by administrative courts in the administrative procedure. For such violations only penal sanctions are applicable.

§2. Penal Sanctions

428. The system of sanctioning is divided among several institutions, including the Police, the State Prosecution and the Courts, depending on the fact whether the irregular migrants are considered offenders of misdemeanours or perpetrators of the criminal offence, i.e., illegal crossing of the state border.

429. In case of a misdemeanour, irregular migrants are being prosecuted as follows: the Police issue a misdemeanour order to the migrant due to the violation of the Law on Misdemeanors (e.g., entering the country without a valid travel document, illegal residing in the country, etc.). The foreigner has the option to pay a fine within the eight-day period prescribed by the order for the initiation of the misdemeanour proceeding. If the migrant does not pay a fine at this stage, the proceeding will be initiated before the competent misdemeanour court. If the fine is sentenced during that proceeding and the migrant is not able to pay it, a fine will be replaced with the imprisonment sentence, for a certain period of time. The court may order that a foreign national who committed a misdemeanour as a result of which his/her further stay in the country is unwelcome be deported from the territory of Montenegro and prohibited from returning for a period of up to one year. When deliberating whether to impose this measure, the court shall take into account the nature and severity of the committed offence, the motives for committing the misdemeanour, the manner in which the misdemeanour was committed, and other circumstances that indicate that a foreign national's further stay in Montenegro is undesirable. Duration of the imposed measure shall run from the date the decision took effect as final and legally binding, whereby time spent in prison shall not be deducted from the time length of this measure. The measure of deportation may not be imposed on an offender that enjoys protection in accordance with ratified international treaties.[433]

430. If the migrant is suspected of committing a criminal offence (e.g., illegal crossing of the state border of smuggling of persons), he/she shall be prosecuted in accordance with the Criminal Procedure Code.[434] In that case, if there is a

433. Article 48 of the Law on Misdemeanors.
434. *Zakonik o krivičnom postupku*, 'Official Gazette of Montenegro', Nos 49/2010, 47/2014, 2/2015, 35/2015, 58/2015.

reasonable suspicion that a criminal offence has been committed, the state prosecutor submits an indictment to the competent court to initiate a criminal proceeding. According to Article 76 of the Criminal Code of Montenegro, a foreign national who committed a criminal offence may be expelled from the territory of Montenegro under a court judgment for a term from one to ten years, and where a foreign national is a repeat perpetrator, he may be expelled for good (for more detailed information regarding criminal acts *see* Chapter 2).

431. Sanctions for the violation of entry into, exit from, movement throughout, stay and work of foreign nationals and/or cross-border regime are provided by the Law on Border Control and the Law on Foreign Nationals.

I. Sanctions Against Natural Persons

432. A fine of EUR 100 up to EUR 1,100 will be imposed on a natural person who crosses the state border outside the designated border crossing or crosses or tries to cross the border checkpoint without valid travel documents or off-hour border crossing or contrary to the purpose of border crossing.[435]

433. A fine of EUR 100 up to EUR 1,100 shall be punished for an offence unless he or she does not inspect the documents prescribed for crossing the state border or does not undergo a border check or leave the border crossing area until a border check is made or avoids or attempts to avoid the border check.[436]

434. A fine of EUR 50 to EUR 300 shall be imposed on a natural person for an offence if he or she moves outside a certain area of the border crossing area or fails to comply warns or does not execute the orders of police officers exercising border control.[437]

435. A fine of EUR 50 to EUR 300 shall be imposed on a physical person for an offence if the means of transport crossing the state border does not stop at a certain area of the border crossing at which a border check is performed.[438]

436. A fine of EUR 50 to EUR 300 shall be imposed on a natural person for offence in case that he or she does not leave the border crossing area with its means of transport, after the end of the border check.[439]

437. A foreign national shall be punished for the misdemeanour with a fine in the amount from EUR 200 to EUR 1,200 if:

435. Article 67 para. 1 item 1 of the Law on Border Control.
436. Article 67 para. 1 item 2 of the Law on Border Control.
437. Article 68 para. 1 item 3 of the Law on Border Control.
438. Article 68 para. 1 item 4 of the Law on Border Control.
439. Article 68 para. 1 item 5 of the Law on Border Control.

- he or she enters, stays and moves in Montenegro without a valid foreign travel document which contains a visa or without a valid foreign travel document with which he or she has a temporary residence permit, a temporary residence and work permit, i.e., a permanent residence permit;
- he or she fails to observe the restriction or prohibition of movement at a particular area of Montenegro;
- he or she fails to use the travel document with which he or she has entered Montenegro;
- he or she stays in Montenegro contrary to the purpose for which the visa has been issued to him or her;
- he or she fails to stay in Montenegro in accordance with the purpose for which the temporary residence has been granted to him or her;
- the foreign student works longer than fifteen hours a week;
- the foreign researcher works longer than fifteen hours a week;
- he or she does not work pursuant to a temporary residence and work permit or work registration certificate;
- he or she does not work in Montenegro on the jobs for which temporary residence and work permit or the work registration certificate has been issued to him or her and for the employer who employs him or her;
- he or she has illegally entered or stays in Montenegro or fails to promptly leave its territory or within the period defined for him or her;
- fails to observe the rules of stay in the Reception Centre or leaves the Reception Centre without permission;
- does not carry with him or her, or upon the request of an authorized official, refuses to present the document evidencing his or her identity;
- gives his or her ID to another person for use, or uses invalid or other person's document as his or her own;
- does not use his or her personal name which is entered in a foreign travel document, a valid identity card issued by a competent authority of another state, a temporary residence permit, a temporary residence and work permit, and a permanent residence permit.[440]

438. A foreign national shall be punished with a fine in the amount from EUR 60 to EUR 600 if:

- he or she fails to file the application for the extension of permanent residence permit, within eight days from the date of expiry of the permit validity period;
- he or she has been issued visa for a longer stay (visa D) or stays in Montenegro for up to ninety days and fails to file to the police the application for registration in the place where he or she intends to stay or if he or she intends to stay in another place for longer than twenty-four hours, within twenty-four hours from the arrival to the place of residence;
- he or she has been issued a temporary residence permit, a temporary residence and work permit, or a permanent residence permit, and fails to file to the police

440. Article 213 of the Law on Foreign Nationals.

the application for registration of residence in the event that he or she temporarily resides in another place in Montenegro for longer than three days;
- he or she fails to file to the police the application for deregistration of residence within twenty-four hours prior to leaving the place of residence;
- he or she fails to file the application for registration and deregistration of residence for a child;
- in the event of the change in his or her personal data, or if the document is damaged or in a worn-out condition and may no longer serve its purpose or in the case when a photograph does not correspond to the foreign national's appearance, he or she fails to file the application for the replacement of a temporary residence permit, a temporary residence and work permit, and a permanent residence permit within eight days from the date of the occurrence of these reasons;
- fails to return the temporary residence permit, temporary residence and work permit, and permanent residence permit if such permit has ceased to be valid or he or she has acquired Montenegrin citizenship or is moving out of Montenegro;
- fails to report the missing ID;
- during the stay in Montenegro moves in a foreign military uniform, except in the following cases (if they are staying as members of a diplomatic or consular mission of a foreign country or in some other foreign mission with a diplomatic status in Montenegro as military representatives while the mission is underway; if they are on an official visit as members of a foreign military mission or foreign military delegation; if they are studying at military school; if they are passing through the territory of Montenegro as members of foreign military missions or foreign military delegations with diplomatic or official travel documents; they are participating in a military exercise and training.);
- during the residence in Montenegro moves in a foreign police uniform or a foreign customs uniform, except in the following cases (if they are on an official visit as members of delegations of foreign police or customs authorities; if they are carrying out their duties on the basis of an international treaty; if they are studying at a police academy; if they are passing through the territory of Montenegro as members of foreign police or foreign customs delegations with diplomatic or official travel documents).[441]

439. A natural person, upon whose invitation a foreign national has been issued visa or granted entry to Montenegro, shall be punished with a fine in the amount from EUR 500 to EUR 2,000, when such foreign national has been subject to the forced removal in accordance with the Law on Foreign Nationals if such natural person fails to assume the costs incurred during the stay and return of the foreign national.[442]

A national of the EU Member State and a member of his or her family shall be punished for a misdemeanour with a fine in the amount from EUR 200 to EUR 1,200 if they do not carry or upon the request of an authorized official refuse to present the document evidencing their identity.

441. Article 214 of the Law on Foreign Nationals.
442. Article 211 of the Law on Foreign Nationals.

An EU Blue Card holder shall be punished for the offence with a fine in the amount from EUR 200 to EUR 1,200 if:

- he or she works on the jobs for which he has not been issued the EU Blue Card or works for an employer by whom he or she has not been employed;
- he or she has failed to notify the Ministry of Interior in the event of termination of the employment contract or other conditions based on which the EU Blue Card was issued;
- he or she has failed to file the application for the extension of the EU Blue Card, not later than within thirty days prior to the expiry of the EU Blue Card validity period;
- upon the expiry of the period of two years, he or she fails to notify the Ministry of Interior of the change of employer within eight days from the date of the change of employer.[443]

II. Sanctions Against Legal Entities

440. An employer-legal entity shall be punished for misdemeanour with a fine in the amount from EUR 1,000 to EUR 10,000, if:

- a student works longer than fifteen hours a week;
- a foreign national researcher works as a lecturer or professor longer than fifteen hours a week;
- assigns a foreign national to jobs for which a temporary residence and work permit, i.e., a work registration certificate, was not issued to him or her;
- does not keep in business premises or workplace of a foreign national, a copy of the residence and work permit, i.e., a copy of a work registration certificate of a foreign national employed by them;
- fails to inform the Ministry of Interior of the termination of foreign national's employment prior to the expiry of the residence and work permit validity period, not later than within eight days from the date of termination of foreign national's employment;
- employs or uses the work of a foreign national who illegally stays in Montenegro;
- does not keep in business premises, i.e., workplace of a foreign national a copy of a temporary residence permit, a copy of a work registration certificate, i.e., evidence on the granted asylum or subsidiary protection or temporary protection;
- within eight days from the date of employment or beginning of foreign national's work, i.e., the termination of foreign national's employment, fails to inform the Ministry of Interior thereof;
- within eight days from the date of the issuing of a temporary residence and work permit for employment or seasonal employment, fails to conclude employment contract with a foreign national and register such a foreign national for compulsory social insurance;

443. Article 215 of the Law on Foreign Nationals.

- fails to notify the Ministry of Interior, not later than within three days, that a foreign national has not started working, for the purpose of annulment of the residence and work permit;
- fails to submit the work registration certificate to the Ministry of Interior, prior to the beginning of work of the foreign national under the work registration certificate;
- employs the EU Blue Card holder on the jobs for which the EU Blue Card was not issued;
- does not keep the copy of the EU Blue Card in the business premises, i.e., workplace of a foreign national;
- fails to inform the Ministry of Interior in the event of termination of the employment contract and other conditions based on which the EU Blue Card was issued, not later than within eight days from the date of occurrence of such circumstances.

For the above-mentioned misdemeanours, a person responsible for the legal entity shall also be punished with a fine in the amount from EUR 300 to EUR 2,000. For the above-mentioned misdemeanours, an entrepreneur shall be punished by a fine in the amount from EUR 300 to EUR 6,000. Also, for the above-mentioned misdemeanours, a protective measure of the prohibition of performing the business activity may also be pronounced in the duration of up to six months.[444]

441. A legal entity shall be punished for a misdemeanour with a fine in the amount from EUR 3,000 to EUR 5,000 if:

- it brings to the border crossing point or to the territory of Montenegro a foreign national who does not meet the conditions for entry into Montenegro (this refers to carriers);
- it fails to transport a foreign national who is not permitted to enter Montenegro from the border crossing point, at its own expense, or fails to find another modality of transportation or fails to assume the costs incurred during the stay and return of such foreign national (this refers to carriers);
- it fails to bear the costs incurred by forced removal of that foreign national from Montenegro, including the costs incurred due to the foreign national's stay in a reception centre for foreigners if the foreign national has been subjected to forced removal in accordance with this law, and does not have sufficient resources to compensate for the costs (this refers to an organizer of tourist or business travels or any legal entity who delivers services to a foreign national and upon whose invitation a foreign national has been either issued a visa or granted entry in Montenegro who also have the obligation bear the costs if these costs cannot be compensated by the foreign national concerned).

For the above-mentioned misdemeanours, a person responsible for the legal entity shall also be punished with a fine in the amount from EUR 300 to EUR 1,200. For the above-mentioned misdemeanours, an entrepreneur shall also be punished

444. Article 210 of the Law on Foreign Nationals.

with a fine in the amount from EUR 300 to EUR 1,200. Also, for the above-mentioned misdemeanours, a protective measure of the prohibition of performing the business activity may be pronounced in the duration of up to six months.[445]

442. A legal entity shall be punished for a misdemeanour with a fine in the amount from EUR 500 to EUR 3,000 if it:

– fails to file the application to the police for registration or deregistration of foreign national, in the place where the residence of foreign national is registered, within twelve hours from the arrival (this refers to accommodation provider);
– fails to check the truthfulness of data by inspecting a foreign travel document of the person to whom it provides accommodation services, and provides untrue data in the application for registration and deregistration of residence filed to the police;
– fails to keep records of foreign nationals to whom it provides accommodation services;
– fails to keep data in records on foreign nationals to whom provides the accommodation services two years from the date of entry;
– fails to enable the police to inspect the records of foreign nationals to whom it provides accommodation services;
– when registering, i.e., deregistering the residence of a foreign national, fails to submit the certificate on a prescribed form and in writing;
– fails to submit to the police the registration, i.e., the deregistration electronically;
– fails to submit to the police the registration or the deregistration for a foreign national with a stay of up to ninety days, to whom it provides the accommodation for longer than twelve hours, within twelve hours from the arrival, i.e., departure of a foreign national;
– fails to submit to the police the certificate of residence registration for a foreign national who was admitted for medical treatment, within twelve hours from the hour of admission;
– fails to submit to the police the deregistration of the residence of foreign national after the completed medical treatment, within twelve hours from the completion of treatment.

For the above-mentioned misdemeanours, a person responsible for the legal entity shall also be punished with a fine in the amount from EUR 150 to EUR 500. For the above-mentioned misdemeanours, a natural person who provides the accommodation services shall also be punished with a fine in the amount from EUR 150 to EUR 500. Also, for the above-mentioned misdemeanours, an entrepreneur shall be punished with a fine in the amount from EUR 300 to EUR 1,500.[446]

445. Article 211 of the Law on Foreign Nationals.
446. Article 212 of the Law on Foreign Nationals.

§3. Detention

443. In principle, according to existing legislation on foreigners, a foreign person may enter, move across and stay in Montenegro with a valid travel document, with a visa entered into, or a valid travel document accompanied with a temporary residence permit, temporary residence and work permit, or permanent residence permit, unless otherwise provided under the law or an international treaty. However, restriction or prohibition of freedom of movement of a foreign national is possible for the whole territory of the country or for a particular area in the country.

444. A foreign national may be deprived of liberty, brought in, and detained for up to twenty-four hours, only if that is necessary to ensure his or her presence in the procedure of cancellation of stay of up to ninety days and in the procedure of annulment of temporary postponement of forced removal. A foreign national, subject to forced removal, may be deprived of liberty, brought in, and detained for up to forty-eight hours. The police are in charge of issuing the decision on the deprivation of liberty of the foreign national. After deprivation of liberty, a foreign national must be immediately notified of the reasons for deprivation of liberty and that he or she may request the diplomatic or consular mission of the state of his/her nationality to be notified of such deprivation of liberty, unless that is otherwise provided for by an international treaty. The competent centre for social work and the diplomatic or consular mission of the state of nationality shall be promptly notified of the deprivation of liberty of an unaccompanied foreign national minor. Against the decision on the deprivation of liberty, a complaint may be lodged to the Administrative Court. A foreign national shall be released as soon as the grounds for deprivation of liberty and detention cease to exist, and not later than upon the expiry of the twenty-four hours, i.e., forty-eight hours, except when actions are taken to enforce forced removal, or when the decision on accommodation in the Reception Centre has been issued.[447]

445. The police can restrict the freedom of movement for a foreign national for whom it is not possible to be removed forcibly or whose return may not be ensured by the enforcement of milder measures, by accommodating such a foreign national in the Reception Centre for foreign nationals,[448] and particularly if there is a risk that the obligation to leave Montenegro shall be evaded or if the foreign national

447. Article 124 of the Law on Foreign Nationals.

448. The Reception Centre for foreign nationals, with a reception capacity of forty-six persons, was formally put into operation on 13 Dec. 2013. The Centre is located in Spuž, Municipality of Danilovgrad. The construction of the Reception Centre was conducted through the IPA 2008 Project 'Support to Migration Management in Montenegro'. Out of the total funds spent on its construction, 50% was coming from the EU funds, and 50% were funds of the state budget for 2011 (national contribution of Montenegro). The EU financial contribution for the construction of the Centre amounted to EUR 450,000, while the funds allocated by the Government of Montenegro (from the state budget for capital investment) amounted to EUR 450,000. In the period from May 2006 to December 2013, when the Reception Centre was established, the placement of irregular migrants who were apprehended in the territory of Montenegro was solved differently, from case to case, by placing them in facilities such as NGO shelters and hotels, or by renting private residential facilities with security provided by the Police.

prevents the enforcement of forced removal and return. The circumstances indicating the existence of a risk that the obligation of foreign national to leave Montenegro shall be evaded are that the foreign national:

- has not left Montenegro within the deadline defined in the decision;
- has entered Montenegro prior to the expiry of the entry and stay ban;
- does not possess or has destroyed the document evidencing his or her identity;
- has used a forged or other person's document;
- has stated that he or she shall not meet the obligation to leave Montenegro;
- does not have sufficient financial means;
- does not have an ensured accommodation;
- has been convicted for a criminal offence.

For the purpose of the previous mentioned conditions, the foreign national shall be considered to have prevented the enforcement of the forced removal and return if he or she failed to observe the obligations defined in the decision on the enforcement of milder measures or he or she has refused to provide personal data and documents necessary for forced removal or has provided false data.[449]

446. When it comes to detention, the following milder measures can be taken:

- depositing of travel instruments, travel documents and travel tickets;
- depositing of particular financial means;
- prohibition to leave particular address where his or her accommodation is;
- reporting to the police at a particular time.

The police is in charge of issuing the decision on the enforcement of milder measures. The decision shall determine the above-mentioned obligations which are appropriate for the circumstances of that particular case, and which shall be effective until the forced removal. Against the decision on the enforcement of milder measures, a complaint may be filed to the Administrative Court, within five days from the date of the decision delivery. During the enforcement of milder measures, the police may ensure the accommodation and support, funds and other financial means for the foreign national, or regarding such measures conclude agreements with international organizations or NGOs. In the event of a large-scale entry or illegal stay in Montenegro, the Government may issue the decision on ensuring the temporary accommodation of foreign nationals who are subject to milder measures.[450]

447. The police are in charge of issuing the decision on the accommodation of a foreign national in the Reception Centre. The accommodation in the Reception Centre may last only for the time required for forced removal and during the performance of activities aimed at forced removal, and not longer than six months. Against the decision on the accommodation in the Reception Centre, a complaint

449. Article 125 of the Law on Foreign Nationals.
450. Article 126 of the Law on Foreign Nationals.

may be lodged to the Administrative Court, within five days from the date of submission of the decision. The accommodation in the Reception Centre may be shortened or extended for a maximum of twelve more months if the foreign national refuses to cooperate or is late with the obtainment of necessary documents from another country. The police are also in charge of issuing this decision, and against the decision a complaint may be lodged to the Administrative Court, within five days from the date of decision delivery.[451]

448. The representatives of state authorities and foreign diplomatic and consular missions whose nationals have been accommodated in the Reception Centre, and the representatives of international and NGOs dealing with the protection of human rights of persons whose freedom of movement is restricted, can visit the Reception Centre and inspect the conditions in the Reception Centre and the extent to which human rights are observed.[452]

449. In the procedure of forced removal or accommodation of a foreign national in the Reception Centre, the police officers are authorized to search a foreign national and his/her personal possessions without a court warrant if the foreign national is suspected of possessing weapons or objects that might be used in an attack, or is suspected that he or she would discard, hide or destroy the objects that may be used as evidence in criminal or misdemeanour proceedings and in the procedure of forced removal. The foreign national who illegally stays and does not have an ID or there is a doubt as to his or her identity, fingerprints and a photograph may be taken, without his or her approval, if that is in the interest of national, i.e., internal security, protection of the economic interests of the country, protection of health and moral values, or protection of rights and freedoms of others.[453]

450. A foreign national cannot leave the Reception Centre without permission and have to observe the rules of stay of the Reception Centre. A foreign national in the Reception Centre is entitled to healthcare in accordance with the regulation on healthcare. A foreign national who believes that he or she has been subjected to torture or other cruel, inhuman or degrading treatment or punishment by the staff or other detainees of the Reception Centre may address the Protector of Human Rights and Freedoms.[454]

451. To a foreign national accommodated in the Reception Centre, stricter police supervision may be imposed if he or she:

- leaves the Reception Centre without permission or if there is a reasonable doubt that he or she will attempt to leave the Reception Centre;
- physically attacks other foreign nationals, police officers, or other employees of the Reception Centre;

---

451. Articles 127 and 128 of the Law on Foreign Nationals.
452. Article 129 of the Law on Foreign Nationals.
453. Article 130 of the Law on Foreign Nationals.
454. Article 131 of the Law on Foreign Nationals.

- attempts to harm himself or herself;
- behaves inappropriately, grossly offends and disparages other foreign nationals, police officers or other employees of the Reception Centre on any grounds;
- prepares or fabricates the objects for attack, self-harm or escape from the Reception Centre;
- engages in the preparation of intoxicating drugs in the Reception Centre;
- intentionally damages clothes and other objects and means he or she has been given in the Reception Centre for use;
- intentionally damages technical and other equipment in the Reception Centre;
- intentionally interferes with the operation of technical equipment (audiovisual and lighting) installed in the premises for the purpose of physical and technical protection;
- constantly refuses to obey orders of the police officers and fails to observe the effective legal regulations or otherwise grossly breaches the rules of stay of the Reception Centre.

A stricter police supervision includes the restriction of freedom of movement of the foreign national in the Reception Centre and may be imposed for not longer than seven days. The police are in charge of issuing the decision on a stricter police supervision. Upon the issuing of this decision, the police is obliged to promptly submit to the Ministry of Interior the case files on the stricter police supervision, on the same day, or if the decision was issued on a non-business day, on the first business day. The Ministry of Interior is in charge to decide on the removal or extension of a stricter police supervision on the first subsequent business day at the latest from the date of submission of the case files. The decision shall be delivered to the foreign national who, against such decision, may file a complaint to the Administrative Court, within five days from the date of delivery. The police shall lift stricter police supervision after the reasons for imposing cease to exist. If the Ministry of Interior decides to extend the stricter police supervision, upon the expiry of each seven days of such supervision, the police and the Ministry of Interior have to act in accordance with previous.[455]

452. A foreign national shall be promptly released from the Reception Centre if the reasons for the accommodation in the Reception Centre no longer exist and if it is reasonably expected that it shall not be possible to forcibly remove the foreign national within the deadlines defined in the Law on Foreign Nationals. The police have to submit to the Ministry of Interior the case files on the accommodation of a foreign national in the Reception Centre, not later than ten days prior to the expiry of three months from the date of accommodation of the foreign national in the Reception Centre. Within ten days from the date of receipt of the case files, the Ministry of Interior is obliged to decide under the decision on the release of the foreign national from the Reception Centre. In the event of prompt release, a foreign national who was accommodated in the Reception Centre for the total duration of eighteen months may be accommodated in the Reception Centre again if due to the

455. Article 132 of the Law on Foreign Nationals.

changed circumstances it can be reasonably expected that he or she shall be able to be forcibly removed, and the reasons for restriction of the freedom of movement still exist.[456]

453. An unaccompanied foreign national minor and a foreign national minor younger than fourteen years of age may be accommodated in the appropriate institution only if the forced removal cannot be ensured in any other way. A foreign national minor older than fourteen years of age, accompanied by a family member, may be accommodated in the Reception Centre only if the forced removal cannot be ensured in any other way. A foreign national minor has to be accommodated in the premises suitable for the accommodation of a minor. The members of the same family shall be accommodated in the Reception Centre, in the separate common room. Stricter police supervision may be imposed on a foreign national minor, but only if he or she is accompanied by a parent or a legal guardian, whereby the attention must be paid to the best interests of the child. The foreign national minor shall be provided with conditions appropriate for his or her age, and with the right to education in accordance with regulations governing education. If there is a reasonable doubt as to whether the foreign national is under age, the age of such person may be investigated.[457]

454. The costs of accommodation in the Reception Centre and the costs occurred during the forced removal are obliged to bear a foreign national. The costs shall be settled from the funds taken from a foreign national on his or her admission to the Reception Centre, and from the other funds in possession of a foreign national. If a foreign national does not possess any funds to settle the costs of accommodation in the Reception Centre and the costs occurred during the forced removal, the costs shall be settled by:

- a natural person or legal entity who assumed the obligation to bear the costs of a foreign national's stay;
- the carrier who has not transported a foreign national in accordance with the Law on Foreign Nationals;
- the organizer of tourist or business travels who delivers services to a foreign national;
- an employer who has employed a foreign national contrary to the Law on Foreign Nationals.

455. The amount of the costs of accommodation in the Reception Centre and the costs which have occurred on the occasion of the forced removal shall be determined by the police through a decision according to actual costs. The costs which cannot be collected from a foreign national in the above-mentioned manner shall be borne by the budget of Montenegro.[458]

456. Article 133 of the Law on Foreign Nationals.
457. Article 134 of the Law on Foreign Nationals.
458. Article 135 of the Law on Foreign Nationals.

456. It should be taken into consideration that the largest number of detainees is represented by migrants who have been prosecuted for any of the violations prescribed by the Law on Foreign Nationals and the Law on Border Control (e.g., entry to Montenegro without valid travel document, illegal residence, illegal work, etc.) for which they were fined. If they did not have the means to pay, the fine could be replaced by a prison sentence.

457. Pursuant to the Law on Asylum which was applicable until 1 January 2018, the asylum seekers were placed in the Centre for reception and accommodation of asylum seekers[459] (so-called Asylum Centre – from 1 January 2018 it is called 'Reception Centre', same as the Reception Centre established in accordance with the Law on Foreign Nationals and these are two separate objects side by side) and located therein until the end of the asylum procedure. An asylum seeker was also entitled to use other accommodation options (renting an apartment or hotel accommodation, etc.), at his/her own expense. Once the asylum procedure was finished and the negative decision became final, that person moved from the umbrella of the asylum system under the umbrella of the Law on Foreign Nationals, meaning that, from that moment, according to the Law on Misdemeanors, it was possible to order detention for an irregular migrant suspected of committing a particular offence(s).

458. Although the Law on Asylum guaranteed full freedom of movement for asylum seekers, one exception was observed in practice – de facto limitation of the movement of minor asylum seekers. Namely, until the opening of the Centre for reception and accommodation of asylum seekers in 2014, minor migrants and asylum seekers have been placed in the Centre 'Ljubovic'[460] even in those cases where the legal conditions for potential limitation of their freedom of movement were not

459. The Centre is an open-type facility, which functions as an organizational unit of the Ministry of Interior. It was officially opened on 3 Feb. 2014 and put into operation on 20 Feb. 2014. The Centre has the capacity of seventeen rooms for accommodating sixty-five people. It is located in Spuž (Municipality Danilovgrad). The construction of the Centre for the reception of asylum seekers was financed from the State Budget of Montenegro (national contribution), the European Union (IPA 2009) and UNHCR. Through IPA 2009, the European Union donated EUR 450,000 for the construction of the Centre, while UNHCR donated EUR 370,000. The national contribution of Montenegro amounted EUR 800,000, so that the total value of the project was EUR 1,620,000. The Centre provides a range of services, including psychosocial assistance, translation services, internet, and cable television.

460. The Center Ljubovic is a public institution established in 2006, with the aim to provide accommodation and assistance to children and youth who needs enhanced supervision and upbringing. It is a semi-open type of institution because it hosts juveniles in conflict with the law who were designated to the specialized institutions because of the perpetration of criminal offences, and who are subjected to the measure of placement in the upbringing and educational institution and have limited freedom of movement.

fulfilled.[461] The Government claimed that there are no other more appropriate reception centres or other more appropriate institutions to accommodate minor unaccompanied migrants. However, no legal basis for placing those minors in the Centre Ljubovic ever existed. Such a practice was openly criticized by UNHCR.

459. The Law on International and Temporary Protection of Foreigners, which began with the implementation on 1 January 2018, brings one novelty, namely the possibility of a foreigner seeking international protection to be restricted of his/her freedom of movement. If an irregular migrant residing at the Reception Centre for a foreign national intends to apply for international protection or apply for international protection, he/she cannot leave the Reception Centre for a foreign national until the end of the proceedings upon his/ her request (this is a difference in relation to the previous Law on Asylum, by which an irregular migrant was allowed to leave the Reception Centre for a foreign national and move to the Asylum Centre, which is an open-type facility) (for more detailed information *see* Part III Chapter 6).

460. In accordance with the above mentioned, there were no asylum seekers who were restricted by the freedom of movement to accommodation in closed-type facilities because the earlier Law on Asylum (which was applicable until 1 January 2018) did not prescribe the possibility of asylum seekers to be 'detained'. As of 1 January 2018, since the new Law on International and Temporary Protection of Foreigners has been applied, there is a possibility that a foreigner seeking international protection may be restricted of his or her freedom of movement by being placed in the Reception Centre for foreign nationals, and few such cases appeared from January 2018 till now, according to information obtained from the Ministry of Interior.

461. Table 5 shows data on detained foreign nationals in 2019 and their nationality.

461. Article 31 of the Law on Asylum, adopted in 2006, stipulated three situations for possible limitation of the freedom of movement till the end of the asylum procedure: (1) if there is a need to determine the identity of the person; (2) if the person has destroyed the travel document or has a false document with the intention of abusing its procedural rights; (3) if that is necessary in order to protect the community's security.

Table 5 Structure of Detained Foreign Nationals by Months in 2019[462]

Nationality	*January*	*February*	*March*	*April*	*May*	*June*	*July*	*August*	*September*	*October*	*November*	*December*	*Total*
Serbia	5	2	2	4	4	3	3	1	1	3		3	31
B&H			1	1			1	1					4
Libya	5	14	1	4	6	8	3	14	17	5			77
Syria	30	35	98	57	59	42	13	21	48	22			425
Morocco	7	18	29	21	37	59	48	83	109	28	2		441
Algeria	9	32	15	10	21	43	51	64	31	19			295
Iran		2	7	13	1	9	5	11	8	6			62
Pakistan		5	13	10	4	20	9	20	6	6			93
Turkey	1	2	1	4	1	3	1		3	3	6		25
Egypt		4	8	1			2	5	11	1			32
Palestine	9	27	9	21	7	12	2	4	9	1			101
Iraq	16	19	76	74	41		11	6	11				254
Yemen			1	1		1	1		7	1			12
Croatia	1				1								1
Kosovo	1		1	2	2	2	3		1	2	2	3	17
Cuba				1									1
Russia	2			1		2		1		2			8
Lebanon				1									1
Germany				2									2

462. Report on the implementation of the Action Plan for the Implementation of the Strategy for Integrated Migration Management for 2019.

Nationality	*January*	*February*	*March*	*April*	*May*	*June*	*July*	*August*	*September*	*October*	*November*	*December*	*Total*
Romania	1				1		1						3
West Sahara			2					3					5
Ecuador		1										3	4
India					2		4					1	7
Nepal					1	5							6
Albania					1	1	1					1	4
Ukraine						1				1			2
Kyrgyzstan											1		1
Jordan													1
Tunisia						2		2				1	5
Cameroon						1							1
China							1						1
Sudan						4			1				5
Bangladesh							4		10				14
Afghanistan						4	4		11	9		1	29
Poland						1							1
Belarus		1											1
USA								1					1
North Macedonia		1								1			2
Total:	**87**	**163**	**264**	**228**	**189**	**223**	**169**	**237**	**284**	**110**	**11**	**13**	**1,981**

§4. EXPULSION AND REMOVAL

462. In essence, the deportation procedure has always been based on confirmed international readmission agreements and the Law on Foreign Nationals. According to applicable regulations, when a foreign national who has an illegal residence in Montenegro cannot be returned according to readmission agreement, removal of such foreign national shall be made in accordance with the Law on Foreign Nationals.

463. A foreign national who has illegally entered, i.e., illegally stays in Montenegro, must leave its territory promptly or within the period determined by the police. An illegal entry to Montenegro is considered if the foreign national crosses the state border outside the place or time designated for crossing of the state border or avoids or attempts to avoid the border control. An illegal stay in Montenegro is considered the stay of the foreign national who fails to fulfil or no longer fulfils the conditions for entry and stay prescribed by the Law on Foreign Nationals. The measures for ensuring the return of a foreign national are:

- voluntary departure from Montenegro;
- expulsion of the foreign national;
- entry and stay ban;
- forced removal;
- restriction on freedom of movement;
- obligation of the foreign national in the return procedure.[463]

464. The competent state authority who has initiated the misdemeanour proceedings or criminal proceedings against a foreign national for the acts prosecutable ex officio have to promptly inform the police of the initiation and completion of the proceedings. The competent state authority who has issued a decision under which a foreign national is found guilty of a committed misdemeanour or criminal offence prosecutable ex officio have to promptly, upon issuing the decision, inform the police thereof. The administrative authority in charge of enforcement of the imprisonment sentence has to, at least forty-eight hours before releasing the foreign national, inform the police thereof.[464]

465. The police are in charge of issuing and delivering the decision on return to the foreign national who illegally stays in Montenegro. The decision determines the period within which a foreign national is obliged to leave Montenegro voluntarily and which may not be shorter than seven days or longer than thirty days. The period for voluntary leaving of Montenegro defined in the decision on return may be extended by the police, upon the request of a foreign national, however not longer than ninety days, taking into account the circumstances of that particular case, notably the duration of stay, family and social ties, or whether the foreign national has children who attend school. If prior to leaving Montenegro a foreign national, for

463. Articles 104 and 106 of the Law on Foreign Nationals.
464. Article 105 of the Law on Foreign Nationals.

whom the decision on return was issued, has been granted residence, the decision on return shall cease to be valid upon the issuing of the decision on granting residence. In the decision on return, the police may pronounce to a foreign national the entry and stay ban, taking into account relevant circumstances of each individual case, and such ban may not be shorter than thirty days or longer than five years.

466. The decision on return may be issued even without conducting the misdemeanour proceedings against the foreign national who illegally stays in Montenegro. A foreign national shall not be issued the decision on return if:

- he or she has been pronounced an additional security measure for the expulsion of foreign national from Montenegro or protective measure of expulsion of foreign national from the territory of Montenegro due to a criminal offence or misdemeanour with elements of violence;
- he or she has illegally entered Montenegro and the circumstances based on which he or she would be allowed to stay in Montenegro do not exist;
- he or she has been issued the decision on the refusal of entry in Montenegro;
- the procedure for his or her extradition is pending under an international treaty;
- there is a risk of evasion of obligation to leave Montenegro or if the foreign national prevents the enforcement of forced removal and return;
- his or her application for temporary residence permit has been rejected as evidently unfounded or such rejection is required for the reasons of national, i.e., internal security of Montenegro.[465] Against the decision on return, an appeal may be lodged to the Ministry of Interior, within five days from the date of receipt of the decision. The Ministry of Interior is obliged to decide within fifteen days from the date of receipt of the appeal.[466]

467. Voluntary departure from Montenegro defined in the decision on return means the departure of a foreign national to the country of origin, the country from which he or she has entered Montenegro, or another country where he or she shall be admitted. A foreign national who illegally stays in Montenegro has the right to apply for voluntary departure from Montenegro. In that case, a foreign national has the right to ask for the assistance of an international or NGO dealing with providing aid to foreign nationals who voluntarily depart from Montenegro. In order to encourage voluntary departure from Montenegro:

- the Ministry of Interior may conclude agreements with the competent authorities of other countries and with international organizations for the implementation of international treaties, as well as with NGOs;
- the police may annul the decision on the expulsion of foreign national, i.e., annul or shorten the entry and stay ban;
- the police may provide a travel document and a travel ticket for return, and necessary financial assistance.

---

465. Article 107 of the Law on Foreign Nationals.
466. Article 108 of the Law on Foreign Nationals.

If a foreign national who illegally stays in Montenegro has applied for voluntary departure from Montenegro after the decision on expulsion, in that case, the police can issue a decision on voluntary return.[467]

468. If a foreign national fails to leave Montenegro within the time limit defined in the decision on return, the police have to issue the decision on the expulsion of a foreign national. The police may issue the decision on expulsion of a foreign national under a final decision of the competent state authority, if a foreign national:

- violates regulations governing employment and work of foreign nationals;
- aids in the illegal entry, transit or stay;
- enters a marriage of convenience;
- breaches the regulations governing prevention of violence at sports events, public law and order, weapons, or drug abuse;
- evades tax liabilities;
- commits a criminal offence prosecutable ex officio;
- has been convicted of a criminal offence in the first degree in another country, which is also punishable under Montenegrin regulations;
- repeats misdemeanours;
- commits a misdemeanour with the elements of violence.

469. The entry and stay ban in Montenegro shall be pronounced under the decision on expulsion of a foreign national, which may not be shorter than three months or longer than twenty years, and in that case, forced removal from Montenegro shall be determined. The decision on expulsion may be issued even without the conducting of the misdemeanour proceedings against a foreign national who illegally stays in Montenegro. In the course of the procedure for issuing the decision on expulsion, a foreign national who has illegally stayed and worked shall be informed of the possibilities to receive wage allowances and payment of contributions he or she is entitled to in accordance with the labour regulations, as well as of the legal remedies for the protection of such rights. Against the decision on expulsion of a foreign national, an appeal may be lodged to the Ministry of Interior, within five days from the date of receipt of the decision.[468]

470. The decision on expulsion of a foreign national may not be issued in the cases when he or she has to be removed to a country where his or her life or freedom would be jeopardized on account of his or her race, religion or nationality, membership in a particular social group or political opinion or where he or she might be exposed to torture or inhuman and degrading treatment or punishment, or where he or she could be subject to a death penalty, and to a country where he or she would be in danger of being subject to forced removal to the country of origin, or if that would be contrary to the Convention for the Protection of Human Rights and Fundamental Freedoms, the European Convention for the Prevention of Torture and Inhuman or Degrading Treatment or Punishment, the Convention on the Rights

467. Article 109 of the Law on Foreign Nationals.
468. Article 110 of the Law on Foreign Nationals.

of the Child, and the Convention on the Exercise of Children's Rights. In these cases, it is prohibited to forcibly remove a foreign national. When issuing a decision on expulsion, duration of stay is taken into account, as well as private or family life, economic connections and the level of social and cultural integration of a foreign national in Montenegro, as well as his connections with the country of origin. When it comes to an unaccompanied foreign national minor, and taking into account the best interests of the child, an unaccompanied foreign national minor shall be subject to forced removal to a state in which he or she shall be handed over to a member of his or her family, to an appointed guardian, or to an institution for receiving children. The decision on expulsion of a foreign national who has been granted a permanent residence in Montenegro, three years of temporary residence for family reunification with Montenegrin national or with a foreign national with permanent residence, may be issued only if:

- due to an intentionally committed criminal offence, the foreign national has been convicted by a final judgment pronouncing a non-suspended term of imprisonment exceeding one year;
- due to an intentionally committed criminal offence, the foreign national has been convicted several times in the period of five years, by a final judgment to a term of imprisonment in the total duration of minimum three years;
- due to a criminal offence against the values protected by the international law, the foreign national has been convicted of an unconditional term of imprisonment;
- it is required for the reasons of national security.[469]

In the procedure before the Administrative Court in connection with the decision on expulsion, a foreign national is entitled to free legal aid in accordance with the law governing free legal aid.[470]

471. A foreign national can be subject to forced removal from Montenegro if the decision on his or her expulsion has been issued and in the following events:

- if he or she has been pronounced an additional security measure for the expulsion of foreign national from Montenegro or protective measure of expulsion of foreign national from the territory of Montenegro due to a criminal offence or misdemeanour with elements of violence;
- if he or she has illegally entered Montenegro and the circumstances based on which he or she would be allowed to stay in Montenegro do not exist;
- if he or she has been issued the decision on the refusal of entry into the country;
- if the procedure for his or her extradition is pending under an international treaty.

472. In previous cases, a foreign national shall be escorted by the police officers for the purpose of leaving Montenegro. A foreign national subject to forced removal shall not hinder the forced removal in any way. In order to ensure that the forced

469. Articles 111 and 116 of the Law on Foreign Nationals.
470. Article 113 of the Law on Foreign Nationals.

removal is carried out with the observance of the fundamental human rights of a foreign national subject to forced removal, a forced removal may be technically recorded, and a foreign national has to be informed of the purpose of recording. Carrying out of forced removal and of measures for the protection of human rights and freedoms of a foreign national who is subject to forced removal is monitored by the Protector of Human Rights and Freedoms, and the police are obliged to cooperate with the Protector of Human Rights and Freedoms. In the course of forced removal, the police may cooperate with state administration authorities, competent authorities of other states, or with international and NGOs. For efficient supervision over forced removal, the Ministry of Interior may conclude agreements with the competent bodies of other states and international organizations for the purpose of implementation of international treaties, as well as with NGOs. A foreign national may be forcibly removed to the country of his or her origin, to the country from which he or she came to Montenegro or to another country where he or she shall be accepted, upon his or her consent.[471]

473. A foreign national with the granted temporary residence in Montenegro shall be subject to forced removal if it is established that the EU Member State has issued against him or her a legally effective decision on expulsion because he or she was convicted of a criminal offence and pronounced the term of imprisonment of minimum one year because he or she is suspected to have committed or intended to commit a criminal offence in the first degree or because of the violation of the provisions on entry and stay of the law of such state. The EU Member State which has issued the decision on expulsion has to be informed of the forced removal of a foreign national. This does not apply to the nationals of an EU Member State, their family members, and to the family members of Montenegrin nationals.[472,473]

474. A forced removal may be temporarily postponed if a foreign national's identity has not been established, if his or her forced removal would produce serious consequences on his or her health, due to the impossibility of transportation, or for other justified reasons due to which a foreign national may not be subject to forced removal. The police are in charge of issuing the decision on the temporary postponement of forced removal. This decision may define the following obligations:

- depositing travel instruments, travel documents and travel tickets;
- depositing particular financial means;
- prohibition to leave particular address where his or her accommodation is;
- reporting to the police at a particular time.

471. Article 114 of the Law on Foreign Nationals.
472. Article 115 of the Law on Foreign Nationals.
473. This provision of the Law on Foreign Nationals shall be applied from the date of accession of Montenegro to the European Union.

475. The decision determines the time of postponement, which may not be longer than six months. During temporary postponement of forced removal, a foreign national is entitled to the right to healthcare in accordance with the regulations governing healthcare. Also, a foreign national minor is entitled to the right to education for the period for which his or her forced removal has been temporarily postponed, in accordance with the regulations governing the area of education. Temporary postponement of forced removal may be annulled if the reasons for temporary postponement of forced removal have ceased to exist, or a foreign national fails to meet the obligations on depositing travel instruments, travel documents and travel tickets, particular financial means or if he or she left particular address where his or her accommodation is and in case if he or she does not report to the police at a particular time. Against the decision on the annulment of temporary postponement of forced removal, an appeal may be lodged to the Ministry of Interior, within eight days from the date of receipt of the decision. This appeal does not postpone the execution of the decision. Temporary postponement of forced removal shall terminate upon the expiry of the time for which a foreign national was imposed temporary postponement of forced removal, upon the annulment of the decision on temporary postponement of forced removal and if the residence of a foreign national has become legal. In the first and second case, a foreign national shall be subject to forced removal.[474]

476. The Ministry of Interior can organize and take part in joint flights of the EU Member States for the purpose of forced removal by air. At the request of the competent authority of an EU Member State, the police are obliged to provide assistance in the case of transit for the purpose of forced removal by air. The request for assistance may be rejected if:

- a foreign national who is subject to forced removal was accused in Montenegro of having committed a criminal offence or if a warrant of his or her deprivation of liberty was issued, so that he or she might start serving his or her prison sentence;
- it is not possible to organize transit through other states or admission in the country of destination;
- it is necessary to change flights in Montenegro from one airport to another;
- forced removal is not possible for practical reasons;
- that is required for the reasons of national, i.e., internal security or public health, or if that would be contrary to the international interests of Montenegro;
- in case of forced removal to a state where his or her life or freedom would be jeopardized on account of his or her race, religion or nationality, membership in a particular social group or political opinion or where he or she might be exposed to torture or inhuman and degrading treatment or punishment, or where he or she could be subject to a death penalty, and to a state where he or she would be in danger of being subject to forced removal to the country of origin, and if that would be contrary to the international documents (Convention for the Protection

474. Articles 117, 118 and 119 of the Law on Foreign Nationals.

of Human Rights and Fundamental Freedoms, the European Convention for the Prevention of Torture and Inhuman or Degrading Treatment or Punishment, etc.).

477. The request for assistance in the case of transit for the purpose of forced removal by air may be also rejected due to procedural reasons:

- if a foreign national may be subject to forced removal by a direct flight to the country of destination;
- if the request was not submitted at the latest two days before transit;
- if the request was not submitted on a prescribed form;
- if the request is incomplete;
- if the transit will take longer than twenty-four hours.

Notification of actions upon the request for assistance has to be submitted within two days, and in justified cases, this period may be extended by two more days and the notification rejecting the request for assistance has to include the reasons for rejection.[475,476]

478. For a foreign national who illegally stays in Montenegro and to whom the residence is granted in an EU Member State, the police have to issue the decision under which he or she is obliged to leave Montenegro and return to the EU Member State where his or her residence is granted, and to determine the deadline within which he or she has to leave Montenegro. In case that a foreign national for whom the decision was issued fails to leave Montenegro within the deadline defined in such decision, the police shall issue the decision on return. Prior to issuing the decision on return, the police is obliged to check if a foreign national still has a granted residence in the EU Member State. In case that a foreign national for whom the decision on return was issued fails to leave Montenegro within the deadline defined in such decision, he or she shall be subject to forced removal. A foreign national whose residence in Montenegro has terminated for the reasons of national, i.e., internal security or who has been convicted after a final judgment for a criminal offence may also be subject to forced removal to another state. For a foreign national whose permanent residence in Montenegro has terminated and who was granted international protection in an EU Member State, the decision on leaving Montenegro shall be issued. In case that such foreign national fails to leave Montenegro within the deadline defined in the decision, he or she shall be subject to forced removal. A foreign national whose permanent residence in Montenegro has terminated for the reasons of national or internal security or who has been convicted after a final judgment for a criminal offence and who has granted international protection in an EU Member State may also be subject to forced removal to another state.[477]

475. Articles 120, 121 and 122 of the Law on Foreign Nationals.
476. This provision of the Law on Foreign Nationals shall be applied from the date of accession of Montenegro to the European Union.
477. Articles 136 and 137 of the Law on Foreign Nationals.

479. When applying the measures for ensuring the return of a foreign national, the best interest of a foreign national minor and other vulnerable persons has to be taken into account, as well as family life and health condition of a foreign national who is subject to such measures. During the procedure of forced removal of a foreign national, particular attention has to be paid to foreign national minors, unaccompanied foreign national minors, persons with special needs, persons with disabilities, elderly persons, pregnant women, single parents with minor children, and the persons who were exposed to torture, rape or other severe forms of psychological, physical or sexual violence. When applying the measures for the return of an unaccompanied foreign national minor, the competent centre for social work and a diplomatic or consular mission of the state whose national the minor is have to be promptly informed thereof.[478]

480. When it comes to a foreigner seeking international protection whose application has been rejected, the procedure is the same as in the case of irregular migrants. This is because a foreigner seeking international protection (after his/her application is rejected and becomes final) falls under the Law on Foreign Nationals, meaning that he/she is being treated in the same way as any other irregular migrant who is illegally residing in Montenegro. The return policy and procedures, including the voluntary return programme, are also being applied to foreigners seeking international protection as to any other irregular migrants.

481. Table 6 shows detailed data on irregular migration in 2017 and 2018.

Table 6 Statistical Data on Irregular Migration[479]

Activity	*2017*	*2018*
Registered traffic of passengers	18,515,709	19,494,734
Entry ban	2,360	1,358
Foreigners in an illegal stay	733	881
Cancellation of stay	2,129	2,373
Decision on return	732	766
Forced removal	235	133
Expulsion	No data	160

478. Article 138 of the Law on Foreign Nationals.
479. Ministry of Interior work reports for 2017 and 2018.

Chapter 2. Sanctions Against Persons Helping Illegal Immigrants or Residents

§1. Human Smuggling

482. Article 405 of the Criminal Code of Montenegro lays down the criminal offence 'Illegal Crossing of State Border and Smuggling of Persons' within the group of criminal offences against public law and order. Anyone who, without the required permission, crosses or attempts to cross the state border of Montenegro under arms or by use of force shall be punished by a prison term of up to one year.[480] Anyone who is engaged in illegal transfer of other persons across the border of Montenegro or who enables another person in return for a gain to illegally cross the border or to illegally stay or transit shall be punished by a prison term from three months to five years.[481] Where the offence was committed by several persons in an organized manner, through misuse of one's office, or in a manner that endangers the life or health of persons whose illegal border crossing, stay or transit is enabled or where a number of people are smuggled, the perpetrator shall be punished by a prison term from one to ten years.[482] Where the criminal offence has been committed by a criminal organization,[483] then the perpetrators of criminal offence shall be charged with committing the criminal offence of illegal crossing of state border in concurrence with the criminal offence of trafficking in human beings punished by a prison term from one to fifteen years.

483. Therefore, this criminal offence, in addition to the act of illegal crossing of the state border, also includes actions pertaining to the smuggling of migrants. With the ratification of the Protocol against the Smuggling of Migrants by Land, Sea and Air, representing an amendment to the UN Convention against Transnational Organized Crime, a commitment has been assumed to criminalize certain actions as a criminal offence.[484]

484. Pursuant to the document of the Police Administration 'Serious and Organized Crime Threat Assessment in Montenegro – SOCTA' – illegal migrations in Montenegro are still having transiting features through the territory of Montenegro from Albania and Kosovo to Croatia, B&H and Serbia. In the previous period, these were mostly economic migrants from Pakistan, Algeria, Morocco, Afghanistan, Syria, Tunisia, or migrants of Kurdish origin, who from their countries, affected by poverty and other economic problems, are moving to Western Europe in search of a better life for their families and themselves.[485] In the previous period, the Montenegrin police conducted several investigations and prosecuted some organized

480. Article 405 para. 1 of the Criminal Code of Montenegro.
481. *Ibid.*, Art. 405 para. 2.
482. *Ibid.*, Art. 405 para. 3.
483. *See* Art. 401a Establishment of criminal organization of the Criminal Code.
484. Zoran Stojanović, *Comment to the Criminal Code of Montenegro,* OSCE Mission to Montenegro (Podgorica, 2010), p. 785.
485. *'Serious and Organized Crime Treat Assessment in Montenegro'*, Police Administration – publically available, 2014, p. 9.

groups of smugglers, who enabled migrants to illegally cross the state border and to be transported across the territory of Montenegro.[486] In some cases, taxi carriers were also used. Two years ago, the police had information that immigrants were smuggled through Montenegro by organized groups at the price of EUR 3,500 to EUR 4,000 per person.[487]

§2. Human Trafficking

485. Article 444 of the Criminal Code of Montenegro lays down the criminal offence 'Trafficking in Human Beings' within the group of criminal offences against humanity and other values guaranteed by international law. Anyone who by use of force or threat, deceiving or keeping in deception, abuse of power, trust, dependence, position of vulnerability of another person, dispossession of personal documents or giving or receiving payments or other undue advantages to achieve the consent of a person having control over another person commits any of the following: recruits, transports, transfers, surrenders, sells, buys, mediates in sale, conceals or keeps another person for the purpose of exploitation of his labour, forced labour, submission to servitude, commission of criminal activity, prostitution or other types of sexual exploitation, beggary, exploitation for pornographic purposes, unlawful extraction of organs for transplantation, or for exploitation in armed conflicts shall be punished by a prison term from one to ten years.[488] The acts under paragraph 1 of this Article shall constitute criminal offences when committed against minors even where the perpetrator did not use force, threat or any other of the methods listed above.[489] Where the offence under paragraph 1 of this Article was committed against a minor by an authorized officer while carrying out his official duty or where a life of a person or several persons has been threatened with wrongful intent, the perpetrator shall be punished by a prison term of not shorter than three years.[490] Where the offence resulted in a serious bodily injury of a person, the perpetrator shall be punished by a prison term from one to twelve years.[491] Where the offence resulted in the death of one or more persons, the perpetrator shall be punished by a prison term not shorter than ten years.[492] Anyone who regularly engages in the commission of the criminal offences or where the offence was committed by several persons in an organized manner shall be punished by a prison term not shorter than ten years.[493] Furthermore, anyone who uses the services of a person knowing that the person is a victim of the offence under paragraph 1 above shall be punished by a prison term from six months to five years, whereas if an offence was committed

486. *Ibid.*
487. This data has been taken from the website of the Centre for investigative journalism of Montenegro, http://www.cin-cg.me/azilanti-crna-gora-tranzitna-zona-za-izbjeglice-hiljade-traze-azil-pa-se-svercuju-ka-eu/.
488. Article 444 para. 1, of the Criminal Code of Montenegro.
489. *Ibid.*, Art. 444 para. 2.
490. *Ibid.*, Art. 444 para. 3.
491. *Ibid.*, Art. 444 para. 4.
492. *Ibid.*, Art. 444 para. 5.
493. *Ibid.*, Art. 444 para. 6.

against a minor, the perpetrator shall be punished by a prison term from three to fifteen years.[494] It is important to emphasize the consent of the victim without prejudice to the existence of this crime.[495]

486. Article 3 of the Protocol to Prevent, Suppress and Punish Trafficking in Human Beings, Especially Women and Children, which complements the UN Convention against Transnational Organized Crime, and whose provisions were not clearly formulated due to both their complexity and partial ambiguity, is not easy to implement in the national criminal law.[496] Therefore, the legal formulation of this criminal offence referred to in Article 444 of the Criminal Code is quite complex, and in a negative sense atypical, although it was sought to formulate it more clearly and in accordance with criminal law standards enshrined in the Protocol.[497]

487. Article 445 of the Criminal Code of Montenegro lays down the criminal offence 'Trafficking in Children for Adoption', establishing that anyone who abducts for adoption a person who has not reached the age of 14 in breach of valid regulations or anyone who adopts such a person or mediates in such adoption or whoever for that purpose buys, sells or surrenders another person who has not reached the age of 14 or who transports, provides accommodation for or conceals such a person shall be punished by a prison term from one to five years. Anyone who regularly engages in the commission of the offences or participates in their organized commission together with several other persons shall be punished by a prison term not shorter than three years.[498]

488. Moreover, the Criminal Code is sanctioning anyone who, in breach of rules of international law, submits another person to slavery or other similar position or keeps another person in such a position, or who buys, sells, surrenders to another person or mediates in buying, selling or surrendering of such a person or who incites another person to sell his own freedom or freedom of persons he supports or cares for.[499] This criminal offence titled 'Submission to slavery and transportation of enslaved persons' has been specified in Article 446 of the Criminal Code and it carries a prison term from one to ten years. Anyone who transports persons in the position of slavery or other similar position from one country to another shall be punished by a prison term from six months to five years, while a perpetrator who commits the offences against a minor shall be punished by a prison term from five to fifteen years.[500]

489. A criminal offence related to trafficking in human beings, often the result of trafficking in human beings, is the criminal offence of pandering under Article

494. *Ibid.*, Art. 444 para. 8.
495. *Ibid.*, Art. 444 para. 9.
496. Zoran Stojanović, *Comment to the Criminal Code of Montenegro,* OSCE Mission to Montenegro (Podgorica, 2010), p. 862.
497. *Ibid.*
498. *Ibid.*, Art. 445 para. 2.
499. *Ibid.*, Art. 446 para. 1.
500. *Ibid.*, Art. 446 paras 2 and 3.

210 of the Criminal Code. Pandering shall mean soliciting another for sexual activity whereby money or any other form of remuneration or reward has been promised or given as the payment for soliciting that person in sexual activities, regardless of whether that payment, promise or reward is given to that person or to a third party.[501] This offence consists of soliciting or instigating another for prostitution or participating in or handing over a person to another for prostitution and is quite similar with the offence of trafficking in human beings. The criminal offence of pondering is quite often qualified by the prosecutors as the criminal offence of trafficking in human beings due to the fact that the victims for the fear of retaliation are reluctant to admit that they are forced to provide sexual services, thus instead of being treated as victims, they are subjected to misdemeanour charges for committing acts against public law and order,[502] and sometimes the victims are even charged with the offence of association for prostitution. However, prostitution and the entertainment industry, which entails sexual exploitation, especially in coastal cities during the tourist season, pose a potential risk and fertile ground for the occurrence of human trafficking offences.[503] When it comes to human trafficking, it is important to mention the underage Roma, which is the population at risk requiring special attention.[504]

---

501. *Ibid.*, Art. 210 para. 4.
502. Anyone involved in prostitution in a public place or engages in activities that incite to prostitution shall be fined from EUR 20,000 to EUR 1,000 or imprisoned for up to thirty days; *see* Art. 27 of the Law on Public Peace and Order, 'Official Gazette of Montenegro', No. 064/11 of 29.12.2011.
503. *'Serious and Organized Crime Treat Assessment in Montenegro',* Police Administration – publically available, 2014. p. 9.
504. *Ibid.*

Part VI. Legal Remedies and Procedural Safeguards

Chapter 1. Legal Remedies in Case of Refusal of Right to Enter, Stay or Reside

§1. Administrative Legal Framework

490. Decisions rendered by the competent authorities in the area of migration law represent administrative act adopted in administrative procedure; thus, it is necessary to present the basic principles of administrative procedure defined by the Law on Administrative Proceedings,[505] being applied by these authorities when deciding on the rights of foreign nationals. Moreover, the rights of foreign nationals are also subjected to the misdemeanour proceedings instituted before the misdemeanour courts, which are applying the Misdemeanor Law.[506]

491. An administrative matter shall mean any specific situation in which a public authority renders an administrative act to decide or performs another administrative activity to determine or otherwise influence the rights, obligations or legal interests of a natural person, legal entity or other party, as well as any other legal situation that is legally defined as an administrative matter.[507] An administrative act shall mean a written act of a competent state authority, usually titled 'Decision', by which that authority decides on the rights, obligations or legal interests of a party in an administrative matter.[508]

492. Therefore, a foreign national, like any other natural person, or like every citizen of Montenegro, enjoys legal protection when the competent state authority is deciding on his rights and interests based on the law. Legal protection is reflected, above all, in the respect of the principle of two-instance procedure when deciding on his rights, i.e., possibility of lodging an appeal against decisions of first-instance state authorities, as well as the possibility of judicial review of administrative acts.

505. Law on Administrative Proceedings, 'Official Gazette of Montenegro', Nos 056/14 of 24.12.2014, 020/15 of 24.4.2015, 040/16 of 30.6.2016, 037/17 of 14.6.2017.
506. Law on Misdemeanors, 'Official Gazette of Montenegro', Nos 001/11 of 11.1.2011, 006/11 of 25.1.2011, 039/11 of 4.8.2011, 032/14 of 30.7.2014, 043/17 of 4.7.2017, 051/17 of 3.8.2017.
507. Article 2 of the Law on Administrative Proceedings.
508. Article 18 of the Law on Administrative Proceedings.

This legal protection is guaranteed by the Constitution of Montenegro, which guarantees the right of appeal. Article 22 of the Constitution stipulates that everyone, even a foreign national, shall have the right to a legal remedy against a decision deciding on his right or on a legitimate interest. In addition to the Constitution, legal protection in the field of migration law is also regulated by the Law on Administrative Proceedings and the Law on Administrative Dispute.[509]

493. The basic principles of administrative procedure prescribed by the Law on Administrative Procedure applicable to every person and also to a foreigner are as follows: principle of legality and justified expectations of the parties, proportionality principle, party's right to legal protection, principle of active assistance to a party, principle of cost-economy and effectiveness of the procedure, principle of establishing the truth, principle of independence and discretionary assessment of evidence, principle of obtaining data ex officio, the party's right to declare, prohibition of abuse of rights, right to inspect the files, and one of the most important principle is the principle of two-instance procedure, or the principle of deciding in two instances, which includes the right to a legal remedy, representing the right relevant to the migration law of foreigners.

494. Principle of two-instance procedure, under the Law on Administrative Proceedings, implies that a party who believes that its rights and/or legal interests were violated by administrative activity in the administrative matter of a public authority shall be entitled to a legal remedy, being as follows: appeal, repeating the procedure and the objection.[510] The party shall be entitled to appeal against the decision rendered in the first instance, except that the appeal is not allowed by law.[511] An appeal against the first-instance decision of the ministry may be lodged only when so prescribed by law.[512] General deadline for lodging an appeal is fifteen days, unless the law prescribes otherwise. The right of appeal also exists when the first-instance authority failed to render a decision within the statutory deadline at the request of the party (silence of the administration).[513] The second-instance authority must render a decision as soon as possible, and at latest within forty-five days, unless the law prescribes otherwise. An appeal may not be lodged against decisions of second-instance authorities.

495. The decisions of the administrative authorities shall be appealed to the competent ministry, and the decisions of the ministries, when prescribed by the law, shall be appealed to the Appeals Commission. The Appeals Commission has a president and four members, who are appointed and dismissed by the Government, at the proposal of the Ministry of Public Administration, following a public competition.[514] The Appeals Commission is independent and autonomous in its work,

509. *Zakon o upravnom postuku*, 'Official Gazette of Montenegro', No. 054/16 of 15.8.2016.
510. Article 118 of the Law on Administrative Proceedings.
511. Article 119 of the Law on Administrative Proceedings.
512. *Ibid.*
513. Article 129 of the Law on Administrative Proceedings.
514. Law on Civil Servants and State Employees (*Zakon o državnim službenicima i namještenicima*), 'Official Gazette of Montenegro', Nos 002/18 of 10.1.2018, 034/19 of 21.6.2019, Art. 141.

adopts the Rules of Procedure governing its method of work and decision-making and has a seal developed in accordance with the regulation governing the seal of state authorities.[515] There is no right of appeal against the decisions of the Government, but a complaint may be lodged before the Administrative Court. Thus, the decisions of the Government are not subject to the right of appeal, but there is a possibility of judicial review of the Government's decisions before the Administrative Court.

496. When it comes to the work of second-instance authorities (ministries, Appeals Commission) on appeal, they may adopt the appeal, dismiss the decision of the first-instance authorities, repeat the proceedings, dismiss an appeal and confirm the decision of the first-instance authorities, or possibly, which is a rare situation, accept an appeal and resolve the administrative matter themselves by reversing the decision of the first-instance authority. In almost every situation, the second-instance authority will, once it has accepted the appeal, return the case to the first-instance authority for reconsideration. In the past, prior to the amendments to the Law on Administrative Proceedings, there was a possibility of so-called Ping-Pong effect, that the second-instance authority annuls the decision of the first-instance authority and returns it for reconsideration, and that the first-instance authority renders the same decision again. After the amendments to the Law on Administrative Proceedings, this possibility no longer exists because the second-instance authority can now only dismiss the decision of the first-instance authority once and return it for reconsideration, and if the first-instance authority renders the same decision again, then the second-instance authority must reverse it and resolve the administrative matter itself if it considers that the decision of the first-instance authority is without merits. The rules of misdemeanour procedure enable fair conduct of misdemeanour proceedings, protection of human rights, and proper determination of facts and rendering of lawful decision on misdemeanour liability, so that no innocent person is convicted, sentenced or subject to any other misdemeanour charges.[516] The defendant has the right to a defence, and the Criminal Procedure Code shall apply to all issues not regulated by the Misdemeanor Law. The basic principles of misdemeanour proceedings are, *inter alia*, the prohibition of retrial, principle of truth and fairness, and the two-instance–decision-making procedure. A party not satisfied with the misdemeanour court decisions may lodge an appeal within eight days to the second-instance court – the Misdemeanor Council – which may accept the appeal, dismiss the decision and return it to the first-instance court for reconsideration, dismiss the appeal as unfounded and adopt the first-instance decision of the misdemeanour court, or possibly reverse the first-instance decision.[517] An appeal may be lodged on the grounds of a substantive violation of the provisions of the misdemeanour procedure; misapplication of a substantive law prescribing an offence; wrongly or incompletely established facts; decisions on sanction, assets recovery, costs of misdemeanour proceedings and property claim. Appeals against the decisions of the second-instance court – the Misdemeanor

515. *Ibid.*, Art. 143.
516. Law on Misdemeanors, Art. 98.
517. *Ibid.*, Art. 210.

Council – may not be lodged, but extraordinary legal remedies may be used, such as the motion for retrial or a motion for the protection of legality.[518]

§2. Refusal of the Right to Enter

497. There are three situations where a foreign national may be refused to enter Montenegro. The first is when he is refused entry at the border crossing point, while the second is when a foreign national applying for a visa outside Montenegro is denied a visa. A third situation exists where a foreign national's application for asylum has been dismissed.

498. The Police shall adopt a decision on the refusal of entry to a foreign national to whom the entry at a border crossing point has been refused, without hearing the foreign national concerned.[519] An appeal may be lodged against the decision on the refusal of entry via the nearest diplomatic-consular mission of Montenegro abroad (hereinafter referred to as 'the Diplomatic and Consular mission'), within eight days as of the day of receiving the decision. The Ministry of Interior shall decide on the appeal and the appeal shall not postpone the decision enforcement. Exceptionally, an appeal shall postpone the decision enforcement if the Police estimate that they consider that the life or freedom of the foreign national is jeopardized in the country of origin due to his racial, religious or national affiliation, due to the affiliation to a particular social group or due to political opinion, or where he could be subject to torture or inhuman and degrading treatment or punishment, or he could be subject to a death penalty, as well as his returning to a country where there is danger of him being forcibly returned to the country of origin.[520] The refusal of entry shall be affixed to the foreign national's travel document.

499. In reference to the reasons for the refusal of entry to a foreign national at a border crossing point, the most controversy is created by item 9 paragraph 1 of Article 8 of the Law on Foreign Nationals, which stipulates that a foreign national shall not be allowed to enter where national or internal security reasons require that. This provision is set quite broadly so that it gives great discretion to the competent authorities, i.e., Police and the National Security Agency when deciding whether there is a national or internal security threat to a person's entry into the country. Namely, neither the Police nor the National Security Agency is obliged to explain or state the reasons why the entry of a particular foreigner is considered a national security threat. A foreign national who is denied entry on this basis has no opportunity to be informed, nor will he receive a response from the Police as to why his entry into the country is considered a threat to national security. He has the right to appeal to the Ministry of the Internal Affairs and may lodge an appeal against the Ministry's decision to the Administrative Court of Montenegro. The practice has shown that the Administrative Court most often overrules the decisions rendered by

518. For more information, *see* the Law on Misdemeanors.
519. Article 8 of the Law on Foreign Nationals.
520. *Ibid.*

the Ministry of the Internal Affairs and the Police on the grounds that these decisions do not contain the reasons for rendering it, as well as the reason why a person is considered a threat to national security. However, after the Administrative Court dismissed the decisions, the Police again brought the same decision on the refusal of entry, and the entire proceeding is going around in circles. Therefore, in the opinion of the author, amendments to the Law should be considered to allow the court an insight into the acts of the Police and the National Security Agency and to see whether the reasons are justified for refusing the entry to a foreign national for the reasons of national or internal security.

500. An appeal may be lodged against the decision on the refusal of the application for a short-stay visa (C visa) at the border crossing point to the Ministry of Foreign Affairs via the nearest Diplomatic or consular mission, within eight days from receiving the decision.[521] An appeal shall not postpone the execution of the decision.

§3. Refusal of Application for Permanent Residence

501. An appeal against a decision of the Ministry of the Internal Affairs rejecting the visa application for a temporary residence permit may be submitted to the Ministry of Interior within eight days as of receiving the decision.[522] If the Ministry of Interior dismissed the appeal, a foreign national may submit a complaint to the Administrative Court within twenty days as of receiving the decision. It is important to emphasize that when it comes to decisions on rejecting the application for a temporary residence permit and work due to the occupancy of the annual quota, it is not allowed to appeal to the Ministry of Interior, but an administrative dispute can be brought directly before the Administrative Court.[523]

§4. Refusal of Application for Temporary Residence

502. A decision of the Ministry of Interior rejecting a foreigner's application for issuing a permanent residence permit may not be appealed, but an administrative dispute may be initiated.[524] Therefore, a complaint may be lodged to the Administrative Court against the decision of the Ministry of Interior, pursuant to the rules of administrative dispute regulated by the Law on Administrative Dispute. A complaint may be filed within twenty days from receiving the decision. Moreover, an administrative dispute may be initiated against a decision of the Ministry of Interior on the termination of permanent residence of a foreigner to which the same aforementioned rules of administrative dispute apply.[525]

521. Article 32 of the Law on Foreign Nationals.
522. *Ibid.*, Art. 62.
523. *Ibid.*, Art. 80.
524. *Ibid.*, Art. 90.
525. *Ibid.*, Art. 94.

§5. REFUSAL OF APPLICATION FOR ASYLUM

503. A foreign national may lodge an appeal to the Administrative Court against the decision of the Ministry of Interior rejecting the request for international protection within fifteen days from the date of receiving the decision being.[526] Furthermore, within the same deadline, a foreigner can lodge a complaint to the Administrative Court against the decision of the Ministry of Interior determining the termination of the right to asylum.

526. Article 48 of the Law on International and Temporary Protection of Foreigners.

Chapter 2. Legal Remedies in Case of Expulsion and Detention

§1. Time Limit for Leaving Montenegro

504. The Law on Foreign Nationals allows for the possibility of lodging an appeal against a decision on return specifying the deadline within which a foreigner residing illegally must voluntarily leave Montenegro. The complaint shall be lodged with the Ministry of Interior via the Police – authority that issued the decision – within five days from the day the foreigner received the decision.[527] The Ministry of Interior must decide on the appeal lodged within fifteen days. Considering that the deadline by which a foreigner is obliged to voluntarily leave the country cannot be less than seven days, it is noted that the legislator set forth even a shorter deadline (five days) within which he can file an appeal against the decision on return. The Law on Foreign Nationals does not stipulate that an appeal is not postponing the execution of a decision, then the general rules of administrative procedure under which an appeal postpones the execution of a decision applies, thus a foreigner who has been issued a voluntary return decision is not required to leave the country until the decision is final and enforceable, i.e., until the decision on appeal is brought.

§2. Restricting the Freedom of Movement

505. A complaint may be lodged before the Administrative Court against the decision on the deprivation of liberty of the foreign national, brought in and detained up to twenty-four hours, only if that is necessary to ensure his or her presence in the procedure of cancellation of stay of up to ninety days and in the procedure of annulment of temporary postponement of forced removal for up to forty-eight hours.[528] The procedure before the Administrative Court shall be urgent and the complaint may be lodged within the statutory deadline of twenty days from the date of receiving the decision. Pursuant to the rules of the administrative proceeding, a complaint shall not postpone the execution of the decision.

§3. Ordering the Stay in the Immigration Detention Centre

506. An appeal against the Police decision on the placement of a foreign national to the Reception Center for Foreigners may be lodged to the Administrative Court, within five days from the date of receiving the decision.[529] The proceeding before the Administrative Court is conducted in accordance with the Law on Administrative Dispute. The complaint does not postpone the enforcement of the decision. The placement in the Reception Center for Foreigners determined by the Police decision can only last for the time required for forced removal and as long as the activities for forced removal are effective, for a maximum of six months, and

527. Article 108 of the Law on Foreign Nationals.
528. *Ibid.*, Art. 124.
529. *Ibid.*, Art. 127.

may possibly be extended for a maximum of twelve months. For this reason, the procedure before the Administrative Court challenging the decision on the placement of a foreigner in the Reception Center for Foreigners is an urgent procedure.

§4. Imposing Milder Measures

507. Pursuant to Article 126 of the Law on Foreign Nationals, the Police may impose the following milder measures:

(1) depositing of travel instruments, travel documents and travel tickets;
(2) depositing of particular financial means;
(3) prohibition to leave particular address where his or her accommodation is;
(4) reporting to the police at a particular time.

508. An appeal may be lodged before the Administrative Court against the decision on the application of milder measures, within five days from the day of submitting the decision.[530] The complaint does not postpone the execution of the decision.

530. *Ibid.*, Art. 126.

Chapter 3. Procedural Safeguards

§1. Principle and Regulations

509. The Law on Administrative Proceedings includes general procedural safeguards that are important for the lawful and valid exercise of the rights of foreigners in Montenegro. These procedural guarantees do not contravene the special procedural guarantees prescribed by other laws and regulations (Law on Foreign Nationals, Law on International and Temporary Protection of Foreigners, Law on Misdemeanors, Law on Border Control, etc.) which are used as subsidiary sources of law when it comes to exercising the immigration rights of foreigners. Provisions of special laws which, due to the specific nature of administrative matters in certain administrative areas, prescribe the necessary derogations from the rules of administrative procedure may not contravene the principles and purpose of the Law on Administrative Procedure, nor diminish the level of protection of the rights and legal interests of the parties, in this case the foreigners.

I. Administrative Procedure Act

A. *Principles of Procedure*

510. The procedure for exercising the rights of foreigners before the competent state authorities is accomplished in an administrative procedure which is regulated primarily by the Law on Administrative Proceedings entailing basic procedural guarantees significant for all parties to the procedure, including foreigners:

- *The principle of legality* means the obligation of the administration to carry out its duties in accordance with the law and within the framework of the law and thus to contribute to the enforcement of the law.[531] In other words, when deciding on the rights of foreigners, the competent administrative authority must decide on the basis of the laws, other regulations and general acts.[532] When a public authority is authorized by law to decide on an administrative matter at its own discretion, the administrative act must be rendered within the limits of that power, in accordance with the purpose for which the power has been granted and in accordance with previous decisions rendered by the public authority in essentially identical administrative matters.[533] As a part of the principle of legality is also the principle of legal certainty and predictability, which means that actions and decisions of a public body should not cause uncertainty in legal entities.[534]
- *The principle of justified expectation of the parties* means that substantially identical legal situations are handled in a substantially uniform, predictable manner.

531. Sreten Ivanović, *Comment to the Law on Administrative Proceedings*, Podgorica, 2015, p. 38.
532. Article 5 of the Law on Administrative Proceedings.
533. *Ibid.*
534. Sreten Ivanović, *Comment to the Law on Administrative Proceedings*, Podgorica, 2015, p. 39.

When deciding on the rights, obligations and interests of the parties, administration must decide in a neutral, impartial and equal manner.

- *The principle of the protection of legitimate expectations* means that the expectation of the outcome of the proceedings is predictable and legitimately expected, and such legitimacy is drawn from the actions of a public authority in the same or similar legal matters.
- *The proportionality principle* means that the administrative activity of a public authority may limit a party's right only if it is necessary to achieve the statutory purpose if it is proportionate to the goal to be achieved and if it does not violate human rights and freedoms.[535] When obligations are imposed on foreigners and other participants in a procedure, the public authority shall, in relation to the party and other participant in the procedure, apply the prescribed measures that are more favourable for them if these measures achieve the goal of the law.
- In other words, what can be achieved by milder measures for a party and which are disposable to the authority does not need to resort to more severe and restrictive measures if those milder measures may achieve the objectives set by the regulation.[536]
- *Party's right to legal protection* means that a party shall be guaranteed with protection against the administrative activity of a public authority when the latter decides the rights, obligations or interests of the party. The party has the right to a lawyer during the administrative procedure, while the decision by which the competent authority decides on the rights, obligations or interests of the party has the right to appeal to the second-instance body. If the appeal is not allowed, the party has the right to lodge a complaint before the Administrative Court in Podgorica.
- *The principle of active assistance to a party* means when an authorized person acting in official capacity who conducts an administrative procedure and renders an administrative act finds out or estimates that a party or another participant in the administrative procedure has grounds for exercising a right or legal interest, he/she shall warn the party or other participant of the legal consequences of their actions or omissions. The ignorance or lack of awareness of the party or other participant in the administrative procedure cannot be at the expense of the protection of their rights and legal interests.[537]
- *Principle of cost-efficiency and effectiveness of procedure* means that the administrative procedure must be conducted without delay and as little cost as possible, but in such a manner that all the facts and circumstances relevant to the successful and complete exercise and protection of the rights and legal interests of the parties or other participants in the procedure are properly and fully established.[538]

535. Article 6 of the Law on Administrative Proceedings.
536. Sreten Ivanović, *Komentar zakona o upravnom postupku*, Podgorica, 2015, p. 43.
537. Article 8 of the Law on Administrative Proceedings.
538. *Ibid.*, Art. 10.

- *Principle of establishing the truth* means that all the facts and circumstances relevant to the lawful and proper decision-making on the administrative matter must be properly and fully established in the administrative procedure.[539]
- *Principle of independence and discretionary assessment of evidence* means that the authorized official shall establish the facts and circumstances in the administrative procedure independently and shall decide on the administrative matter on the basis of established facts and circumstances.[540]
- *Principle of obtaining data ex officio* means that when deciding on the administrative procedure, the public authority shall, while acting ex officio, inspect, obtain and process data from official records and registers kept by that public authority or other competent authority, unless access to such data is limited in accordance with the law.[541]
- *Party's right to declare* means that the party shall be entitled to participate in the administrative procedure with the aim of establishing the facts and circumstances relevant for rendering an administrative act. Before an administrative act is rendered, the party shall be entitled to declare on the results of the examination procedure.[542] An administrative act can be rendered without the party's declaration only in the cases prescribed by law.
- *Prohibition of abuse of rights* means that the public authority must prevent any abuse of the party's rights in the administrative procedure.[543]
- *Right to inspect files* means that the public authority shall enable parties or other participants in the administrative procedure to inspect the files and be notified about the course of the procedure, in accordance with the law.[544]

B. Use of Language and Alphabet in the Procedure

511. A public authority shall conduct the administrative procedure in the Montenegrin language. If a party or other participant in the administrative procedure does not understand the Montenegrin language, the public authority shall, in the administrative procedure, provide for translation of the course of procedure into their language or language they understand, as well as for the delivery of summons and other notices in their language and alphabet.[545]

C. Costs of the Procedure

512. A foreigner may be exempted from paying the costs when this is provided for in an international treaty, and if there is no such treaty, under the condition of

539. *Ibid.*, Art. 11.
540. *Ibid.*, Art. 12.
541. *Ibid.*, Art. 13.
542. *Ibid.*, Art. 14.
543. *Ibid.*, Art. 15.
544. *Ibid.*, Art. 16.
545. *Ibid.*, Art. 9.

reciprocity.[546] The party's request for exemption from payment of costs shall be decided upon by a decision, against which the party has the right to appeal.

II. Law on International and Temporary Protection of Foreigners

513. The Law on International and Temporary Protection of Foreigners contains the following procedural safeguards that are of importance for securing the rights of foreigners:

- *Prohibition of expulsion or return (non-refoulement)* means that it is forbidden to expel or in any way return a third-country national or a stateless person to a country: where his life would be threatened on account of his race, religion, nationality, membership of a particular social group or political opinion, or where he could be subjected to torture, inhuman or degrading treatment, or which could extradite him to another country where his life would be threatened on account of his race, religion, nationality, membership of a particular social group or political opinion, or where he could be subjected to torture, inhuman or degrading treatment.[547]
- *Principle of family unity* means that a foreigner seeking international protection, an asylee, a foreigner granted subsidiary protection and a foreigner granted temporary protection shall be entitled to family unity.[548]
- *Principle of best interests of a minor* means that in pursuing the best interest of an unaccompanied minor, the minor's guardian shall undertake all the necessary actions, including contacts and interactions with state authorities, state administration bodies, foreign bodies, international and non-governmental organizations in order to reunite the minor with his family if that is in the best interest of the minor.[549]
- *Exclusion of the public* means that the public shall be excluded from the process of granting international protection. Exceptionally, the interview may be attended by a representative of the UNHCR or other organizations dealing with the protection of human rights and the rights of refugees, or asylees, if the foreigner seeking international protection does not object to that.[550]
- *Provision of interpretation to a foreigner* who does not understand the Montenegrin language is laid down in Article 18 of the Law on International and Temporary Protection of Foreigners, prescribing that where a foreigner seeking international protection does not understand the Montenegrin language, he will be provided with an interpreter for a language which is reasonably assumed to be understood and in which can communicate. A foreigner who believes that the involvement of a particular interpreter could lead to incomplete and inaccurate presentation of his reasons for seeking international protection shall be obliged to

546. *Ibid.*, Art. 96.
547. Article 11 of the Law on International and Temporary Protection of Foreigners.
548. *Ibid.*, Art. 14.
549. *Ibid.*, Art. 15.
550. *Ibid.*, Art. 17.

provide valid reasons thereof. If the Ministry of the Internal Affairs deems these reasons justified, it shall provide the foreigner with another interpreter.

- Special procedural safeguards shall be afforded to a foreigner seeking international protection who, due to personal features and circumstances (age, sex, sexual orientation, gender identity, severe illness, mental health or consequences of torture, rape or other severe forms of psychological, physical or gender-based violence), is not fully able to pursue own rights and perform duties under this Law without adequate assistance.[551] Special procedural safeguards shall mean appropriate support to a foreigner for the purpose of pursuing rights and executing duties under the Law on International and Temporary Protection.
- *Principle of personal interview* has been prescribed by Article 42 Law on International and Temporary Protection, and it is similar to the party's right to declare defined by the Law on Administrative Procedure. Upon the application for international protection, the Ministry shall, as soon as feasible, conduct the examination procedure and allow the foreigner seeking international protection to be heard in person regarding all the facts and circumstances relevant to the procedure for granting international protection. A foreigner seeking international protection is obliged to personally attend and participate in the interview regardless of whether he has a legal representative, a guardian and/or an attorney.[552]
- *Right to information and counselling* has been defined by Article 68 defining that at the Reception Centre, upon the request of the foreigner seeking international protection, he shall be provided with information relevant for his residence, counselling regarding the procedure upon his application for international protection, as well as free legal assistance, in a language he is reasonably assumed to understand and in which he can communicate.
- *Free legal assistance* shall be provided to a foreigner seeking international protection and a foreigner in transfer shall enjoy the right to free legal assistance in an administrative dispute concerning the application for international protection, at personal request, provided that he does not have money or valuables, and that the complaint is not manifestly unfounded.[553] Free legal assistance shall include assistance in making the complaint; representation before the Administrative Court; exemption from the payment of costs of the administrative dispute.[554] The decision on granting free legal assistance shall be taken by the Ministry and furnished to the Administrative Court. An appeal may be lodged before the Administrative Court within eight days against the decision of the Ministry rejecting the request for free legal assistance. The proceedings before the Administrative Court shall be completed within fifteen days from the day of filing the complaint.
- *Cooperation with the UNHCR* has been regulated by Article 16 of the Law on International and Temporary Protection, setting forth that the Ministry of Interior shall at the request of the UNHCR supply information on foreigners seeking international protection. The Ministry shall, with the consent of the foreigner

551. *Ibid.*, Art. 20.
552. *Ibid.*, Art. 42.
553. *Ibid.*, Art. 69.
554. *Ibid.*

seeking international protection, provide the UNHCR access to information relating to his application for international protection, the course of the proceeding and the decision taken with regard to the application.[555]

III. Law on Misdemeanors

514. One of the procedural safeguards relevant to the exercise of foreigners' immigration rights is also included in the Law on Misdemeanors:

- *The principle of legality in determining misdemeanours and imposing misdemeanour penalties* means that no person may be given a misdemeanour sanction for an act that did not constitute a misdemeanour or for which a sanction was not provided under the law or other piece of legislation at the time when it was committed.[556] Misdemeanours and misdemeanour sanctions may be prescribed by law, decree of the Government and decision of the local government unit.
- *Fair conduct of proceedings* means that the rules on misdemeanour proceedings ensure the just conduct of misdemeanour proceedings, the protection of human rights, accurate determination of facts and lawful determination of misdemeanour liability, so that no innocent person is convicted, and so that the offender is pronounced with a sentence or imposed another misdemeanour sanction.[557] If certain matters regarding misdemeanour proceedings are not regulated by the Law on Misdemeanors, the provisions of the Criminal Procedure Code shall apply to such matters.
- Law on Misdemeanors entails procedural safeguard of the *right of defence and other rights of the accused*, meaning that the defendant shall have the right to be notified as soon as possible, in detail and in a language he understands, of the misdemeanour he is accused of committing, to be provided the possibility and adequate time to prepare a defence, to conduct his own defence or with the expert assistance of a defence counsel that he chooses, or in the event he lacks sufficient means to pay for his defence, a court appointed defence counsel must be provided to him when the interests of justice so require; to be able to respond to all facts and evidence presented against him and to present facts and evidence in his favour; to use his own language or be provided with interpretation in a language that he understands during the proceedings.[558]
- *Ne bis in idem principle* means that no person may be retried for a misdemeanour that he was convicted or acquitted of committing by a final and legally binding judicial decision. This prohibition does not exclude the reopening of proceedings in accordance with the Law on Misdemeanors.[559]
- *Principle of truth and fairness* means that the court is obliged to truthfully and fully establish all facts that are of significance for rendering a lawful and fair

555. Article 16 of the Law on International and Temporary Protection of Foreigners.
556. Article 2 of the Law on Misdemeanors.
557. *Ibid.*, Art. 98.
558. *Ibid.*, Art. 99.
559. *Ibid.*, Art. 100.

decision, and to dedicate equal attention to both the facts against and the facts in favour of the defendant when examining and establishing such facts.[560]

- *Principle of the free evaluation of evidence* means that the existence or lack of facts upon which it bases its decision shall be freely ascertained by the court and shall not be limited by special formal rules, whereas the court may not base its decision on evidence obtained in violation of human rights and fundamental freedoms guaranteed by the Constitution or ratified international treaties.[561]
- The Law on Misdemeanors entails *procedural safeguard for a lay party*, meaning that the court shall inform a defendant or other person that is participating in the proceedings, who due to ignorance may omit to undertake an action or utilize their rights, of his rights under this Law, as well as of the consequences of omitting an action.[562]
- *Principle of efficiency of proceedings* means that the court is obliged to conduct proceedings without stalling and to prevent any abuse of the rights of the persons taking part in the proceedings.[563]
- *Principle of two-instance misdemeanour proceedings* means that an appeal may be filed against the first-instance decision unless otherwise provided by the Law on Misdemeanors.[564]
- The Law on Misdemeanors includes the principle that a person who is unlawfully deprived of his liberty or otherwise punished must be *compensated for the damage*. In such case, a person shall address to the Ministry of Justice with a claim for compensation, which is obliged to determine the manner and amount of compensation for the damage. In the event that a person is not satisfied with the amount of damage, he may initiate a procedure against the state of Montenegro before the basic court.

---

560. *Ibid.*, Art. 101.
561. *Ibid.*, Art. 102.
562. *Ibid.*, Art. 103.
563. *Ibid.*, Art. 104.
564. *Ibid.*, Art. 105.

Part VII. Access to the Labour Market

Chapter 1. Overview of Applicable Legislation

515. Employment and work of foreigners in Montenegro is generally regulated by the Law on Labor and, largely, by the Law on Foreign Nationals, as well as the Law on International and Temporary Protection of Foreigners, which in one part deals with the employment of this category of foreigners. With the implementation of the new Law on Foreign Nationals from 1 April 2015, the Law on Employment and Work of Foreigners ceased to be valid because the new Law on Foreign Nationals incorporated its provisions. Until that moment, the normative framework regarding the employment and work of foreign nationals was such that a foreign national first had to obtain a work permit, pursuant to the Law on Employment and Work of Foreigners, and only then submitted a request to the Ministry of Interior for temporary residence on the basis of work and employment, pursuant to the Law on Foreign Nationals. So these were two separate proceedings. One of the most significant innovations in the Law on Foreign Nationals, which included all provisions regarding the employment and work of foreign nationals, was the introduction of a single and unique procedure for issuing work and residence permits, as a single document, in accordance with Directive 2011/98/EU of the European Parliament and of the Council of 13 December 2011 on a single application procedure for a single permit for third-country nationals to reside and work in the territory of a Member State and on a common set of rights for third-country workers legally residing in a Member State.

516. In general, the Labor Law applies to national employed citizens as well as to employed foreigners, unless otherwise provided by a special law (Law on Foreign Nationals and Law on International and Temporary Protection of Foreigners).[565] Thus, Article 44 of the Labor Law stipulates that a foreigner may conclude an employment contract if he meets the requirement determined by the Labor Law, a special law and international treaties.

517. The Constitution of Montenegro contains a number of labour-related provisions, which also apply to foreigners employed in Montenegro. Thus, Article 62 of the Constitution stipulates that everyone (including foreigners) shall have the right to work, to free choice of occupation and employment, to fair and humane working conditions and protection during unemployment. The employed shall have

565. Article 2 of the Law on Labor.

the right to adequate salary, limited working hours and paid vacation, protection at work, whereas youth, women and the disabled shall enjoy special protection at work.[566] Furthermore, the employed shall have the right to strike, while social insurance of employed shall be deemed mandatory.[567]

518. Annual number of temporary residence and work permits for foreign nationals – 'annual quota' – is determined by the Government, in accordance with the migration policy, status and movements on the labour market in Montenegro. The annual quota (separately determined for employment and for seasonal employment) determines the business activities and occupations where the foreign nationals may be employed. The Ministry of Labor and Social Welfare proposes the annual quota, upon previously obtained opinions of the Employment Agency of Montenegro, state administration authorities in charge of particular business activities for which annual quota is determined, and the Social Council. The Government may restrict the annual quota, increase the number, or make rearrangements by purposes, if that is conditioned by the changed ratio between labour market supply and demand or due to special conditions in particular business activities.[568]

519. The Decision on Determining the Annual Number of Temporary Residence and Work Permits for Foreigners for 2019[569] determined the number of work permits for foreigners for 2019 in the total number of 20,454. Out of this number, 5,000 work permits have been allocated by the Ministry of Labor and Social Welfare, in accordance with labour market needs. The Ministry of Labor has decided to allocate 3,620 work permits for employment of foreigners; i.e., the total number of work permits allocated is 19,074.[570]

520. In 2019, 27,634 permits were issued for work and employment of foreigners (15,582 in quota and 12,052 out of quota), which is 1,307 or 4.96% more than in 2018 (26,327). Of the total issued permits for foreigners in the quota, by type of permits, 80.30% were issued for employment of foreigners (12,513) and 19.70% for seasonal employment of foreigners (3,069). Of the total number of permits issued, the majority (81.38%) refers to four occupational groups: construction, accommodation services and catering, other service activities and trade. The quota consumption compared to the allocated quota in 2019 is at 81.69%. The use of quotas by type of permit is for employment of foreigners – 89.24% – while for seasonal employment it is 60.75%.[571]

---

566. Article 64 of the Constitution of Montenegro.
567. Articles 66 and 67 of the Constitution of Montenegro.
568. Articles 76 and 77 of the Law on Foreign Nationals.
569. *Odluka o utvrđivanju godišnjeg broja dozvola za privremeni boravak i rad stranaca za 2019. godinu,* 'Official Gazette of Montenegro', No. 2/2019.
570. Government of Montenegro, *Report on the implementation of the Action Plan for the Implementation of the Strategy for Integrated Migration Management for 2019* (Podgorica 2020).
571. *Ibid.*

521. The Decision on Determining the Annual Number of Temporary Residence and Work Permits for Foreigners for 2020,[572] the annual quota for 2020, as well as the activities in which foreigners could be employed was determined in the total number of 20,454 permits for temporary residence and work of foreigners. Out of this number, 5,000 work permits has been allocated by the Ministry of Labor and Social Welfare, in accordance with labour market needs.[573]

522. Table 7 shows activities in which foreign nationals may be employed, with quota data for each individual economic activity.

Table 7 Overview of Activities in Which Foreigners May Be Employed for 2020[574]

Activity	*Employment of Foreigners*	*Seasonal Employment of Foreigners*	*Total*
A. Agriculture, forestry and fishing	160	370	530
B. Mining	90	0	90
C. Manufacturing industry	370	30	400
D. Electricity, gas, steam and air conditioning supply	70	0	70
E. Water supply, waste management, control of waste disposal processes and similar activities	60	0	60
F. Construction	4,525	100	4,625
G. Wholesale and retail trade, repair of motor vehicles and motorcycles	1,000	102	1,102
H. Traffic and storage	370	90	460
I. Accommodation and catering services	2,500	2,478	4,978
J. Information and communication	380	20	400
K. Financial and insurance activities	80	0	80
L. Real estate business	90	10	100

572. *Odluka o utvrđivanju godišnjeg broja dozvola za privremeni boravak i rad stranaca za 2020. godinu*, 'Official Gazette of Montenegro', No. 69/2019.

573. *Ibid.*

574. *Ibid.*

Activity	*Employment of Foreigners*	*Seasonal Employment of Foreigners*	*Total*
M. Professional, scientific, innovation and technical activities	320	10	330
N. Administrative and support service activities	123	8	131
O. Public administration and defence, compulsory social security	0	0	0
P. Education	60	0	60
Q. Health and social care	120	0	120
R. Arts, entertainment and recreation	200	40	240
S. Other service activities	1,300	370	1,670
T. Household activity as an employer; the activity of households producing goods and services for their own use	5	2	7
U. Activities of extraterritorial organizations and bodies	1	0	1
TOTAL	**11,824**	**3,630**	**15,454**

Chapter 2. Conditions for Entitlement to Work in the Country as an Employed Person

523. As a general rule, a foreigner may enter the employment contract if he fulfils certain requirements stipulated by the Labor Law, special law and international treaties.[575] In accordance with the special law – Law on Foreign Nationals – a foreigner may work under a temporary residence and work permit or work registration certificate. A foreign national may work in Montenegro only on jobs for which the temporary residence and work permit or work registration certificate was issued to him or her, and only for an employer who employs him or her. The employer may assign the foreign national only to the jobs for which a temporary residence and work permit or work registration certificate was issued to such a foreign national.[576]

524. A foreign national may work in Montenegro without a temporary residence and work permit or work registration certificate, in the cases he or she provides:

- temporary residence permit for family reunification with a Montenegrin national or with a foreign national who holds a permanent residence permit, temporary residence permit for scientific and research work, or temporary residence and work permit for movement of person within a foreign company;
- temporary residence permit for studying;
- temporary residence permit for humanitarian reasons;
- temporary residence permit for a stateless person;
- certificate of registered residence;
- temporary residence permit for a third-country national to whom permanent residence in another Member State of the EU was granted;
- temporary residence permit for family reunification with the holder of the EU Blue Card;
- granted asylum or subsidiary protection or temporary protection.

525. A foreign national who holds a temporary residence permit for family reunification with a foreign national who holds a temporary residence permit for work may work in Montenegro upon the expiry of one year from the issue date of temporary residence permit. The above-mentioned categories of foreign nationals have a free access to the labour market of Montenegro. In business premises or in the place of work of the foreign national, the employer must keep the copies of the temporary residence permit, work registration certificate, or evidence of the granted asylum or subsidiary protection or temporary protection. The employer who employs these foreign nationals is obliged to inform the Ministry of Interior thereof, within eight days from the date of employment or beginning of work of the foreign national or from the employment termination of the foreign national.[577]

575. Article 44 of the Law on Labor.
576. Article 66 of the Law on Foreign Nationals.
577. Article 67 of the Law on Foreign Nationals.

526. A temporary residence and work permit beyond the annual quota may be issued to a foreign national:

- who carries out business activities in Montenegro under an international treaty concluded between Montenegro and other states, under the condition of reciprocity;
- who teaches in the educational institutions in the language and script of the members of minority nations and other national minority communities;
- who is a professional athlete or sports worker who works in Montenegro in accordance with the law governing sports;
- who is an executive director of a company and an entrepreneur who is registered in Montenegro in accordance with the law governing the form of carrying out business activities and their registration;
- who possesses higher education and is employed by the employer at managerial job positions;
- who is temporarily posted as a manager, a specialist or an intern;
- for the purpose of provision of the agreed services;
- with domicile in a neighbouring country, who is employed and works in Montenegro and at least once a week returns to the place of domicile (daily migrant);
- who is included in the implementation of development projects from the list of development projects determined by the Government, upon the proposal of the administration authority in charge of development projects, not later than until 30 November of the current year for the subsequent year.[578]

527. In 2019, the Law on Mediation for Job Placement and Rights during Unemployment[579] has been adopted. This Law stipulates that the following categories of foreign nationals are also considered as unemployed persons:

- a foreign national with permanent residence permit;
- a foreign national with temporary residence permit for a stateless person;
- a foreign national with temporary residence permit for family reunification with a Montenegrin citizen or with a foreigner holding a permanent residence permit;
- a foreign national with a temporary residence permit for humanitarian reasons;
- a foreign national granted asylum, subsidiary protection or seeking international protection, within a period of nine months from the date of application for international protection.

The above-mentioned categories of foreign nationals may be registered in the unemployment records at the Employment Service of Montenegro and exercise their rights during unemployment, in accordance with Law on Mediation in Employment and Rights during Unemployment.

---

578. Article 78 of the Law on Foreign Nationals.

579. *Zakon o posredovanju prilikom zapošljavanaja i prava tokom nezaposlenosti,* 'Official Gazette of Montenegro', No. 24/19.

528. At the bookstore, these categories of foreign nationals have to buy an employment booklet form and two application forms for its issuing that they need to fill in and sign. Also, they have to bring with themselves personal ID and evidence of recognized education degree in Montenegro. After that, they have to go to the municipal authority responsible for labour affairs according to the address of their residence, where they personally submit the documents. They can collect the fulfilled employment booklet the next day. There is no administrative fee for issuing an employment booklet.

529. Also, they can register in the records of unemployed persons of the Employment Agency of Montenegro – Labor Bureau – if they are between 15 and 67 years of age, and capable or partially able to work, and if they are actively seeking employment.

530. As unemployed persons, they have the following possibilities:

- informing about the possibilities and conditions for employment;
- counselling in order to increase employability and employment;
- professional orientation;
- mediation in employment;
- exercising the right to monetary compensation during unemployment in accordance with the law;
- exercising the right to monetary assistance and reimbursement of transportation costs during education and training and inclusion in other measures aimed at increasing employment, i.e., reducing unemployment, in accordance with the law and the act of the state administration body competent for labour affairs.

531. As unemployed persons, they have the following obligations:

- to actively seek employment;
- to be available for work;
- to conclude with the Employment Agency an individual employment plan and carry out the obligations determined by the individual employment plan;
- to participate in active employment policy programmes;
- to accept the offered employment;
- to inform the Employment Agency on every change affecting the obtaining or losing of rights, i.e., obligations according to the law, no later than eight days from the day of the occurrence of the change.

The Employment Agency publishes vacancies on the website http://www.zzzcg.me, and they are also published in daily newspapers on Mondays, Wednesdays and Fridays.

Chapter 3. Sanctions Against Illegal Participation in the Labour Market

§1. Sanctions Against Employers

532. An employer-legal entity shall be punished for misdemeanour with a fine in the amount from EUR 1,000 to EUR 10,000, if:

- a student works longer than fifteen hours a week;
- a foreign national researcher works as a lecturer or professor longer than fifteen hours a week;
- assigns a foreign national jobs for which a temporary residence and work permit, i.e., a work registration certificate, was not issued to him or her;
- it does not keep in business premises or workplace of a foreign national, a copy of the residence and work permit, i.e., a copy of a work registration certificate of a foreign national employed by them;
- it fails to inform the Ministry of Interior of the termination of foreign national's employment prior to the expiry of the residence and work permit validity period, not later than within eight days from the date of termination of foreign national's employment;
- it employs or uses the work of a foreign national who illegally stays in Montenegro;
- it does not keep in business premises, i.e., workplace of a foreign national a copy of a temporary residence permit, a copy of a work registration certificate, i.e., evidence on the granted asylum or subsidiary protection or temporary protection;
- within eight days from the date of employment or beginning of foreign national's work, i.e., the termination of foreign national's employment, it fails to inform the Ministry of Interior thereof;
- within eight days from the date of the issuing of a temporary residence and work permit for employment or seasonal employment, it fails to conclude employment contract with a foreign national and register such a foreign national for compulsory social insurance;
- it fails to notify the Ministry of Interior, not later than within three days, that a foreign national has not started working, for the purpose of annulment of the residence and work permit;
- it fails to submit the work registration certificate to the Ministry of Interior, prior to the beginning of work of a foreign national;
- it employs the EU Blue Card holder on the jobs for which the EU Blue Card was not issued;
- it does not keep the copy of the EU Blue Card in the business premises, i.e., workplace of a foreign national;
- it fails to inform the Ministry of Interior in the event of termination of the employment contract and other conditions based on which the EU Blue Card was issued, not later than within eight days from the date of occurrence of such circumstances.

For the above-mentioned misdemeanour, a person responsible for the legal entity shall also be punished with a fine in the amount from EUR 300 to EUR 2,000.

For the above-mentioned misdemeanour, an entrepreneur shall be punished by a fine in the amount from EUR 300 to EUR 6,000.

For the above-mentioned misdemeanour, a protective measure of the prohibition of performing the business activity may also be pronounced in the duration of up to six months.[580]

533. According to the data of the Inspection Directorate, in 2018, 637 controls were carried out, 546 employers were fined, 1,260 measures were taken, of which 210 recommendations and 1,050 misdemeanour orders were issued (for legal entity – 427, for responsible person in legal entity – 479, for the entrepreneur – 144). The amount of fines imposed on misdemeanour warrants was EUR 613,900,00. During 2019, a total of 743 controls were carried out, 738 violations were established, 215 recommendations were issued, 1 decision on elimination of irregularities was issued, 1,221 misdemeanour orders were issued, EUR 716,700,00 of fines were issued in 690 companies. Employment is legalized for 206 foreign nationals.[581]

534. The criminal offence 'Unlawful Employment' was introduced in the Criminal Code of Montenegro in 2013. According to the Criminal Code, anyone who employs a foreign national who is not a national of a Member State of the EU and does not enjoy the right to freedom of movement in the EU, and who unlawfully resides in the territory of Montenegro, under conditions of work which they are exploiting or knowing that they are victims of trafficking in human beings or younger than 18 years for a longer period of time, or re-employs them or at the same time employ those persons in a larger number, shall be punished by a prison term from six months up to five years.[582]

§2. Sanctions Against Workers

535. A foreign national shall be punished for the misdemeanour with a fine in the amount from EUR 200 to EUR 1,200 if:

- a foreign student works longer than fifteen hours a week;
- a foreign national researcher works as a lecturer or professor longer than fifteen hours a week;
- he or she does not work pursuant to a temporary residence and work permit or work registration certificate;

580. Article 210 of the Law on Foreign Nationals.
581. Government of Montenegro, *Report on the Implementation of the Action Plan for the Implementation of the Strategy for Integrated Migration Management for 2019* (Podgorica 2020).
582. Article 225a of the Criminal Code of Montenegro.

- he or she does not work in Montenegro on the jobs for which temporary residence and work permit or the work registration certificate has been issued to him or her and for the employer who employs him or her.[583]

536. An EU Blue Card holder shall be punished for the offence with a fine in the amount from EUR 200 to EUR 1,200 if:

- he or she works on the jobs for which he has not been issued the EU Blue Card or works for an employer by whom he or she has not been employed;
- he or she has failed to notify the Ministry of Interior in the event of termination of the employment contract or other conditions based on which the EU Blue Card was issued;
- he or she has failed to file the application for the extension of the EU Blue Card, not later than within thirty days prior to the expiry of the EU Blue Card validity period;
- upon the expiry of the period of two years, he or she fails to notify the Ministry of Interior of the change of employer within eight days from the date of the change of employer.[584]

537. If the police or labour inspection establishes that a foreign national carries out business activities for which he/she does not have the temporary residence and work permit or a foreign national does not use his/her residence in Montenegro for the purpose for which the residence was granted to him/her, the sanction shall be annulment of his/her residence and work permit.

583. Article 213 of the Law on Foreign Nationals.
584. Article 215 of the Law on Foreign Nationals.

Chapter 4. Legal Remedies and Procedural Safeguards

538. The Police are in charge of control of the movement, work and stay of foreigners, while the Inspection Directorate (labour inspection) controls the work of business entities and employees, that is, whether they operate in accordance with the laws and regulations. Pursuant to the Decree on the Organization and Functioning of the State Administration, the Directorate for Inspection Affairs is an independent administrative authority integrating all types of inspection services, including labour inspection of both nationals and foreigners. Inspection supervision is an administrative function that includes supervision over the application of laws and other regulations, i.e., oversight of legality, and less frequently of effectiveness.[585]

539. In case of a misdemeanour, foreign nationals are being prosecuted as follows: the Police issue a misdemeanour order to the foreign national due to the violation of the Law on Misdemeanors.[586] A foreign national has the option to pay a fine within the eight-day period prescribed by the order for the initiation of the misdemeanour proceeding. If a foreign national does not pay a fine at this stage, the proceeding will be initiated before the competent misdemeanour court. If the fine is sentenced during that proceeding and the foreign national is not able to pay it, a fine will be replaced with the imprisonment sentence, for a certain period of time. Also, a misdemeanour judge may, in accordance with the Law on Misdemeanors, order a deportation from the territory of Montenegro for up to one year.

540. Pursuant to the Law on Inspection Supervision,[587] in case the inspector of the Inspection Directorate finds any irregularity in the work of the subject of supervision, he/she is authorized to:

- point out the identified irregularities and set a deadline for their elimination;
- order appropriate measures and actions to be taken within the time limit he/she specified;
- temporarily prohibit the activity of the subject of supervision;
- impose fines, in accordance with the law and other regulations;
- issue a misdemeanour warrant;
- file criminal or other appropriate charges;
- exercise other powers and obligations in accordance with the regulations.

An authorized inspector may file a request for misdemeanour proceedings.[588]

585. Đorđe Blažić, *Inspekcije* (Udruženje pravnika, Podgorica 2000), p. 269.
586. *Zakon o prekršajima,* 'Official Gazette of Montenegro', Nos 01/2011, 06/2011, 39/2011, 32/2014, 43/2017, 51/2017.
587. *Zakon o inspekcijskom nadzoru*, 'Official Gazette of Montenegro', Nos 76/2009, 57/2011, 18/2014, 11/2015, 52/2016.
588. Article 15 of the Law on Inspection Supervision.

541. An appeal may be lodged against the inspector's decision within eight days from the day the decision was served. The ministry responsible for the administrative area to which the decision relates shall decide upon appeal. The appeal shall not postpone the Decision enforcement.[589]

542. Exceptionally, the execution of the decision may be postponed until the decision on appeal is taken, if the nature of the relationship permits it, if the delay does not contravene the public interest and if the execution of the decision would cause damage to the subject of supervision. The request to postpone enforcement has to be stated in the appeal. The inspector shall decide on the request within three days from the day the appeal is submitted.[590]

543. The subject of supervision is obliged to execute the decision within the deadline specified in the decision. If the supervised entity fails to execute the decision within the time limit set for voluntary enforcement, administrative execution of the decision shall be initiated. The inspector shall inform the subject of the time and manner of administrative execution. The inspector monitors and/or ensures the implementation of the measures ordered.[591]

544. The inspector's decision shall be administered through other persons, by a fine or by direct coercion. In the process of administrative enforcement, the inspector will evaluate how the target and purpose of enforcement can be achieved in the easiest way for the supervised entity.[592]

545. An administrative dispute may be brought against a decision rendered in the second-instance and against a first-instance decision against which no appeal is allowed in administrative proceedings. An administrative dispute may also be initiated when a public-law body has not issued a decision, that is, has not decided on a party's complaint or failed to take an administrative activity – the so-called silence of the administration. The decision may be contested for violation of the rules of procedure, wrong and incompletely established facts, and incorrect application of substantive law. The lawsuit may be lodged to the Administrative Court within twenty days from the date of receipt of the decision.

589. Article 40 of the Law on Inspection Supervision.
590. Article 41 of the Law on Inspection Supervision.
591. Article 56 of the Law on Inspection Supervision.
592. Article 57 of the Law on Inspection Supervision.

Part VIII. Access to Self-Employed Activities

Chapter 1. Overview of Applicable Legislation

546. Montenegrin legislation vaguely recognizes the term 'Self-employed Activities', as well as the term 'Self-employed worker', and therefore does not specifically regulate self-employment of foreigners. The only exception is the Law on Pension and Disability Insurance,[593] which in the light of this law recognizes the term of persons performing an independent activity, which means persons who independently perform economic or other activity, persons who perform work on the basis of employment contract, i.e., work on the basis of service contracts, as well as jobs on the basis of other contracts, priests, religious officials, monks, provided that all of them are not compulsorily insured on another basis.[594]

547. The Law on Foreign Nationals does not recognize the term 'self-employed worker', but it does recognize the terms 'entrepreneurs' and 'executive directors' in companies in which they are the sole owners or owners of more than 51% of capital, prescribing for them sometimes different conditions from employed persons and it may be concluded that this category could include persons who perform economic activity as entrepreneurs and executive directors in companies in which they are the sole owners or majority owners of capital, which are established and registered in accordance with the Law on Business Organizations, as well as persons who perform professional activity such as lawyers, public enforcement officers and others in accordance with special laws. In the light of the above, the Law on Foreign Nationals prescribes that an entrepreneur and executive director of a company in which he is the sole or majority owner, unlike persons employed by another employer, do not have to submit a written employment offer from the employer

593. *Zakon o penzijskom i invalidskom osiguranju*, 'Official Gazette of the Republic of Montenegro', Nos 054/03 of 29.9.2003, 039/04 of 9.6.2004, 061/04 of 7.10.2004, 079/04 of 23.12.2004, 081/04 of 30.12.2004, 029/05 of 9.5.2005, 014/07 of 12.3.2007, 047/07 of 7.8.2007, 'Official Gazette of Montenegro', Nos 012/07 of 14.12.2007, 013/07 of 18.12.2007, 079/08 of 23.12.2008, 014/10 of 17.3.2010, 078/10 of 29.12.2010, 034/11 of 12.7.2011, 039/11 of 4.8.2011, 040/11 of 8.8.2011, 066/12 of 31.12.2012, 036/13 of 26.7.2013, 038/13 of 2.8.2013, 061/13 of 30.12.2013, 006/14 of 4.2.2014, 060/14 of 31.12.2014, 060/14 of 31.12.2014, 010/15 of 10.3.2015, 044/15 of 7.8.2015, 042/16 of 11.7.2016, 055/16 of 17.8.2016.

594. Article 11 of the Law on Pension and Disability Insurance.

when applying for a temporary residence and work permit, as well as that they can be issued a temporary residence and work permit even after completing the age of 67.[595]

548. The Labor Law also does not recognize the term 'self-employed worker', but prescribes that it also applies to physical persons engaged in economic activity for the purpose of generating profit, and not performing that activity on behalf of another,[596] which would include entrepreneurs within the meaning of the Law on Business Organizations. Moreover, it is important to emphasize that the Labor Law also applies to employed foreigners who work for an employer in the territory of Montenegro, unless otherwise prescribed by the Law on Foreign Nationals.[597]

549. The Law on Business Organizations[598] stipulates that an entrepreneur shall mean any physical person engaged in economic activity in Montenegro for the purpose of gaining profit, and who does not perform that activity on behalf of another.[599] Moreover, a person who performs the activity of an independent profession regulated by special regulations shall be considered an entrepreneur under this law if these regulations regulate it that way.[600] An entrepreneur shall not be obliged to register, unless he performs the activity under someone else's name. The entrepreneur shall register by submitting the registration statements to the Central Registry of the Commercial Court, on the basis of which he is issued a certificate of registration. In addition to entrepreneurs, foreigners in Montenegro, as self-employed persons, can also perform economic activity through the establishment of their own companies, primarily limited liability companies and joint-stock companies.

595. Article 69 of the Law on Foreign Nationals.
596. Article 2 of the Labor Law.
597. *Ibid.*
598. *Zakon o privrednim društvima*, 'Official Gazette of Montenegro', No. 006/02 of 8.2.2002, 'Official Gazette of Montenegro', Nos 017/07 of 31.12.2007, 080/08 of 26.12.2008, 040/10 of 22.7.2010, 036/11 of 27.7.2011, 040/11 of 8.8.2011.
599. Article 5 of the Law on Business Organizations.
600. *Ibid.*

Chapter 2. Condition for Entitlement to Work in the Country as Self-Employed

§1. General Conditions

550. When it comes to self-employment of foreigners in Montenegro, it is important to emphasize that this issue has been regulated by the same legal sources that regulate the general employment of foreigners with another employer, and therefore, Montenegrin legislation does not contain significantly different or discriminatory provisions when it comes to the right of foreign physical persons and legal entities to establish companies in Montenegro and perform economic activity in comparison with the rights and obligations of national citizens. The only difference when founding a company would be proving the identity of the founders of foreigners (for individuals, photocopies of passports, and for foreign legal entities, an excerpt from the register of the country in which they are registered). Therefore, there are no special requirements, different from the general conditions, language and citizenship of the founders prescribed by the founding act of the company, which can affect and limit the right of foreigners to establish 'self-employed companies' in Montenegro.

§2. Administrative Rules and Procedures

551. A foreigner may establish a company in Montenegro under the same conditions as nationals and has the right to be employed in it. He or she can be the only employee in it when he/she performs the work of the executive director (single-owner companies), and he/she can also be one of the employees in his/her company. Under the Law on Business Organizations, a foreigner can independently perform economic activity in Montenegro as an entrepreneur, and also as the sole or majority owner (more than 51%) of a limited liability company or joint-stock company.

552. A limited liability company may be formed by physical persons and legal entities who shall make a monetary or non-monetary contribution in the company for the purpose of generating gain, and its founders shall be liable for the obligations of the limited liability company to the amount of their contributions. The contributions shall constitute the limited liability company's initial capital.[601] The amount of the minimum initial capital is EUR 100, and the company must limit the maximum number of its members to thirty. A limited liability company may have a sole member when it is formed and also when all its parts are acquired by a single person. The sole member of the company shall have the powers of the general meeting of the company, and the decisions taken by the sole member shall be recorded

601. Article 77 of the Law on Business Organizations.

in the books of the company. The liability of a single-member company shall be limited to the amount of contribution in the company and he shall perform the duty of the executive director.[602]

553. A joint-stock company shall mean a company made of physical persons or legal entities formed for the purpose of conducting economic activity, and the ownership of which is represented by shares. The founders of a joint-stock company shall be physical persons or legal entities who have executed the company foundation agreement in accordance with the provisions of this Law. Founders may be domestic and foreign physical persons or legal entities. By executing the foundation agreement of a joint-stock company, the founders shall become the shareholders. The minimum initial capital of a joint-stock company shall be EUR 25,000. A single-member–joint-stock company shall mean a joint-stock company established by a single shareholder, i.e., when all shares upon the establishment are acquired by one physical person or legal entities.[603] A shareholder of a single-member–joint-stock company shall have the authorizations of the general meeting of shareholders of the company and shall make all decisions in a written form. Decisions shall be entered in the book of decisions of the company in a chronological order.[604]

554. Unlike entrepreneurs, limited liability companies and joint-stock companies are obliged to register by submitting an application to the Central Register of Commercial Entities. Along with the application, the companies are obliged to submit all the necessary documentation required by the Law on Business Organizations for nationals (memorandum and articles of associations or contract, statute, rulebooks, name, company's seat, names and surnames of the founders, board members, etc.), provided however that if the founders are foreigners, they must submit a photocopy of the passport instead of the ID card, whereas foreign legal entities must submit an excerpt from the register of the country in which they are registered.

555. The procedure under which a self-employed foreigner applies for and obtains temporary work and residence permits is almost identical to the procedure under which a foreigner employed with another employer does so and is described in Part V Chapters 1–4 and Part VII. In the light of the above, in order to obtain a temporary residence and work permit, a foreigner who is self-employed (entrepreneur or executive director in his own company) must meet all the conditions required for employment of foreigners with another employer, except instead of a written offer of employment, a foreigner must submit proof of ownership and registration.[605] Unlike foreigners employed by another employer, self-employed foreigners can obtain a temporary residence and work permit even after 67 years of age. Specifically, in accordance with the Labor Law, the employment of every

602. *Ibid.*
603. Article 18a of the Law on Business Organizations.
604. *Ibid.*
605. Article 69 of the Law on Foreign Nationals.

employee, even an employed foreigner in Montenegro, ends at the age of 67. However, when it comes to self-employed foreigners, they can work after the age of 67, so they can be issued a temporary residence and work permit.[606] Moreover, unlike foreigners employed by another employer, self-employed foreigners holding a temporary residence and work permit can be extended for a period longer than two years, as long as they meet the conditions for issuing a permit under Article 43 of the Law on Foreign Nationals. It is important to emphasize that self-employed foreigners – entrepreneurs and the executive director of a company – are issued a temporary residence and work permit outside the annual quota for the work of foreigners.

556. An application for residence registration for the purpose of work or entrepreneurial activity a national of an EU Member State shall personally submit to the Ministry of Interior, in the place of his/her residence, on a prescribed form, which he/she received from the Ministry of Interior.[607] In addition to the application, the national of an EU Member State shall submit a valid travel document or personal identity card issued by the competent authority of such state, as well as the evidence that he or she has been registered as an entrepreneur.

---

606. *Ibid.*
607. Article 153 of the Law on Foreign Nationals.

Chapter 3. Sanctions Against Illegal Exercise of Self-Employment

557. Sanctions against illegal exercise of self-employment are the same which are applicable to violation of law on employment of foreigners in general (*See* Chapter 7). Thus, the Law on Foreign Nationals prescribes that a monetary fine shall be imposed on legal entity ranging from EUR 300 to EUR 600 for violation of provisions of this Law related to work without prior solving the residence status and the work permit.[608]

558. The Labor Law stipulates that a monetary fine ranging from EUR 1,000 to EUR 10,000 shall be imposed on any legal entity (national and foreign), or EUR 500 to EUR 5,000 on an entrepreneur who fails to protect the rights of employees from various forms of discrimination.[609] These are the following forms of discrimination, which are prohibited to the national and foreign persons:

- Article 7 of the Labor Law (direct and indirect discrimination against job seekers and employees shall be prohibited, with regard to race, colour, nationality, social or ethnic origin, affiliation to a minority people or minority national community, language, religion or belief, political or other opinions, gender, change of gender, gender identity, sexual orientation, health status, disability, age, property, marital or family status, pregnancy, affiliation to a group or assumption of affiliation to a group, a political party, trade union or another organization, or some other personal trait).
- Article 9 of the Labor Law (discrimination shall be prohibited as regards: terms and conditions of employment and the selection of candidates to perform a particular job; working conditions and employment rights; education, training and development; promotion at work and the termination of contracts of employment). The provisions of the contracts of employment determining discrimination on any of the above grounds shall be considered null and void.
- Article 10 of the Labor Law (harassment and sexual harassment at work and in connection with work shall be prohibited; as well as in relation to training, education and capacity building; promotion at work; employment conditions; termination of employment or other issues arising from employment).
- Article 12 of the Labor Law (discrimination is prohibited in relation to access to all types and levels of professional orientation, professional training and professional development and retraining, including practical work experience).
- Article 13 of the Labor Law (discrimination against membership in organizations of employees and employers is prohibited; in relation to membership and participation in organizations of employees or employers or any organization that brings together members of a particular profession, including benefits provided by those organizations).

608. Article 210 of the Law on Foreign Nationals.
609. Article 209 of the Labor Law.

Chapter 4. Legal Remedies and Procedural Safeguards

559. There are no specific legal remedies and procedural safeguards relating to the legal status of self-employed aliens that are different from those regarding employment of aliens in general (*see* Part V, Chapters 1–4 and Part VII).

Selected Bibliography

Books and Articles

Blažić, Đ. *Inspections.* Association of Lawyers, Podgorica, 2000.

Dimitrijević, D. *Regulation of Citizenship in the Former SFR Yugoslavia.* International Problems LX, No. 2-3. Belgrade, 2008.

Fassmann, H. & Miinz R. *East-West Migration in Europe from 1918-92.* Migration Themes 11, 1995.

Friganović M. *Migration as a Constant of Geospace.* Papers, Vol. 24, 19–30, Zagreb, 1989.

Grečić, V., Vekarić, V. & Todić, D. *Serbia. Migration Law.* Wolters Kluwer Law, The Netherlands, 2016.

Đonović, J. *Constitutional and Political Struggles in Montenegro 1905-1910.* Belgrade, 1939.

Goldner Lang, I. *Freedom of Movement of People in the EU, the Context of the Association Agreement.* Školska kniga, Zagreb, 2007.

Ivanović, S. *Commentary on the Law on Administrative Procedure.* Official Gazette of Montenegro, Podgorica, 2015.

Kreća, M. *International Public Law.* Eight Edition, Faculty of Law, University of Belgrade, Belgrade, 2016.

Lakočević*, B. Protection of the Right to a Trial Within a Reasonable Time.* Judges' Days, Association of Judges of Montenegro, Budva, 2018.

Lekić, B. *Contributions to the Knowledge of Settlements and Settlements of Vojvodina.* Matica srpska. Novi Sad, 1974.

Lilić, S. & Cerović, D. *Administrative Procedure Law.* Faculty of Law, University of Montenegro, Posgorica, 2013.

Matica 1. *Montenegrin Emigrants.* Vol. I. Republic Secretariat for Information of Montenegro, Podgorica – Cetinje, 1997.

Medojević, S. *Colonization of Montenegrins in Vojvodina 1945-46.* Montenegrin matica, Cetinje, 2010.

Miljić, M. *Montenegrin Emigration Through History.* Diaspora Administration of Montenegro, http://www.dijaspora.mvpei.gov.me/O_nama/Istorija_crnogorskih_i seljavanja (accessed 1 November 2019).

Selected Bibliography

Pejin-Stokić, L.J. & V. Grečić. *Social Impact of Emigration and Rural-Urban Migration in Central and Eastern Europe*. Final Country Report – Serbia, Brussels: The European Commission, DG Employment, Social Affairs and Inclusion and GVG, 2012, available at, http://ec.europa.eu/social/BlobServlet?docId=8824&langId=en.

Rastoder, Š. *Montenegrin Emigrants in Turkey, Damages and Claims after World War I*. Matica 1, Cetinje, 2000.

Stojanović, Z. *Commentary on the Criminal Code of Montenegro*. OSCE Mission to Montenegro, Podgorica, 2010.

Stojović, G. *Montenegrin Emigrants in the New World*. Montenegrin Matica, Podgorica 2016.

Škulić, M. *Commentary on the Criminal Procedure Code*. OSCE Mission to Montenegro, Podgorica, 2009.

Vukčević, M. *Internal Market of the EU & Four Freedoms*. TRIM MNE – EU Approximation in Trade and Single Market Policies, Podgorica, 2009.

Vukčević, M. *Judicial Protection in the EU*. Faculty of Law, Mediterranean University, Podgorica, 2015.

National Legislation

Amendments I to XVI to the Constitution of Montenegro (*Amandmani I do XVI na Ustav Crne Gore*), 'Official Gazette of MNE', No. 038/13 of 2.8.2013.

Constitution of Montenegro (*Ustav Crne Gore*), 'Official Gazette of Montenegro', Nos 001/07 of 25.10.2007, 038/13 of 2.8.2013.

Constitution of the Federal Republic of Yugoslavia (*Ustav Savezne Republike Jugoslavije*), 'Official Gazette of the Federal Republic of Yugoslavia', No. 1/1992.

Criminal Code of Montenegro (*Krivični zakonik Crne Gore*), 'Official Gazette of the Republic of Montenegro', Nos 070/03 of 25.12.2003, 013/04 of 26.2.2004, 047/06 of 25.7.2006, 'Official Gazette of Montenegro', Nos 040/08 of 27.6.2008, 025/10 of 5.5.2010, 073/10 of 10.12.2010, 032/11 of 1.7.2011, 064/11 of 29.12.2011, 040/13 of 13.8.2013, 056/13 of 6.12.2013, 014/15 of 26.3.2015, 042/15 of 29.7.2015, 058/15 of 9.10.2015, 044/17 of 6.7.2017, 049/18 of 17.7.2018, 003/20 of 23.1.2020.

Decision on determining the annual number of permits for temporary residence and work of foreigners in 2020 (*Odluka o utvrđivanju godišnjeg broja dozvola za privremeni boravak i rad stranaca za 2020. godinu*), 'Official Gazette of Montenegro', No. 069/19 of 18.12.2019.

Decision on the criteria, manner and procedure for selection of persons who can acquire Montenegrin citizenship by admission for the purpose of implementation of a special investment programme of special importance for the business and economic Interest of Montenegro (*Odluka o kriterijumima, načinu i postupku izbora lica koje može steći crnogorsko državljanstvo prijemom radi realizacije posebnog programa ulaganja od posebnog značaja za privredni i ekonomski interes Crne Gore*), 'Official Gazette of Montenegro', Nos 079/18 of 7.12.2018, 012/20 of 11.3.2020.

Decree on the amount of financial assistance to a foreigner seeking international protection and to an asylum seeker and a foreigner under subsidiary protection (*Uredba o visini novčane pomoći strancu koji traži međunarodnu zaštitu i azilantu i strancu pod subsdijarnom zaštitom*), 'Official Gazette of Montenegro', No. 028/18 of 27.4.2018.

Decree on the criteria and procedure for determining the annual number of permits for temporary residence and work of foreigners (*Uredba o kriterijumima i postupku zautvrđivanje godišnjeg broja dozvola za privremeni boravak i rad stranaca*), 'Official Gazette of Montenegro', No. 020/19 of 4.4.2019.

Decree on the Organization and Functioning of the State Administration (Uredba o organizaciji i nadležnosti državne uprave), 'Official Gazette of Montenegro', Nos 087/18 from 31.12.2018, 002/19 from 11.1.2019, 038/19 of 5.7.2019.

Law on the Movement and Stay of Foreigners (*Zakon o kretanju i boravku stranaca*), 'Official Gazette of the SFRY', Nos 056/80 of 3.10.1980, 053/85 of 4.10.1985, 030/89 of 16.5.1989, 026/90 of 18.5.1990, 053/91 of 12.7.1991, 'Official Gazette of the SRY', Nos 024/94 of 18.4.1994, 028/96 of 21.6.1996, 068/02 of 19.12.2002, 'Official Gazette of Serbia and Montenegro', No. 012/05 of 25.3.2005.

Law on crossing the state border and moving within the border zone (*Zakon o prelaženju državne granice i kretanju u graničnom pojasu*), 'Official Gazette of the SFRY', Nos 34/1979, 56/1980 and 53/1985.

Law on conditions for the establishment of employment relationship with foreign nationals (*Zakon o uslovima za zasnivanje radnog odnosa sa stranim državljanima*), 'Official Gazette of the SFRY', Nos 11/1978, 64/1989, 42/1992, 24/1994 and 28/1996.

Law on Yugoslav Citizenship (Zakon o jugoslovenskom državljanstvu), 'Official Gazette of the SRY', Nos 33/1996, 9/2001.

Law on Travel Documents of Yugoslav Nationals (*Zakon o putnim ispravama jugoslovenskih državljana*), 'Official Gazette of the SRY', Nos 033/96 of 19.7.1996, 049/96 of 25.10.1996, 012/98 of 6.3.1998, 044/99 of 25.6.1999, 015/00 of 7.4.2000, 007/01 of 16.2.2001, 071/01 of 28.12.2001, 023/02 of 27.4.2002, 053/02 of 27.9.2002, 068/02 of 19.12.2002, 005/03 of 25.1.2003.

Law on Asylum (Zakon o azilu), 'Official Gazette of SaM', No. 012/05.

Law on International and Temporary Protection of Foreigners (*Zakon o međunarodnoj i privremenoj zaštiti stranaca*), 'Official Gazette of Montenegro', Nos 002/17 of 10.1.2017, 003/19 of 15.1.2019.

Law on Foreign Nationals (*Zakon o strancima*), 'Official Gazette of Montenegro', Nos 082/08 of 31.12.2008, 072/09 of 30.10.2009, 032/11 of 1.7.2011, 053/11 of 11.11.2011, 027/13 of 11.6.2013, 061/13 of 30.12.2013, 56/14.

Law on employment and work of foreigners (*Zakon o zapošljavanju i radu stranaca*), 'Official Gazette of Montenegro', Nos 22/08 and 32/11.

Law on Montenegrin Citizenship (*Zakon o crnogorskom državljanstvu*), 'Official Gazette of Montenegro', Nos 013/08 of 26.2.2008, 040/10 of 22.7.2010, 028/11 of 10.6.2011, 046/11 of 16.9.2011, 020/14 of 25.4.2014, 054/16 of 15.8.2016, 073/19 of 27.12.2019.

Law on Border Control (*Zakon o graničnoj kontroli*), 'Official Gazette of Montenegro', Nos 072/09 from 30.10.2009, 020/11 of 15.4.2011, 040/11 of 8.8.2011, 039/13 of 7.8.2013, 017/19 of 19.3.2019.

Law on Public Administration (*Zakon o državnoj upravi*), 'Official Gazette of Montenegro', No. 078/18 of 4.12.2018.

Selected Bibliography

Law on Constitutional Court of Montenegro (*Zakon o Ustavnom sudu Crne Gore*), 'Official Gazette of Montenegro', Nos 011/15 of 12.3.2015, 055/19 of 27.9.2019.

Law on the Protector of Human Rights and Freedoms (*Zakon o zaštitniku ljudskih prava i sloboda*), 'Official Gazette of Montenegro', Nos 042/11 of 15.8.2011, 032/14 of 30.7.2014, 021/17 of 31.3.2017.

Law on Border Control (*Zakon o graničnoj kontroli*), 'Official Gazette of Montenegro', Nos 072/09 of 30.10.2009, 020/11 of 15.4.2011, 040/11 of 8.8.2011, 039/13 of 7.8.2013, 017/19 of 19.3.2019.

Law on Social and Child Protection (*Zakon o socijalnoj i dječijoj zaštiti*), 'Official Gazette of Montenegro', Nos 27/13, 01/15, 42/15, 47/15, 56/16, 66/16, 01/17, 31/17, 42/17, 50/17.

Rulebook on the method of issuing and the form of permanent residence permit (*Pravilnik o načinu izdavanja i obrascu dozvole za stalni boravak*), 'Official Gazette of Montenegro', No. 20/2019.

Law on Health Insurance (*Zakon o zdrastvenoj zaštiti*), 'Official Gazette of Montenegro', Nos 06/16, 02/17.

Law on Montenegrin Citizenship (*Zakon o crnogorskom državljanstvu*), 'Official Gazette of Montenegro', Nos 13/2008, 40/2010, 28/2011, 46/2011, 20/2014, 54/2016.

Law on international and temporary protection of foreigners (*Zakon o međunarodnoj i privremenoj zaštiti stranaca*), 'Official Gazette of Montenegro', Nos 2/2017, 3/2019.

Law on Courts (*Zakon o sudovima*), 'Official Gazette of Montenegro', No. 011/15 of 12.3.2015.

Law on Administrative Proceedings (*Zakon o upravnom postupku*), 'Official Gazette of Montenegro', Nos 056/14 of 24.12.2014, 020/15 of 24.4.2015, 040/16 of 30.6.2016, 037/17 of 14.6.2017.

Law on Misdemeanors (*Zakon o prekršajima*), 'Official Gazette of Montenegro', Nos 001/11 of 11.1.2011, 006/11 of 25.1.2011, 039/11 of 4.8.2011, 032/14 of 30.7.2014, 043/17 of 4.7.2017, 051/17 of 3.8.2017.

Law on Administrative Disputes (*Zakon o upravnom sporu*), 'Official Gazette of Montenegro', No. 054/16 of 15.8.2016.

Law on Civil Servants and State Employees (*Zakon o državnim službenicima i namještenicima*), 'Official Gazette of Montenegro', Nos 002/18 of 10.1.2018, 034/19 of 21.6.2019.

Law on Mediation for Job Placement and Rights During Unemployment (*Zakon o posredovanju pri zapošljavanju i pravima za vrijeme nezaposlenosti*), 'Official Gazette of Montenegro', No. 24/19.

Law on Inspection Supervision (*Zakon o inspekcijskom nadzoru*), 'Official Gazette of Montenegro', Nos 76/2009, 57/2011, 18/2014, 11/2015, 52/2016.

Law on Pension and Disability Insurance (*Zakona o penzijskom i invalidskom osiguranju*), 'Official Gazette of the Republic of Montenegro', Nos 054/03 of 29.9.2003, 039/04 of 9.6.2004, 061/04 of 7.10.2004, 079/04 of 23.12.2004, 081/04 of 30.12.2004, 029/05 of 9.5.2005, 014/07 of 12.3.2007, 047/07 of 7.8.2007, 'Official Gazette of Montenegro', Nos 012/07 of 14.12.2007, 013/07 of 18.12.2007, 079/08 of 23.12.2008, 014/10 of 17.3.2010, 078/10 of 29.12.2010, 034/11 of 12.7.2011, 039/11 of 4.8.2011, 040/11 of 8.8.2011, 066/12 of

31.12.2012, 036/13 of 26.7.2013, 038/13 of 2.8.2013, 061/13 of 30.12.2013, 006/14 of 4.2.2014, 060/14 of 31.12.2014, 060/14 of 31.12.2014, 010/15 of 10.3.2015, 044/15 of 7.8.2015, 042/16 of 11.7.2016, 055/16 of 17.8.2016.

Law on Business Organizations (*Zakon o privrednim društvima),* 'Službeni list Republike Crne Gore', No. 006/02 of 8.2.2002, 'Official Gazette of Montenegro', Nos 017/07 of 31.12.2007, 080/08 of 26.12.2008, 040/10 of 22.7.2010, 036/11 of 27.7.2011, 040/11 of 8.8.2011.

Labor Law (*Zakona o radu*), 'Official Gazette of Montenegro', No. 074/19 of 30.12.2019.

Organic Law on registration of permanent and temporary residence and residence of citizens (*Osnovni zakon o evidenciji prebivališta i boravišta građana*), 'Official Gazette of the SFRY', Nos 008/65, 029/71.

Rulebook on more detailed manner and procedure of forced removal of foreigners (*Pravilnik o bližem načinu i postupku prinudnog udaljenja stranca*), 'Official Gazette of Montenegro', No. 043/18 of 3.7.2018.

Rulebook on more detailed manner and implementation of the special protection procedure for juvenile foreigners in ensuring the implementation of return measure (*Pravilnik o bližem načinu i sprovođenju postupka posebne zaštite maloljetnih stranaca prilikom obezbjeđenja primjene mjera za povratak*), 'Official Gazette of Montenegro', No. 073/18 of 19.11.2018.

Rulebook on more detailed manner of submitting the application and cancellation of the residence of foreigners through a tourist organization, or a competent local government authority (*Pravilnik o bližem načinu podnošenja prijave i odjave boravka stranaca preko turističke organizacije, odnosno nadležnog organa lokalne uprave*), 'Official Gazette of Montenegro', No. 070/18 of 31.10.2018.

Rulebook on the layout and content of the form and the manner of issuing documents for foreigners who have applied for international protection, asylum seekers and foreigners under subsidiary protection (*Pravilnik o bližem načinu uzimanja otisaka prstiju i fotografije od stranca koji izražava namjeru za podnošenje zahtjeva za međunarodnu zaštitu),* 'Official Gazette of Montenegro', No. 072/17 of 1.11.2017.

Rulebook on the conditions of accommodation and the manner of providing accommodation for asylum seekers and foreigners under subsidiary protection *(Pravilnik o uslovima smještaja i načinu obezbjeđivanja smještaja azilanata i stranaca pod supsdijarnom zaštitom),* 'Official Gazette of Montenegro', No. 087/17 of 22.12.2017.

Rulebook on determining the list of safe countries of origin of foreigners seeking international protection (*Pravilnik o utvrđivanju liste sigurnih zemalja porjekla stranaca koji traže međunarodnu zaštitu*), 'Official Gazette of Montenegro', No. 069/19 of 18.12.2019.

Rulebook on more detailed conditions and manner of issuing a temporary residence permit for conducting scientific research work (Pravilnik o bližim uslovima i načinu izdavanja dozvole za privremeni boravak radi naučno istraživačkog rada), 'Official Gazette of Montenegro', No. 073/18 of 19.11.2018.

Rulebook on more detailed conditions and manner of issuing a temporary residence permit for participation in international student fellowship and student exchange programmes or other youth programmes (*Pravilnik o bližim uslovima i načinu izdavanja dozvole za privremeni boravak radi učestvovanja u programima međunarodne razmjene učenika i studenata ili drugim programima mladih*), 'Official Gazette of the Montenegro', No. 077/18 of 30.11.2018.

Rulebook on more detailed conditions for issuing a work registration certificate of foreigners and application forms for registering work and the certificate on registration of work of foreigners (*Pravilnik o bližim uslovima za izdavanje potvrde o prijavi rada stranaca i obrascima prijave rada i potvrde o prijavi rada stranaca*), 'Official Gazette of Montenegro', No. 043/18 of 3.7.2018.

Rulebook on the voluntary departure of foreigners (*Pravilnik o dobrovoljnom odlasku stranaca*), 'Official Gazette of the Montenegro', No. 068/18 of 19.10.2018.

Rulebook on the manner of issuing and the form of a permanent residence permit (*Pravilnik o načinu izdavanja i obrascu dozvole za stalni boravak*), 'Official Gazette of Montenegro', No. 020/19 of 4.4.2019.

Rulebook on the rules of stay and house rules at the Foreigners Reception Center (*Pravilnik o pravilima boravka i kućnom redu u Prihvatilištu za strance*), 'Official Gazette of Montenegro', Nos 061/17 of 2.10.2017, 040/19 of 19.7.2019.

Rulebook on implementation of the procedure on the application for determining whether the applicant is a stateless person (*Pravilnik o sprovođenju postupka po zahtjevu za utvrđivanje da je podnosilac zahtjeva lice bez državljanstva*), 'Official Gazette of Montenegro', No. 072/18 of 13.11.2018.

Rulebook on organization and systematization of employees posts in the Ministry of Interior (*Pravilnik o organizaciji i sistematizaciji radnih mjesta MUP-a*), Ministry of Interior, www.mup.gov.me.

Rulebook on the manner of carrying out certain police tasks and the exercise of powers in carrying out these tasks (*Pravilnik o načinu obavljanja određenih policijskih poslova iprimjeni ovlašćenja u obavljanju tih poslova*), 'Official Gazette of Montenegro', Nos 021/14 of 6.5.2014, 066/15 of 26.11.2015.

Rulebook on registering entry ban and cancellation of stay of a foreign national in a foreign travel document (*Pravilnik o unošenju zabrane ulaska i otkaza boravka stranca u stranu putnu ispravu*), 'Official Gazette of Montenegro', Nos 043/18 of 3.7.2018, 044/18 of 6.7.2018.

Rulebook on Visas and Visa Forms (*Pravilnik o vizama i obrascima za vize*) 'Official Gazette of Montenegro', No. 36/2015.

Rulebook on Residence Permit and the Temporary Residence and Work Permit (*Pravilniko obrascima, bližim uslovima i načinu izdavanja dozvole za privremeni boravak i dozvole za privremeni boravak i rad*), 'Official Gazette of Montenegro', No. 25/2019.

Visa Regime Decree (*Uredba o viznom režimu*), 'Official Gazette of Montenegro', No. 033/19 of 14.6.2019.

Strategies and Reports

European Commission, Montenegro, Progress report, Brussels, 2019.

European Commission, Montenegro, Non – paper, Brussel, 2018.

First report of the Republic of Montenegro on the implementation of the Framework Convention for the Protection of National Minorities (Vlada Crne Gore, Prvi izvještaj Republike Crne Gore o ostvarivanju Okvirne Konvencije za zaštitu nacionalnih manjina), Podgorica, 2007.

Government of Montenegro, *Report on the Implementation of the Action Plan for the Implementation of the Strategy for Integrated Migration Management for 2017-2020, for 2019 (Vlada Crne Gore, Izvještaj o implementaciji Strategije za integrisano upravljanje granicom za 2019)*, Podgorica, 2020.

Government of Montenegro, *Report on the Implementation of the Action Plan for the Implementation of the Strategy for Integrated Migration Management for 2017-2020, for 2018 (Vlada Crne Gore, Izvještaj o implementaciji Strategije za integrisano upravljanje granicom za 2017-2020, za 2018)*, Podgorica, 2020.

Government of Montenegro, *Strategy for Integrated Migration Management in Montenegro for the period 2017-2020 (Vlada Crne Gore, Strategija za integrisano upravljanje granicom za 2017-2020)*, Podgorica, 2016.

Government of Montenegro, *Reintegration Strategy for Persons Retuned under the Readmission Agreements for the Period 2016-2020 (Vlada Crne Gore, Strategija reintegracije lica vraćenihna osnovu Sporazuma o readmisiji za period 2016-2020)*, Podgorica, 2015.

Government of Montenegro, *Integrated Border Management Strategy for 2014-2018 (Vlada Crne Gore, Strategija za integrisano upravljanje granicom)*, Podgorica, 2013.

Government of Montenegro, *Strategy for Permanent Resolution of the Problems of Displaced and Internally Displaced Persons in Montenegro, with Special Reference on the Konik Area, for the Period 2017-2019 (Vlada Crne Gore, Strategija za trajno rješavanje problema raseljenih i interno raseljenih lica u Crnoj Gori, sa posebnim osvtom na Konik za period 2017-2019)*, Podgorica, 2016.

Government of Montenegro, *Strategy for Integrated Migration Management in Montenegro for the Period 2011-2016 (Vlada Crne Gore, Strategija za integrisano upravljanje granicom za 2011-2016)*, Podgorica, 2010.

Government of Montenegro, *Program of Accession of Montenegro to EU 2014-2018 (Vlada Crne Gore, Program pristupanja Crne Gore EU 2014-2018)*, Podgorica, 2013.

Government of Montenegro, *Strategy for Combating Trafficking in Human Beings 2019-2024 (Vlada Crne Gore, Strategija za borbu protiv trgovine ljudima 2019-2024)*, Podgorica, 2018.

Government of Montenegro, *Report on the Implementation of the Action Plan for the Implementation of the Strategy for Reintegration of Persons Returned on the Basis of Readmission Agreements for the Period 2016-2020, for 2018 (Vlada Crne Gore, Strategija reintegracije lica vraćenih na osnovu Sporazuma o readmisiji za period 2016-2020, za 2018)*, Podgorica, 2019.

Government of Montenegro, *Schengen Action Plan (Vlada Crne Gore, Šengen Akcioni Plan)*, Podgorica, 2017.

Police Administration, Serious and organized crime threat assessment in Montenegro – SOCTA, (Procjena opasnosti od teškog i organizovanog kriminala u Crnoj Gori – SOCTA), Podgorica, 2014.

Selected Bibliography

Index

The numbers here refer to paragraph numbers.

Index

Index